Italian Racing Red

Italian Racing Red

Drivers, Cars and Triumphs of Italian Motor Racing

Karl Ludvigsen

Karl Ludvigsen

Karl Ludvigsen – Author

In addition to his motor industry activities as an executive (with GM, Fiat and Ford) and head of a consulting company, Karl Ludvigsen has been active for over 50 years as an author and historian. As an author, co-author or editor he has some fifty books to his credit – all of them about cars and the motor industry, Karl's life long passion.

Since 1997 Karl Ludvigsen has been drawing on the photographic resources of the Ludvigsen Library to write and illustrate books on the great racing drivers, including Stirling Moss, Jackie Stewart, Juan Manuel Fangio, Dan Gurney, Alberto Ascari, Bruce McLaren, and Emerson Fittipaldi.

He has written about road racing in America, the cars of the Can-Am series, the AAR Eagle racing cars, the GT40 Fords and *Prime Movers*, the story of Britain's Ilmor Engineering.

His introduction to *At Speed*, a book of Jesse Alexander's racing photography, won the Ken W. Purdy Award for Excellence in Automotive Journalism. He has written three times about Mercedes-Benz, twice about its racing cars. His books on the latter subject have won the Montagu Trophy (once) and the Nicholas-Joseph Cugnot Award (twice), both recognising outstanding automotive historical writing. In 2001 he again received the Cugnot award from the Society of Automotive Historians for his book about the early years of the Volkswagen, *Battle for the Beetle*. In 2002 the Society gave him its highest accolade, Friend of Automotive History.

Resident in England since 1980, Karl Ludvigsen is respected as a close and knowledgeable observer of, and participant in, the world motor industry. On motor industry topics Karl has written books about high-performance engines, the Wankel rotary engine, the histories of American auto makers and the V12 Engine.

He is a former technical editor of *Sports Cars Illustrated* (1956-57), editor of *Car and Driver* (1960-1962) and east coast editor of *Motor Trend* (1970s). His articles have been published in America by *Road & Track* and *Automobile Quarterly*, among others, while in Europe he writes frequently for *The Automobile*. He is a columnist for *Hemmings Sports & Exotic Cars* and Just-Auto.com and a senior writer for Autosport-Atlas.com, a leading motor racing website.

Italian Racing Red © 2008

ISBN (13) 978 1 7110 3331 3

Produced by Chevron Publishing Limited
Concept: Robert Forsyth
Project Editors: Robert Forsyth/Chevron Publishing
and Karl Ludvigsen
Cover and book design: Mark Nelson
© Text: Karl Ludvigsen
© Colour profiles: Steven Cavalieri

Published by Ian Allan Publishing
an imprint of Ian Allan Publishing Ltd. Hersham, Surrey, KT12 4RG

Printed by Ian Allan Publishing Ltd. Hersham, Surrey, KT12 4RG

Visit the Ian Allan Publishing website at:
www.ianallanpublishing.com

Ian Allan
PUBLISHING

CONTENTS

FOREWORD

This book, one of an unique series from Ian Allan Publishing, was conceived to introduce the reader to the cars, circuits, companies and characters of one of the great motor-sporting nations. Soon after the first races of 1895 the issue of nationality loomed large in Europe, birthplace of motoring. In fact the first major international motor race, the Gordon Bennett Cup of 1900 to 1905, was contested not by companies but by trios of cars representing their nations. Every part of every car had to be manufactured in the respective countries.

By the 1920s cars from France, Germany, Great Britain, the United States, Italy and Austria were prominent in international motor sports, distinguished by their official national colours. With the rebirth of assertive nationalism in the 1930s their colours took on new significance as the flag-bearers of European nations took to the tracks to demonstrate their skills and superiority.

After World War Two their colours bespoke the nationality of racing cars until the late 1960s, when liveries were allowed to reflect sponsorship. Though this relaxation of constraints did produce fabulous-looking racing cars, some competitors continued to reflect their countries of construction in their choice of colours. Because national identities are blurred when French racing cars are made in Britain and German cars are produced in Switzerland – as they are in the 21st Century – the new paradigm can be seen to have its merits.

Introduced, explained and illustrated in these pages are the companies, engineers, executives and enthusiasts whose powerful competitive spirit and dauntless courage drove them to dominate in motor racing. It has been my pleasure to reveal the dramatic stories behind their successes and failures in the great classic endurance races and Grand Prix contests in which they dominated – or faced disaster. Motor racing, which has no equal in the ecstasy of victory and agony of defeat, comes vividly to life in this volume's colourful pages.

Karl Ludvigsen

MANUFACTURING SITES:

1. **TORINO:** Chiribiri, Fiat, Siata, Moretti, Abarth, Lancia, Pininfarina, Ansaldo, Cisitalia, Diatto, Ceirano, Scat, Itala, Spa, Nazzaro

2. **MARANELLO:** Ferrari

3. **VOLPIANO:** Osella

4. **VARANO:** Dallara

5. **BRESCIA:** OM

6. **FERRARA:** Morelli

7. **LIVORNO:** Bizzarrini

8. **FORLI:** Bandini

9. **PADOVA:** Bernardi

10. **MILAN:** Prinetti & Stucchi, Alfa Romeo, Bianchi, Isotta-Fraschini, Zagato, Touring, Pirelli, Autodelta

11. **TRIESTE:** San Giusto

12. **MODENA:** Maserati, Stanguellini, Scaglietti, De Tomaso, Lamborghini

13. **BOLOGNA:** Maserati, Osca, ATS, Tecno

14. **FAENZA:** Minardi

15. **FIRENZE:** Barsanti & Matteucci

16. **ROME:** Giannini

17. **NAPLES:** Darracq assembly

CIRCUITS & HILL CLIMBS:

18. **AUTOSTRADA:** Records

19. **SAN REMO**

20. **SESTRIERE:** Hill climb

21. **MONCENISIO:** Hill climb

22. **BERNARDO:** Hill climb

23. **BALOCCO:** Test circuit

24. **TORINO**

25. **CREMONA**

26. **BRESCIA:** Mille Miglia

27. **SALO**

28. **MONZA**

29. **BOLZANO:** Hill climb

30. **PARMA:** Hill climb

31. **IMOLA**

32. **MUGELLO**

33. **MODENA**

34. **RAVENNA:** Hill climb

35. **LIVORNO**

36. **PESCARA**

37. **NAPLES**

38. **BARI**

39. **PALERMO:** Targa Florio

40. **CATANIA:** Hill climb

41. **SIRACUSA**

Italian manufacturing sites of racing cars – past and present – and the racing circuits and hill climbs used

CHAPTER I

Italy Revs its Engines

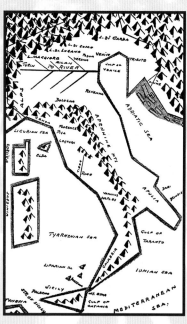

Historian Hendrik Willem van Loon created this schematic depiction of Italy's isolation from its neighbours.

RED is the colour you want on your racing car. It is the most aggressive possible hue, the angry colour that thrusts to the fore. When you glance in your mirror to see who's chasing you, red gets your attention. Whether sunny or grey, rainy or dry, red cuts through the haze to give maximum visibility. Photographing well in any medium, red looks terrific on sports and racing cars. Sponsors love the attention red gets while racing drivers adore red cars because they know they will have the best chance to slash a swathe through the field when those ahead get a glimpse of who's chasing them.

So how did Italy get so lucky? How did red become the official hue of Italy's racing cars? It took a while, partly because Italy was a relative latecomer to the international racing scene. When the *New York Herald*'s James Gordon-Bennett established an international challenge trophy for racing cars made in specific countries, Italy was absent. 'The 1900 Gordon Bennett Trophy attracted entries from France, the United States, Germany and Belgium,' wrote historian David Venables. 'The organisers decreed that the cars of each team should be painted in a distinctive colour. The French cars should be painted blue, the American red, the German white and the Belgian yellow.'

Here was an early coup for the United States, Gordon-Bennett's native land. America's advantage with racing red remained in effect in 1903, when any Italian cars competing for his trophy were obliged to be liveried a bleak, depressing black. Not surprisingly none stepped forward to accept the anonymity of black, a non-colour rarely used in motor racing. Things were not much better for the running of the first Grand Prix in 1906, and according to Venables: 'the cars, entered by manufacturers, appeared in a motley selection of colours and the winning Renault was painted red.' Again the superiority of red was underlined.

By 1908, however, the later order had been established. No Grand Prix racers had been willing to accept black. American cars gave up red in favour of white with a red chassis, but the latter changed to blue in 1913 so that Swiss cars could be white and red to match their national colours. Italian cars at last were red, although some in fact had been painted during 1907's season. Red for Italian Grand Prix cars prevailed as long as official colours were required and, thanks to Ferrari's sense of tradition, well beyond that.

In other categories of racing cars the official colours did not apply. 'For the lesser *voiturette* class and for sports cars there were no rules,' wrote David Venables. 'In sports-car racing the Aston Martin team ran in red; in 1935 a red-painted Lagonda won the Le Mans 24-hour race.' Britain's Sunbeam too used red for some of its racing and record-breaking cars. The power of crimson was too great to be denied. Other factors played a part as well. Mercedes in the 1920s and Porsche in the 1960s entered red cars in Sicily's Targa Florio to avoid the menacing attention that the island's mountain bandits sometimes gave to non-Italian entries.

Although its use was not mandatory, out of choice and preference, Italy's entrants of sports-racers and single-seaters stayed with *rosso corsa* as their hue of choice. It varied in brightness and density according to house preference, there being no 'official' Italian crimson. Darker hues were favoured, for example, by the Scuderia Ferrari for its Alfa Romeos in the 1930s and by Lancia for its racing cars in the 1950s. If an Italian car's entrant were of a different nationality, the custom was for the racer to be painted in his country's colours. Frequently, Belgian-entered Ferraris were yellow, for example.

All shades of red were perfect for the palettes of the artists who heralded the arrival of Italy on the stage of world motor sports. These were the Futurists, a group of painters and sculptors who heralded the age of speed with vivid images of dramatic speed and dynamism while rejecting 'the fanatical, senseless and snobbish religion of the past... that spineless worshipping of old canvases, old statues and old bric-a-brac.' Both the aeroplane and the automobile were taken up by the Futurists as symbolic of a new and exciting age.

Futurism was the creation of an Italian poet, Filippo Tommaso Marinetti. In his manifesto formulated in Milan

in 1909 he urged the rejection of what he saw as corruption of the mind and heart in favour of forward-looking values such as 'instinct, strength, courage, sport, war, youth, dynamism and speed as exemplified by modern machines.' Publication of Marinetti's manifesto in Paris inspired artists, among them Giacomo Balla, Umberto Boccioni and Carlo Carrà, to create artworks that glorified the energy and velocity of machines – especially automobiles. More than 50 of their works were on show at the 1911 Milan exhibition which established Futurism as a school of art.

The synthesis of art and machine as expressed by the Futurists betrays an aspect of the Italian psyche that has had a profound influence on that country's racing cars. With remarkably few exceptions, Italian competition cars are gorgeous. This is not simply a function of their coachwork, important though that is. Rather it pervades

This 1913 work by Luigi Russolo, Dynamism of an Automobile, bespeaks Italy's early adoption of the aesthetics of the motor car.

Seen in Turin's automobile museum is one of Virginio Bordino's steam carriages.

One of the first engines built by Barsanti and Matteucci in the mid-19th century was this vertical two-cylinder unit.

every aspect of the machinery that makes up an automobile – their engines, transmissions, brakes, suspensions and structures. From their innermost ribs, castings, machined surfaces, tubes and fabrications they show an artistic as well as engineering spirit at work. This design characteristic – as well as the colour crimson – sets Italian racing cars apart from their contemporaries.

Accelerating global interest in the style and substance of Italy's cars, the Futurist movement gave a welcome impetus to an automotive industry that was lagging behind its European contemporaries. The reason for this was Italy's relative poverty. It had little in the way of natural resources and raw materials. Walled off from the rest of Europe by the Alpine barrier, it had not been able to participate in the economic development of its neighbours.

Through most of the 19th Century Italy's economy was primarily agricultural thanks in large measure to the fertility of its northern plain, watered by the Po River. This meandered from Turin in the west, passing south of Milan and near Piacenza, Cremona, Mantua and Ferrara on its way to the Adriatic between Venice and Ravenna. Elsewhere in the Italian peninsula, however, poverty propelled a diaspora of the talented and ambitious to other parts of the world that offered greater opportunity.

Only united as a nation in 1861, Italy was slow to enjoy the industrial revolution that was beginning to transform the face of Europe. Its national revenue was less than a third of France's and one-quarter of Britain's. Around the time of that unification, however, engineering advances were taking place that could have vaulted Italy forward. 'Only an act of fate,' said historian Lyle Cummins, 'prevented two sons of Italy from being remembered as the founders of the internal-combustion industry.'

Contrasting with the illiteracy which prevailed in 19th-century Italy, pioneers Eugenio Barsanti and Felice Matteucci were well-educated engineers and academics. Working in Florence, where Barsanti was a priest as well as a lecturer in mathematics, they designed and built internal-combustion engines in one- and two-cylinder versions with electric ignition. Putting their power to work though a rack-and-pinion system, their engines enjoyed industrial installations with power clearly in advance of the engines of Germany's Nicolaus Otto, who was aware of their work.

Patents of 1854 and 1857 covered the advances made by Matteucci and Barsanti, who arranged with other companies to produce their engines. In 1864 Barsanti went to Belgium to attend tests of an engine at a potential contractor but was felled by typhus and died at only 42 years of age. With Matteucci not welcomed as a collaborator by the Belgian firm, and unwell in the bargain, their engines faded from the scene. Instead Otto, working with Eugen Langen, was destined to seize the honour of creating the practical four-stroke engine with his power unit shown in Paris in 1867.

Italy's wheeled-vehicle pioneer was a captain of engineers in Piedmont's pre-unification army, Virginio Bordino. Born in 1804, Bordino travelled to England to observe early steam developments and returned to Italy

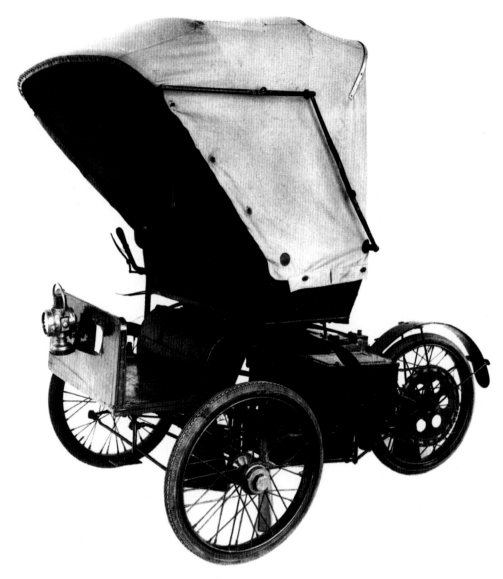

to create vehicles of his own. He worked at Turin's Arsenal, Italy's largest industrial concern in mid-century with its own foundry and 350-strong staff. With the aim of replacing his army's horses Bordino built five experimental steam carriages, the last in 1854. One of his prototypes, a three-wheeler, survives in Turin's automobile museum.

Also still on display in Turin is one of the ingenious internal-combustion tricars designed by Enrico Bernardi of Padua with the assistance of Giustino Cattaneo. Built by that city's Miari & Giusti Company in 1895, the Bernardi is Italy's first indigenous automobile in the modern sense. May 18th of that same year witnessed Italy's first motor-car competition, a 58-mile trial from Turin to Asti and return. Of the five vehicles that left Turin at the 7:30 a.m. start, three made it back from Asti, two motor bicycles led home by a four-seater Daimler. In another longer trial from Turin in 1898 one of the Miari & Giustis acquitted itself well.

Finishing outside the allotted time in the 119-mile 1898 event was Peugeot driver Michele Lanza. A controversial character in Italy's early motorisation, Lanza was a successful candle manufacturer who dabbled in car manufacture as a hobby that pretended to be a business. 'After having seen the first motor cars in use in France,' wrote Carlo Biscaretti di Ruffia, 'he constructed a dozen different models but the zeal of the inventor outweighed his practical judgement. He maintained that

motor technology was still in such a state of evolution that it was impossible for the industrialist to confine himself to one model and mass-produce it.'

Turin was the right city in which to find resources that catered to ambitions like Lanza's. The aforementioned military arsenal both consumed and created metalwork. Italy's major supplier of machine tools was Michele Ansaldo's factory, set up on the Via Ponte Mosca in 1884, while the Diatto works had been an esteemed maker of railway equipment since 1835. Other factories wrought iron and steel, made bolts and fixings and cast type for printing. Drawing on nearby hydroelectric power, Turin led Italy in the electrification of its homes and factories.

Except for Ansaldo, which employed more than 300, most firms were smaller with 150 to 180 employees.

Above left: Padua's Miari & Giusti built this three-wheeler to the designs of Enrico Bernardi and Giustino Catteneo in 1895.

Above: Another version of the 1895 Bernardi, considered Italy's first indigenous automobile, was equipped with a retractable hood.

ANSALDO

As one of Italy's major engineering works, Turin's Ansaldo was recruited to build aero engines for use in the Great War. At first their sixes and twelves were based on Spa designs, but later Ansaldo evolved engines of its own. With demand for aero engines plummeting after the armistice, engineer Guido Soria recommended to his president Pio Perrone that Ansaldo follow the initiative of its Turin neighbour Fiat into the new world of motor-car manufacture.

That Ansaldo cars came from a great maker of armaments was obvious from the crossed cannons on their badge. First appearing in 1919, Ansaldos had sporting potential with their 2.0-litre overhead-cam fours. In 1921 an Ansaldo was being campaigned by Corrado Lotti, who enjoyed some class successes in hill climbs and was the outright winner of the 68-mile Circuit of Montenero at Leghorn. He even defeated Tazio Nuvolari in one of the latter's first four-wheel competitions at Garda.

Class successes continued to come to Ansaldo drivers through the 1920s, in both hill climbs and circuit races, until the products of OM and Diatto rose to the fore in the 2.0-litre category. However Ansaldo was disinclined to take motor sports seriously. After Guido Soria left in 1927, his patrimony to the company a new model range with sixes and eights, Ansaldo's auto activity declined. Its last new cars were sold off during the early 1930s.

Although not at the cutting edge of competition, this Ansaldo was being rallied near Rhyader in Wales in the 1920s.

'The small size of the average firm,' wrote Antonio Fossati, 'reflects the prudent and cautious attitude peculiar to the Piedmontese, who tended to assess realistically the country's possibilities and insure themselves as far as possible against the recurrence of booms and slumps such as those which had hit the banking world a few years earlier.'

One such small firm, on the Via Vanchiglia on the city's east side near the Po River, was the workshop of Giovanni and Giuseppe Martina. It was said of the Martinas that 'they were both highly intelligent and expert, whose most ambitious ideas were always tempered by that grain of common sense which helped their realisation.' While Michele Lanza had the inspirations, he turned to the Martinas to make his many prototypes, the first of which was completed in 1895.

Milan in Lombardy was not without its pioneers. One such was Prinetti & Stucchi, which since 1874 had been making sewing machines and bicycles. Like so many such companies it easily made the transition in 1898 to small three- and four-wheelers powered by the ubiquitous French de Dion air-cooled singles. Its guiding spirit in automobile design was Ludovico Prinetti.

In 1898 a 17-year-old volunteer apprentice at Prinetti & Stucchi had the bright idea of driving the rear wheels of one of its tricycles with a pair of de Dion engines. This produced a simple yet potent racer with which the apprentice, a certain Ettore Bugatti, won the major 100-mile race from Verona to Brescia and Mantua and return on 14 March 1899.

Bugatti's biographer, W.F. Bradley, credited him with victories in eight of ten local races with his twin-engined racer in 1899. Most importantly, Bradley says that Bugatti entered his personal Prinetti & Stucchi in the race from Paris to Bordeaux over 351 miles, starting on 24 May of 1899. Although showing well in the early stages, young Bugatti had to retire after an encounter with a dog left his machine too battered to continue. Nevertheless this was historic as the first entry of an Italian racing car in a major competition abroad.

If two engines were good, four would be better, Bugatti decided, and built such a machine at the Milan works. Not surprisingly it suffered from gear-selection problems. Refused further help by Prinetti & Stucchi, which in any case gave up car manufacture in 1906, Bugatti turned to the noble Gulinelli brothers for backing for a completely new car of his own design.

Featured in a Milan exhibition of 1901, the four-cylinder Bugatti drew the attention of the De Dietrich motor company in the province of Alsace. Moving there in 1902 to take up an engineering post at De Dietrich, Bugatti left Italy behind. When Alsace became French instead of German after World War One, erstwhile Italian Bugatti soon became renowned as a maker of fine French racing and road cars. Meanwhile Italy herself would not be found wanting in automotive engineers and entrepreneurs.

One of the varied creations of Michele Lanza, at the controls here, was this 1899 Victoria.

Twin vertical de Dion engines powered this Prinetti & Stucchi tricycle, driven in competition by Ettore Bugatti in 1899.

Ettore Bugatti's 1901 creation, a four-cylinder auto, was his ticket to an engineering job at De Dietrich in Alsace.

CHAPTER 2

Ceirano's Contributions

IN a cast of colourful characters at the founding of Italy's motor industry one of the most outstanding was Giovanni Battista Ceirano. Carlo Biscaretti di Ruffia described him as 'tall, heavily built, with a powerful head and thick black moustache, and was clever, energetic and obstinate to a marked degree.' Moving north to Turin in 1880 at the age of 20 from his native Cuneo, Ceirano opened a bicycle shop at number 9 on the Corso Vittorio Emanuele, the east-west boulevard that passes the main train station.

Giovan Ceirano, as we will know him to distinguish the eldest from his five-years-younger brother Giovanni, soon began making his own bicycles and patenting his improvements to them. He adopted the British-sounding name 'Welleyes' for his products. Assisting the ambitious Giovan were brother Giovanni and the ten-years-younger Matteo Ceirano.

That Giovan Ceirano was eager to participate in the budding automotive age was shown by his entry of a motorised bicycle in the historic trial from Turin to Asti and return in 1895. In fact he placed second in this, Italy's

first motor competition, behind the winning Daimler. In 1898 both he and Ettore Bugatti failed to finish the lengthened version of this trial, also passing through Alessandria, on their Prinetti & Stucchi motor tricycles.

By that time the Ceirano brothers were readying a Welleyes automobile. On 23 October 1898 they founded the Ceirano Giovanni Battista & C. for this purpose. Their general manager was Turinese engineer, Enrico Marchesi, while their chief engineer was Aristide Faccioli, 'one of the few men in Turin who at that time were capable of designing a motor car,' according to Biscaretti. 'Short, thin, black-bearded, small-featured, with a very mobile and intelligent face, he was a victim of those interior struggles which often beset the studious. He was restless and at times difficult to deal with. One could almost say he was instability personified, but his innate goodness and generosity of mind knew no bounds.'

With the valued help of the indispensable Martina brothers, the first Welleyes was completed in March 1899. Its rear-mounted twin-cylinder engine of 663 cc was horizontal, driving through a patented two-speed belt system. It was, recalled Biscaretti, 'a small car of unique design, graceful line and fairly well sprung, which greatly raised the hopes of its producers.' The newcomer excited

With justifiable pride Giovan Ceirano poses with his Welleyes motor car of 1899. It was destined to become the first Fiat.

This Scat, another Ceirano creation, was driven to victory in the 1911 Targa Florio by Ernesto Ceirano.

Based on a production Scat chassis, this purposeful racing version was the 1914 Targa winner with Ernesto Ceirano.

Cyril Snipe won the 1912 Targa Florio in the sister Scat to this entry of Ernesto Ceirano.

A last gasp in racing for Scat was the 1921 Targa Florio, when team drivers Tarabusi, Mocca and Angelini failed to finish.

great interest during the Turin Automobile Club's motoring rally week in April, when 'never before had the people of Turin seen so many cars assembled.'

On 30 April the Welleyes joined the starters for a trial over 56 miles from Orbassano on Turin's outskirts south-west to Pinerolo and Avigliana and return. At the new car's controls for its baptismal outing was a prominent member of the Turin bar, respected and feared criminal lawyer Cesare Goria-Gatti. Also an investor in Ceirano, the 'small, wiry and dark-haired' Goria-Gatti was a motoring enthusiast whose skill as a driver was a considerable asset to the Welleyes debut.

In its class the Welleyes placed second of four finishers with no involuntary stops, rated a signal success for a brand-new Italian car. This made a strong impression on a retired army lieutenant who had for some time been debating how best to enter the nascent motor industry. In March of 1899 he had won his class for two-seater tricycles in the same Verona-based event that saw Ettore

Bugatti win the other category. Although only a spectator in the April race to Pinerolo, the lieutenant esteemed the merits of the Welleyes and its intense and talented designer.

The outcome was that the lieutenant, Giovanni Agnelli, marshalled the financial support of friends and colleagues to buy the Ceirano car operation lock, stock and barrel, complete with Marchesi and Faccioli and the latter's patents. The Welleyes became the basis of the first Fiat car, introduced as such later in 1899. After a brief period of consultation with the new owners, the senior Ceirano left a post as Fiat's head of sales to found Fratelli Ceirano with brother Matteo. For the first time they would build cars under the Ceirano name.

Their first cars were the work of engineer Alberto Ballocco. In 1902 the 8 HP Ceirano enjoyed success, winning its category in the Sassi-Superga and Susa-Moncenisio hill climbs, driven by young Matteo. Yet in 1903 the services of Ballocco were dispensed with when

Aristide Faccioli, too creative for the strict regime at Fiat, returned to work for the Ceiranos. The latter, following their personal stars, began founding separate companies while the Ceirano marque faded away – temporarily – in 1905.

In Turin in 1906, middle brother Giovanni launched Società Ceirano Automobili Torino, with the lively acronym SCAT, which we will know as Scat. This was a serious undertaking with an initial staff of 150 that grew to 600 before the war. Giovanni's right arm in this was his son, also Giovanni but known as Ernesto, who proved to be a handy racing driver as well as tester. Design was the responsibility of former Fiat man Giuseppe Coda.

Although the field for the sixth Targa Florio race in May of 1911 was meagre, it was still a demanding contest over three laps of a Sicilian road circuit totalling 277 miles. Young Ernesto was the winner in a Scat ahead of a Lancia and Mercedes with another Scat fourth.

In 1912 Ernesto was out of luck in the Targa, which was run that year as a gruelling 600-mile lap of the island of Sicily. Also on the team was an Englishman, Cyril Snipe, with Pardini his mechanic. Snipe started so forcefully that at mid-race his Scat had an incredible two-hour lead, whereupon in the early morning 'he flung himself on the ground and declared emphatically that no power on earth could make him go a yard farther,' said W. F. Bradley.

With the passage of two hours and the approach of rivals, added Bradley, 'in desperation Pardini seized a bucket of water and flung it over his sleep-sodden companion. The result was instantaneous, Snipe leaping to his feet with wild cries of anger, vaulting into his seat and with water dripping from him roared away and finished first with the advantage of half an hour over a Lancia.' In a race lasting 37 minutes more than 24 hours his winning average of 24.3 mph gave a hint of the state of the Sicilian roads.

The choleric Snipe, whose English phlegm evaporated under the Italian sun, failed to finish his Scats in the next two round-Sicily races, which were run in two daily stages. Ernesto Ceirano came to the fore in 1914, winning at 38.9 mph with another Scat fourth. The Scats used for

Giovanni Battista Raggio drove this handsome 100 HP Itala to victory in Brescia's Coppa Florio in 1905.

TARGA FLORIO

Motor sport had no greater spectacle nor Italian industry a better shop window for its wares than the astonishing motor race conceived and implemented by one of the greatest enthusiasts in the history of racing, Vincenzo Florio. As the second son of an immensely wealthy Palermo merchant and industrialist, Florio was able to indulge his own enthusiasms, which as he was born in 1883 included all the amazing new motorised activities that the 20th century had to offer.

While boats, balloons and bicycles were among Florio's passions, motor cars soon took pole position. Young Vincenzo bought examples of the first automobiles including a Fiat, which came with a mechanician to show its qualities, Felice Nazzaro. The two got on so well that Nazzaro became Vincenzo's man-of-all-motors for four years, during which he had the opportunity to learn some of the driving skills that made him a future champion.

When at a motor competition in France in 1905 Vincenzo Florio was braced by a question from a leading editor: Why do you not have a motor race in Sicily?'

'Why,' answered the startled Florio, 'because we have no roads.'

Back in Palermo he asked colleagues to look into the matter of roads. They reported that a circuit of 92½ miles was possible based on the north-coast road at the village of Cerda and climbing some 3,700 feet to the heights of the island's raw interior. Known as the Great Madonie circuit, this was covered in three laps for the first race held on 5 May 1906. The winner received a gold plate or targa, hence the Targa Florio. A cup or coppa was the award in certain races or categories, thus the Coppa Florio.

At the age of 23 Vincenzo Florio had created an important event that was to benefit the reputation and economy of Sicily, entirely in the tradition of his father and family. In his role as 'animator, organiser and underwriter' of the whole shebang he had to cope with many challenges, not least the island's famed Mafia and menacing brigands. Various bodies were the official organisers over the years, for example the Auto Club of Sicily from 1914 to 1935.

As one of the sport's premier events, the Targa Florio tied with the French Grand Prix with its founding in 1906. In 1966, when the French event had seen 45 runnings, the Targa celebrated its 50th. In 1973, the last time the Targa raced as part of the world manufacturers' championship, victory went to a Porsche 911 Carrera RSR. German teams always relished the Targa as a supreme test in the warm south; Porsche in particular developed special cars to compete there. After a Lancia Stratos

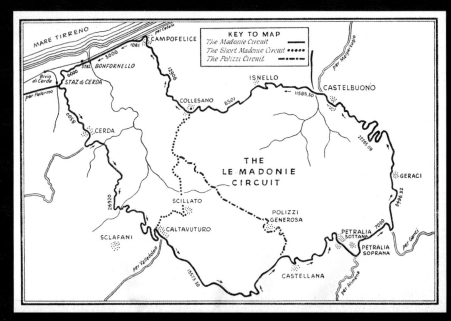

The 'Short' Madonie Circuit for the Targa Florio was made possible by support given the race by Benito Mussolini.

won a local version in 1974 the Targa ceased to be a competitive event.

In the manner of the races of the day the cars were started at intervals; to have done otherwise on these narrow cart tracks would have invited disaster. This remained a feature of the Targa Florio through its active existence, challenging drivers and teams alike to keep track of the timing differences between cars. Save in 1957, when it was run as a regularity trial after the fatal crash of a Ferrari in the Mille Miglia, the classic Targa regularly counted for the sports car world championship.

From 1919 through 1930 the race was run over the Medium Madonie circuit, shortened to 67 miles per lap. In 1932 a 45-mile lap, the Piccolo Madonie, came into use. This required the building of a bypass road, for the funding of which Vincenzo Florio made a successful appeal to Il Duce, Benito Mussolini. After the war many road repairs were needed before the race could be resumed in 1951, when Franco Cortese won in a British Frazer Nash.

Except for the 1936-1940 period, when the Auto Club of Palermo organised the race, the Targa was always the personal fiefdom of Vincenzo Florio. The last race he witnessed was the 1958 event when the Ferrari of Luigi Musso and Olivier Gendebien halted two years of German victories. He died in France in January of 1959.

Alessandro Cagno was a blur as he started the 1906 French Grand Prix in his Itala. After two of the twelve laps all three team Italas retired.

racing were stripped versions of the 4.7-litre 25 HP production car and the 6.3-litre 60 HP, the latter with overhead valves and camshaft.

Although the SCAT company survived the post-war economic crisis its racing days were over, Fiat ultimately absorbing it in 1932. During the 1920s, however, it received an infusion of sporting Ceirano DNA. After the war the Giovanni Ceiranos father and son had left SCAT to set up a new company on Turin's Corso Lecce to revive the production of cars in their own name. This news was welcomed by experts who respected their pioneering role in the industry and considered Giovanni to be a first-rate engineer as well as manager.

The early 1920s saw sporting successes for Ceiranos, whose range included the CS 2 Corsa model with 35 horsepower at 3,000 rpm from its 2,950 cc. With Ernesto again at the wheel, successes were gained on the Mugello circuit and in Italy's popular hill climbs. When the island of Sardinia staged a speed week in May 1922, Ceiranos finished first and third in races over a 52-mile road course.

But after the launch later that year of an overhead-valve six, Giovanni engineered a reunification with the SCAT company which found the latter producing Ceiranos for sale until the end of their road came in 1924.

When last we heard of youngest brother Matteo Ceirano he was racing cars made by Fratelli Ceirano. In 1903 he struck out on his own to found a company in Turin's Via Guastalla, only three blocks west of the resourceful Martina brothers, to make big sporting and racing cars of quality. In 1904 he adopted the name 'Itala' for his products, which that year scored some hill climb successes. Many Italas were distinguished by having shaft drive when chains were still customary for big cars.

When, in 1905, Matteo Ceirano left to found yet another car company, Itala gained a new chief engineer, the Alberto Ballocco with whom Matteo had worked only a couple of years earlier. Destined to remain until 1919, Ballocco began as he meant to go on with the 14.0-litre 100 HP racer which won the Coppa Florio over 312 miles on a circuit near Brescia in September 1905 at the

The frame-lightening techniques used on this 1906 24 HP hill climb Itala would have come in handy for the company's 1913 French Grand Prix entries.

handsome speed of 65.1 mph. The Itala's driver, Giovanni Battista Raggio, had ten minutes in hand over a De Dietrich from the pen of Ettore Bugatti.

Another creation of wealthy enthusiast Vincenzo Florio was Sicily's Targa Florio. When this was first run on 5 May 1906 over 277 miles of mountain roads, 22 cars were expected but shipping problems reduced the starters to ten. Among them, half were Italas with a crack team of drivers. Itala-mounted Alessandro Cagno was the winner with one team car retiring and the others second, fourth and fifth. Although the most undemonstrative of personalities, reported Bradley, with 'the race won, the gold plate his to be carried home, Cagno's pent-up emotion got the better of him, for he applied the brakes with such fierceness that he completely stripped the crown wheel. He could not have run another yard, but it was not necessary to run another yard.'

The name of Itala was etched in motoring legend in 1907 when one of its cars won an epic race from Peking – now Beijing – to Paris. When the Paris daily *Le Matin* announced that it would organise such an audacious contest over more than 8,000 miles of territory – much of it trackless – between China and France, several dozen potential entrants expressed interest. When the transcontinental trial began in June 1907 five cars were ready: two small De Dion-Boutons, an even smaller Tri-Contal three-wheeler, a Dutch Spyker and an Itala from Turin.

The Itala was an entry by Prince Scipione Borghese. For him Alberto Ballocco and Itala managing director, Guido Bigio, prepared a special 40 HP car with reinforced chassis, stiffer springs, a 60-gallon fuel capacity and wheels larger and stronger than standard. Its coachwork was the minimum needed for Borghese, journalist and co-driver, Luigi Barzini, and mechanic Ettore Guizzardi, of whom it was said that 'in intervals of polishing, greasing and testing his beloved Itala, he would lie quietly beneath her, contemplating her piece by piece, for hours on end.'

A book could be written about their adventures on the gruelling trek, which Barzini in fact did. They arrived in Paris after a journey of two months with a margin of two weeks ahead of all rivals. In Berlin Itala provided a trio of its latest models to carry French journalists on the trial's final triumphal leg. When the Itala was the centrepiece of the company's stands at the autumnal motor shows it was in its filthy and battered condition.

Although Itala bravely took part in the first Grand Prix races, starting in 1906, it failed to gain good results. When its cars were presented for the 1913 French Grand Prix they were found to be some 80 kg over the weight limit of 1,100 kg. 'This incident provided quite a lot of excitement,' *The Autocar* reported:

> Out came all the water and all the oil, all the grease from the gear box, and every fitting that could be done without. Another trial showed them still too heavy, but by a very little, so then the grease was washed out from the universal joints, the dirt cleaned from off the tyres, and in one case the handle for screwing down on the spare wheels was shorn of its arms. Then another trial on the scales disclosed the exact weight, not an ounce either over or under.

This effort, no doubt involving faithful mechanic Guizzardi, was in vain for all three Italas retired. Important racing success was denied later products of Itala, whose competition interests suffered a terrible blow when Guido Bigio was killed during tests of a car for the 1913 French Grand Prix. The last Itala left the Turin factory in 1934.

Amazingly we have not yet finished with the Ceiranos. When the youngest brother, the peripatetic Matteo, left Itala in 1905 it was to set up another company, the Società Piemontese Automobili, with the backing of industrialist Michele Ansaldi. Surviving until 1925, when it was absorbed by Fiat, it produced Spa automobiles. Ernesto Ceirano drove one to third place in the 1908 Targa Florio.

In 1909 entries in the Sicilian race fell to only 11 after the earthquake of 28 December 1908, the largest ever to hit Europe, devastated Messina and its surroundings with up to 200,000 dead. To make up the numbers the race's backer Vincenzo Florio decided to drive a Fiat himself, placing second behind the Spa of Francesco Ciuppa. A second Spa of Mario Cortese was fourth. No exceptional successes came to later Spas.

Often overlooked by Giovan Ceirano in his premises at the turn of the century was the unassuming Felice Nazzaro, whom he had taken on as a lad-of-all-work. 'Tall, thin, loose-jointed, slow in movement,' Nazzaro was 'quiet, in spite of occasional fits of temper which were to characterise his whole life.' He proved to have fine mechanical skills and uncanny prowess as a driver.

After a sparkling career behind the wheel for Fiat, Nazzaro set up as a car maker in Turin. His first products appeared in 1912. Only a year later, on 11 and 12 May 1913, he won the Targa Florio in one of his own cars. In 1914 Nazzaro triumphed in the 277-mile Coppa Florio, demoting to second place the Scat of Ernesto Ceirano. Although that helped compensate for failure of a team of specially built Nazzaros in that year's French Grand Prix, Felice broke with his company in 1916.

Thus did the Ceirano workshops on Turin's Corso Vittorio Emanuele serve as the cradle for the creations not only of the brothers themselves but also of many other pioneers of Italy's motor industry. First among these, and by no means least in sporting terms, was Fiat.

Francesco Ciuppa's Spa — another Ceirano creation — was the winner of the 1909 Targa Florio.

CHAPTER 3

Industrialists go Racing

Giovanni Agnelli
13 August 1866 – 16 December 1945

Turin's Giovanni Agnelli was a visionary who had confidence that Italy deserved a producer of automobiles in volume.

FORTUITOUSLY for Italy's automotive pioneers they had help from several developments early in the 20th century. One was the discovery and exploitation of a vein of fine iron ore near the picturesque village of Cogne in the Aosta Valley north-west of Turin. Its exploitation was undertaken by a Belgian, Charles van der Straten Pontoz, who founded Miniere de Cogne and engaged expert Pio Perrone to create a works capable of processing the ore into the finest steels.

Constructed with the help of engineers from both Sweden and Italy, the Cogne works uniquely refined iron and steel by electricity supplied by several generating plants in the region. It produced steel alloys of extremely high quality, just what was needed for the crankshafts, gears ands connecting rods of Italy's racing cars. By the time of the First World War the Cogne mills were in full operation.

As for the cars themselves, Italy had no shortage of pioneering enthusiasts. Nor were they denied the ability to realise their dreams, thanks to the well-established workshop skills of Italy's artisans in Turin in particular. They were sheltered by a government that had turned authoritarian under prime minister Francesco Crispi, who ruled save for two years between 1887 and 1896. Foreign

adventures, including a failed assault on what is modern Ethiopia, led to his replacement by Giovanni Gollitti, who brought social reforms such as a ban on work by children under 12. Nevertheless many Italians had a hankering for the inviting delights of socialism.

That the automobile was a worthy objective for Italian industry was doubted at the turn of the century, when only 326 self-propelled vehicles were on the country's roads. 'Stuff for rich exhibitionists,' derided many. 'We already have horses and they're stronger.' Where was the domestic market for such expensive creations in a country where the majority lived in poverty?

One man who had a vision of what might be possible was the former army lieutenant we met in the previous chapter. Giovanni Agnelli lived in the heart of Turin on the Corso Cavour, where in addition to his stabling he had a large building in which he could conduct experiments to satisfy his mechanical curiosity. Agnelli read about Daimler's activities in Germany and the work in Padua of Enrico Bernardi, whom he visited to discuss his inventions, a visit which fired his enthusiasm for internal combustion.

Thirty-three years old in 1899, Giovanni Agnelli was eager to make his mark in the world of motors. But his vision differed from that of his contemporaries.

He scorned the plurality of Michele Lanza's creations. 'When you realise that he builds his cars piece by piece without the necessary machinery and throws away the dies that cost him a tremendous amount for every new car he manufactures,' Angelli was quoted by Carlo Biscaretti di Ruffia, 'you can imagine the sort of balance sheet he has at the end of the year. He doesn't sell his cars but stores them as museum pieces for the future. Lanza is intelligent but he'll never be a good motor-car manufacturer.'

For Agnelli the challenge was to create a trained workforce working with the most advanced machines to build cars in quantity to consistent designs. 'We are at the very beginning of a huge movement of capital, people and labour,' he said. 'I may be wrong, but I am convinced that the motor car will bring about a fundamental change in human society. I am following the trend closely and I intend to take my part in it when the time comes.'

That time came in 1899 when Agnelli learned that the scion of a prominent Piedmontese family, Count Emanuele Cacherano di Bricherasio, was working with a bank and colleagues to fund the creation of a serious car-making company. This meant availability of the capital that Agnelli knew was essential if his goals were to be achieved. The articles of association of just such a company were signed in Count Emanuele's palace on Turin's Via Lagrange on 1 July 1899. Later Giovanni Agnelli was named company secretary and Ludovico Scarfiotti chairman. With the company name Fabbrica Italiana Automobili Torino, the acronym FIAT or Fiat was the happy result.

The outright purchase of the Ceirano designs, patents and personnel served as the basis of the new company. From Ceirano came managing director Enrico Marchesi and technical director Aristide Faccioli. Their first task was to build and equip a new factory on the Corso Dante near the Po River. Astonishingly, the first Fiats were ready before the end of 1899.

Finding engineer Faccioli lacking in the world vision that he felt necessary, too obstinate to take advantage of the rapid technical advances being made by others, Agnelli manipulated his departure in 1901 and replacement by the 50-year-old Giovanni Enrico. His was an experience both broad and deep in all aspects of engineering. 'He was just both in giving praise and in reprimand,' observed

During the Brescia Week races of 1904 Vincenzo Lancia kicks up a dust trail with his 75 HP Fiat.

Felice Nazzaro's success with his Fiat numbered '8B' in Germany's 1907 Kaiserpreis was a coup for the Turin company.

Biscaretti of Enrico, 'and he could maintain the strictest discipline by his calm and pleasant manner. Well do I remember his piercing glance, his long, grey, elegantly curled waxed moustache, the high collar and white tie and his striking figure, seemingly sparse but robust and well proportioned.'

The first manifestation in metal of Giovanni Enrico's skills was the 1902 range with its 12/16 and 24 HP models. The latter, with its 7.2-litre vertical four and chain drive, was the basis for a short-wheelbase special that made its debut in Fiat's backyard, just the other side of the Po, on 23 June 1902 over the tortuous, steep 2.8-mile hill climb from the village of Sassi to the Superga Basilica. Works tester and mechanic Vincenzo Lancia made the climb in six minutes flat, three-quarters of a minute faster than the acknowledged performance car of the day, the 35 HP Mercedes driven by Carlo Adolfo Billia. Lancia followed up on 27 July with

fastest time of the day on the 14.0-mile Susa-Moncenisio climb. A worthy third fastest was Luigi Storero on a race-prepared 12/16 HP Fiat.

Although these were valuable triumphs at home, Giovanni Agnelli knew it was essential to match his Fiats against the world's fastest in the great events. 'He was always passionately fond of the red Fiat racing cars,' recalled Biscaretti, 'even in the days of the company's greatest expansion.' Giovanni Enrico did not hesitate to follow the lead of Wilhelm Maybach at Daimler with more powerful T-head engines in chain-drive chassis to begin building special Fiats for competition.

The racing Fiat of 1904 was the 75 HP four of 14.1 litres developing 76 bhp at 1,200 rpm. It was an easy winner for Lancia in the Susa-Moncenisio hill climb with Cagno third and Storero fifth. In its black paint, as the rules then required, the 75 HP failed to star in the Gordon Bennett Cup in Germany. Two of the cars raced in America's Vanderbilt Cup that year but without success. Nevertheless Paul Satori's timing of 104.4 mph on New York's Empire State track made a powerful impression. Remaining in the States, one car was driven with distinction by Emanuel Cedrino and Ralph DePalma as the 'Fiat Cyclone' in the popular fairground oval races.

Although dubbed the 100 HP model, 1905's racing Fiat developed 110 bhp from its 16.3 litres. Its four-

Numbered '20B', Nazzaro's Fiat won the Targa Florio in 1907.

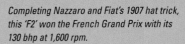

Completing Nazzaro and Fiat's 1907 hat trick, this 'F-2' won the French Grand Prix with its 130 bhp at 1,600 rpm.

In the 1908 French Grand Prix all three Fiats retired including this, the mount of Vincenzo Lancia.

The success of Prince Borghese's Itala in the 1907 Peking-Paris contest produced an international wave of publicity for Pirelli.

Pirelli's Paris branch took full advertising advantage of Campari's victory at Lyon in 1924 driving the Alfa Romeo P2.

PIRELLI

A vital development supporting the successes of Italy's cars at home and abroad was availability of suitable tyres. For Italy this meant Pirelli. After working in the rubber industry in Germany, France and Britain, Giovanni Battista Pirelli founded the company bearing his name in Milan in 1872 at the age of 24 with the aim of making rubber products, which he began the following year. In 1890 he started producing bicycle tyres as prologue to his first tyres specifically for cars in 1901.

Thanks to the bicycle craze many companies made pneumatic tyres, among which Britain's Dunlop and Palmer, France's Michelin and Germany's Continental were prominent in racing. Pirelli's breakthrough to global recognition came in 1907 when it provided the tyres for Prince Borghese's winning Itala in Le Matin's Peking-Paris contest. Understandably Pirelli has kept the telegram from Paris in which the Prince expressed 'extreme satisfaction' with its tyres and added that he had 'consumed' only 16 covers and inner tubes during the journey.

Although Pirelli still had to prove the suitability of its tyres for outright racing, its wares received a boost with the success of Felice Nazzaro on his eponymous mount in the 1913 Targa Florio, run that year in two daily stages as a 606-mile lap of Sicily, and the 1914 Coppa Florio as well. Overshadowing these was the victory in the 1913 French Grand Prix at Amiens by Georges Boillot driving a Pirelli-shod Peugeot. This was an important win for Italian technology in that year's most important race.

In the years to come Pirelli remained an important partner of Italy's racing teams. The Alfas of the 1920s rolled on Pirellis, as did the successful Alfettas of 1950-51 and the Ferraris of champion Alberto Ascari in 1952-53. Ferrari's 1954 Le Mans win was on Pirellis. Its Corsa and Stelvio tyres gave the best control and grip available at the time.

After 1956 Pirelli suspended its Grand Prix racing support, but before shutting down its specialised production it built a season's worth of tyres for loyal user Maserati. Running against Englebert-mounted Ferrari, this contributed materially to Juan Fangio's 1957 world championship on Maserati.

Successes with Lancia in endurance racing and in Formula 2 with Toleman encouraged a return to Formula 1 for Pirelli in 1981. Teams using Pirellis in the early 1980s included Italian squads Osella and Minardi plus Arrows, Fittipaldi, Lotus, Brabham and Benetton. Success was elusive, however. Instead, in addition to its long and successful support of rallying, Pirelli became a force to be reckoned with in the 21st century in endurance events using GT and prototype cars.

cylinder engine was radically new with inclined overhead valves controlled by a spring-returned push-pull rod that operated a rocker arm. When the rod was pulled down by a coil spring it opened the inlet valve and when it was pushed up by the cam the rocker opened the exhaust valve. A transverse leaf spring acted on both valves to close them.

Three of these cars were entered in the second Vanderbilt Cup challenge in 1905 for works drivers Nazzaro and Lancia and for Louis Chevrolet. Leading from the start, after seven laps Vincenzo Lancia was 21 minutes ahead of the second-place Panhard. With less

than 65 miles to go he seemed assured of victory. Pulling out of the Michelin depot following a routine tyre change, his Fiat collided with another car, forcing a 47-minute stop for repairs. A furious Lancia finished fourth. In 1906 he would place second. In September of 1905 Alexandre Cagno's 100 HP Fiat climbed Mount Ventoux in record time to win over Europe's best.

In the late summer of 1907 Giovanni Agnelli sat with friends taking an espresso in Turin's Caffè Allaria, which was newly established as the city's haunt for sporting enthusiasts. On the marble tabletop were three cards which – enigmatic at first glance – bore the legends '20B',

'F2' and '8B'. 'Those who understood smiled,' related Biscaretti, 'others looked somewhat disconcerted.' They symbolised, Agnelli told his friends, 'victories in the three most important races of the year.' These, he added, 'establish our supremacy without question.'

This was no exaggeration. '20B' was Felice Nazzaro's number in the 277-mile Targa Florio on 21 April 1907. The 45-strong field included strong French rivals. In the Sicilian race, said W.F. Bradley, 'the drivers who stood out most prominently were Lancia and Nazzaro, the former bulky, jovial, dominating his car by brute force, the latter slim, elegant, distinguished, delicate of touch, burning with enthusiasm.' Both Fiat-mounted, they took the first two places with Nazzaro leading. Italas were third and fifth.

For the next challenge on 14 June, Germany's Kaiserpreis on a sinuous 73-mile course in the Taunus Mountains, Giovanni Enrico produced cars specially tailored to the event's 8.0-litre engine-size limit. They dominated both the elimination trials and the race proper, Nazzaro winning in car '8B' at 52.6 mph with the other team cars fifth and sixth. Germany's Emperor personally presented the winning trophy.

Enrico developed Fiat's cars for the 2 July 1907 French Grand Prix at Dieppe from his 16.3-litre 100 HP of 1905. They were tuned to cope with a fuel-consumption formula that allowed no more than 30 litres of fuel for every 100 kilometres, equivalent to 9.6 miles per gallon. Only one first-rank competitor fell foul of this limitation: Fiat-mounted Vincenzo Lancia was third on the final lap but pulled up with a dry tank. Felice Nazzaro's Fiat 'F2' was the winner, followed by the Renault of Szisz, the 1906 victor. The fastest lap at 74.6 mph was Nazzaro's as well.

As the rules required, Fiat-mounted Vincenzo Lancia handled his own tyre changes in the 1908 Coppa Florio. He was fifth while team-mate Nazzaro won.

Giovanni Agnelli could take justifiable pride in a season that had seen his cars win the most important races in Italy, Germany and France. In the last-named this was particularly galling for the French, who had created Grand Prix racing with the specific aim of giving more of their manufacturers a shot at victory. 'He realised the enormous publicity value of success by Fiat cars,' Biscaretti said of Agnelli. 'As for the outcome of a race, he was always ready to disarm anyone who did not share his optimism with the usual offer of a 1,000-lire bet, and in those days such a sum was really worth something!'

In the New World too, Fiat finally tasted success. Gentlemanly Ralph DePalma joined the Fiat factory team that captured the 1908 American Grand Prize. Run over a palm-lined 25-mile course on the outskirts of Savannah, this first-ever race in the United States to Grand Prix rules was captured by Louis Wagner, whose Fiat averaged over 65 mph for 403 miles. Felice Nazzaro placed third and DePalma, who led the early laps, was ninth.

Giovanni Enrico, who had never spared himself in his efforts for Agnelli, died in 1909. His successor as technical board member was Turin-born Guido Fornaca, then 39. 'Tall, broad-faced, strong with well-marked features,' Fornaca was described as 'reserved, somewhat introspective, curt almost to the point of seeming rough in manner. He belonged to that strong Piedmontese race of

men who have devoted their efforts to industry and its management and the progress of the nation.'

Fornaca inherited a racing design by Giuseppe Coda under Enrico, for the first time an overhead-camshaft 16-valve four-cylinder engine in the 10.1-litre S61, and evolved it into the 14.1-litre S74 of 1911. Producing 190 bhp at 1,600 rpm, this was the mount of American David Bruce-Brown, still in his teens, when he won the 1911 American Grand Prize at a speed of 74.4 mph for 412 miles. That same year Bruce-Brown drove a Fiat to third place in the inaugural Indianapolis 500-mile race.

Joining Ralph DePalma and Louis Wagner in S74 Fiats at Dieppe for the 1912 running of the French Grand Prix, the young New Yorker made his European debut by taking an early lead and setting the fastest lap. The end of the first day's racing saw Bruce-Brown first, Wagner third and DePalma eighth. In the second day, totalling 956 miles of racing, Bruce-Brown was disqualified. He pushed on to finish an unofficial third with Louis Wagner's Fiat coming in second to George Boillot's Peugeot.

Guido Fornaca's fresh engineering featured in Fiat's entries for the last Grand Prix before the war in 1914. Although unready then, his new ideas would evolve into post-war models that would reassert Fiat as a leader in racing technology.

Bespeaking power and speed, Fiat's Type S74 was the 1911 American Grand Prize winner with David Bruce-Brown.

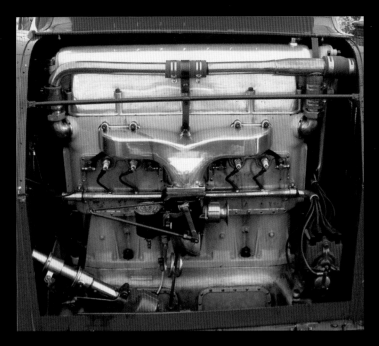

Delivering 190 bhp at 1,600 rpm from its 14.1 litres, the Type 14 engine of Fiat's 1911-12 S74 was an awesome hunk of machinery.

Fiat entries in the 1912 French Grand Prix were for David Bruce-Brown, left, and Louis Wagner. The latter placed his S74 second.

CHAPTER 4

Fiat Sets the Pace

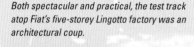

FIAT had a good war. It helped that Italy was on the winning side. Rejecting her alliance with Germany and Austria-Hungary, attracted by the offer of post-war territorial gains, Italy joined the Entente Powers in 1915. Only in her north-east corner was Italian territory occupied during the war. Although the Austro-Hungarian forces forced an incursion, they were thrown back in the battle of Vittorio Veneto, belying the Italian reputation of an ineffectual military.

In this era before strategic bombing, the Fiat factories in Turin worked flat-out during the war on materiel for the fighting forces. Before the war Giovanni Agnelli had bolstered Fiat's position with ancillary enterprises including Riv, to make ball bearings, and joint-venture steel mills. His product portfolio extended into aircraft, ships and railways.

With Fiat outgrowing the Corso Dante factory, a new plant in Turin's Lingotto district was designed by Giacomo Mattè-Trucco. He gave Fiat an epic five-storey manufactory with a test track on its roof.

A new works deserved a new car, which was developed under Guido Fornaca by Carlo Cavalli, who although trained as a lawyer had joined Fiat as a draftsman in 1905. Described as 'pleasant and unassuming', Cavalli contributed as works manager to many of the wartime projects while preparing the Type 501, whose numbering marked a new beginning after the war.

Cavalli's brilliant four-cylinder 501 of 1,460 cc with four-speed transmission established the reputation of Fiat as a maker of lively, versatile and robust family cars. Calling it a car that was 'undoubtedly one of the most remarkable that has ever emanated from this or indeed any other factory,' historian Kent Karslake credited the 501 with 'so perfect a balance in its component parts that it was outstanding among the small cars of its day.'

Remaining in production through 1926, the 501 totted up total production of 66,864 units. It was soon available with a more lively engine and longer gear ratios as the 501 S, of which 2,614 were made. Here was a car that

Both spectacular and practical, the test track atop Fiat's five-storey Lingotto factory was an architectural coup.

FIAT'S TWO-STROKE

Its remarkable U-12 was not the only engine schemed by Fiat's engineers for the new 1.5-litre Grand Prix Formula starting in 1926. They also invested their creativity in a two-stroke engine, one which makes every piston downstroke a firing stroke, unlike the conventional engine that fires only every other stroke. Like some other engineers of the time they felt that this could offer an important advantage.

Based on a concept by Tranquillo Zerbi, Fiat's two-stroke had six vertical cylinders. Within each of them two pistons faced each other crown-to-crown and were connected to two crankshafts, one at the top of the engine and the other at the bottom. The two cranks were geared together at the rear of the engine, where the lower crankshaft drove the clutch.

The layout gave the maximum possible area for the ports, which were apertures in the cylinder walls that were opened and closed by the pistons. The upper pistons controlled the inlet ports, which were fed with air/fuel mixture by a Roots-type blower. The lower pistons uncovered the exhaust ports.

Design work on this Type 451 engine began in 1925. 'The development and experimental testing of this engine constituted a bold endeavour,' wrote Gino Cabutti, 'but one which was not a joy to everyone. Rosso, who was assigned to the test cell, was deafened by it.'

Fiat's two-stroke ran to the remarkable speed of 6,500 rpm and produced a verified 152 bhp. Scipione Treves, who also worked on the project, said that a peak of 170 bhp was achieved. Any value between these numbers would have been respectable power for the first year of the new 1.5-litre Formula. But the Type 451 never reached a level of serviceability that allowed it to be installed in a car, let alone raced. Tragically for posterity it was among the hardware that Fiat scrapped when it stepped out of Grand Prix racing.

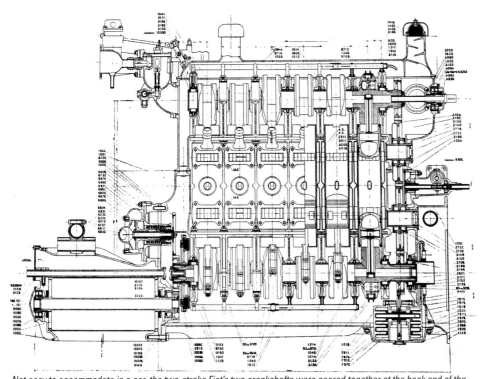

Not easy to accommodate in a car, the two-stroke Fiat's two crankshafts were geared together at the back end of the six-cylinder engine.

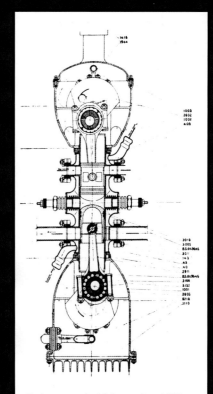

For its two-stroke 1.5-litre engine of 1926 Fiat adopted an opposed-piston layout with inlet ports above and exhaust ports below.

This 501 S Fiat was competing on the Mugello circuit in 1920 between – as the sign said – Florence and Bologna.

Driving a stripped 1914 G.P. Fiat, Antonio Ascari won the 1919 Parma-Poggio di Berceto hill climb.

Italy's motoring enthusiasts could and did take to their hearts for sporting competitions in emulation of the stirring feats of the works cars and drivers. Fiat credits the 501 in all its forms with more than 1,000 such successes.

Some of those stirring Fiat feats were achieved by pre-war cars. One such was the 200 HP racing car. Based on the 1907 Grand Prix model, it was intended for sheer speed for sprints and hill climbs. While keeping the G.P. Fiat's 160 mm stroke its bores were enlarged from 155 to 190 mm to bring displacement to 18,146 cc. Though known as the '200 HP' its actual output was 175 bhp at 1,200 rpm.

In 1908 this awesome car came in handy when the publicity-hungry Selwyn Edge of Napier in Britain invited challengers for his cars over ten laps of the brand-new ultra-fast banked oval at Brooklands in Surrey, by far the world's fastest track. With £250 put up by both parties, a stake of £500 awaited the winner. The challenge was accepted by D'Arcy Baker, Fiat's English importer. For the showdown on Whit Monday, Turin provided not only the 200 HP car but also the skills of Felice Nazzaro.

Edge fielded a Napier named 'Samson' whose six cylinders displaced 17,209 cc, matching it handily against the Fiat thanks to its lighter weight of 3,167 pounds against the Italian car's 3,314 pounds. Both teams had last-minute problems, the Fiat's engine needing a rebuild. Driven by the experienced Frank Newton, the English car made the better start and after two laps was leading Nazzaro, who was making his first competitive start at Brooklands.

During lap three disaster struck 'Samson' in the form of a broken crankshaft. Nazzaro completed the prescribed laps at the modest average of 94.75 mph. On his second lap, however, the track's new electrical timing equipment clocked him at an astonishing 121.64 mph, nearly 19 mph faster than any previous official speed at the track, which had been open since 17 June 1907. Although the subject of immense controversy, some hand timing having been

slower, this stood as the official Brooklands lap record until it was bettered by a Sunbeam V12 in 1922.

In 1921 Brooklands became home to Nazzaro's 200 HP Fiat, which John Duff had found in a London lock-up and bought for £100. In the track's tradition the racer was given a nickname, 'Mephistopheles'. Painted black to suit its name, it compiled an impressive record at the track before being acquired by Ernest Eldridge, who extended its wheelbase and fitted it with a six-cylinder 21,715 cc Fiat A 12 bis aircraft engine of 320 horsepower. April 1924 found Eldridge at Montlhéry where his 146.01 mph two-way average earned Fiat the official international Land Speed Record. This was the first and last time that the celebrated record, the Blue Riband of the automotive world, was held by a car of Italian origin.

Volatile economic conditions after the war were problematic for the creation of new racing cars. Fiat started again with 4.5-litre four-cylinder cars that it had built for the 1914 French Grand Prix, distinguished by being one of the few with four-wheel brakes. In that race two of the three cars had retired while Antonio Fagnano's, running sixth on the penultimate lap, throttled back to 11th and last at the finish.

Fagnano's apparent modesty was attributed to the potentially embarrassing fact that the Fiats had only been allowed to run on the private understanding that if they were successful they would be disqualified. Pre-race checks had shown that over-eager honing of the cylinder bores had made their engines fractionally bigger than the allowable 4.5 litres. Only thanks to Fiat's strong support of the Grand Prix from its first years were its cars permitted to start, this being judged preferable to a mortifying withdrawal.

One of these cars was out as early as August of 1919 when Ferdinando Minoia drove it to the best timing in speed trials on Denmark's Fanø beach. The genial Count Giulio Masetti, who had placed fourth in a Fiat in the 1919 Targa Florio, used one of these Grand Prix models to win the now-classic race in 1921 in record time after a pitched battle with both Mercedes and an up-and-coming Italian marque, Alfa Romeo. This was to be Fiat's one and only Targa success.

Like many other racing-car builders, Fiat was caught on the hop by the reduction in Grand Prix engine size from the 3.0 litres of 1920-21 to 2.0 litres in 1922. Having built new 3.0-litre twin-overhead-cam engines with both four and eight cylinders, Fiat chose the latter, its Type 801, for 1921's two Grands Prix, the French and the newly established Italian race at Brescia. With Italy in the throes of turbulence both economic and political, worker

unrest kept the cars from appearing in France. In Italy they led early, Pietro Bordino setting the fastest lap, but they were hampered by tyre and magneto problems that left Louis Wagner third at the finish behind two French Ballots.

Although too big to race in Europe in 1922, the Type 801 was still useful abroad. Pietro Bordino brought one to America. January 1922 saw Bordino's 115.9 mph take fastest-lap honours on the board track at Beverly Hills. That June he won a 50-mile race at the 1¼-mile Northway bowl at Santa Rosa, also in California.

Rapidly compounding its experience, the Lingotto team under Fornaca was granted great freedom to build new and better racing cars. Carlo Cavalli's contribution was the extensive use of ball and roller crankshaft bearings. Others, such as Delage, had used anti-friction

Updated by Fiat, one of its 1914 Grand Prix cars won the 1921 Targa Florio in the hands of Giulio Masetti.

While Pietro Bordino's Fiat 804 retired from the 1922 French G.P., here, with a broken axle housing, he won that year's Italian Grand Prix.

Monza Park north of Milan. A lone 803 won again at Brescia in June 1923, this time equipped with the novelty of a supercharger. It was thus the first supercharged car to win a race in Europe.

Driving innovation forward at Lingotto under Fornaca and Cavalli were engineers Giulio Cesare Cappa and Tranquillo Zerbi. The last, who joined Fiat in 1919 at the age of 28, was a German-educated engineer who became Cavalli's successor as design chief under Fornaca. Vincenzo Bertarione and Walter Becchia were also in the team with Vittorio Jano, a young engineer who was concerned with racing preparation. Their first racing-car chef-d'oeuvre was the 2.0-litre Type 804 of 1922. Although sixes had been raced before, most successfully by Britain's Napier, this Fiat would be the first car in Grand Prix history to demonstrate that a six could be a competitive racing engine.

Noting the 1914 G.P. success of Mercedes with its engine's water jackets welded of sheet steel around a forged-steel cylinder, Fiat adopted this labour-intensive form of construction for its subsequent racing cars. The 804's six had two groups of three cylinders. It was installed in a superbly profiled body lofted by the company's aeronautical department. Its radiator air inlet was small, to reduce drag. For the same reason its exhaust pipe was contained in a faired shrouding.

Back on Fiat's strength for the 499-mile French Grand Prix on 16 July 1922 was the inimitable Felice Nazzaro, one of the few top drivers who both survived the war and proved able to revive his career after it. After a dominant performance on the road circuit at Strasbourg the winner was Nazzaro's Fiat, which after six hours and seventeen minutes' racing had a margin of nearly an hour over the second-place Bugatti.

Felice Nazzaro took little pleasure in his French success, for his nephew Biagio Nazzaro was killed when a fault in a casting in his 804's rear axle caused an end-over-end crash. So overwhelmingly daunting was the Fiat performance in France that the huge prospective entry for the subsequent Italian G.P. simply melted away. Only Bugattis, Diattos and Heims opposed the Fiats, which won as they pleased with the new star, Pietro Bordino, heading Nazzaro.

In the meantime Fiat's restless racing engineers had been building an even more awesome G.P. car. Cappa led the design of a new 2.0-litre straight eight, the 805. This was akin to the 804 except for its use of a gear train at the rear of the engine, instead of a vertical shaft, to drive two bevel shafts to the overhead cams. Integral with the new engine was the use of a supercharger, an engineering

main bearings in the previous decade, but not for connecting-rod big-end bearings as well. In the new Fiat engines both main bearings and connecting-rod big-ends ran on low-friction rollers, which aided reliability and performance. So novel was this technology that Fiat had to develop precision techniques to make its own rollers.

Half of 3.0 litres being 1.5 litres, Fiat took advantage of some of the components of its Grand Prix car to make four-cylinder engines to compete in the new category for smaller-engined racing cars dubbed *Voiturettes*. Like the larger unit this engine had two overhead valves per cylinder at a vee angle of 102 degrees opening onto a combustion chamber of pure hemispherical form. With good reason this was seen as the most efficient shape, with minimum surface to dissipate heat. Although many pre-war racers had shown four valves per cylinder to be useful, Fiat's successful two-valve designs would establish this as the *beau idéal* for racing-car designers for four decades.

Initially the 1.5-litre four of some 60 horsepower was used in modified 501 chassis as the 501 SS to reap kudos for the new model. Such cars did well in the 1922 Targa Florio. The four also powered a pure racing car, the Type 803, which swept the board, taking the first four places, in a 373-mile race for 1.5-litre cars in the inaugural race meeting on 3 September 1922 at the new circuit in the

1922 FIAT TYPE 804

AN OUTSTANDING TEAM OF ENGINEERS CREATED FIAT'S SIX-CYLINDER TYPE 804 OF 1922. IT SET NEW STANDARDS IN
RACING-CAR DESIGN WITH ITS AERODYNAMICALLY INFLUENCED LINES.

breakthrough that Fiat brought, with its Type 805, to the 1923 French G.P. on a twisty circuit near Tours.

After the war the racing authorities had overlooked reimposition of the ban on forced induction that they had applied in 1914; Fiat was among the first to exploit this loophole. The Wittig vane-type compressor was chosen, driven from the nose of the crankshaft. It brought the 805's power to 130 bhp at 5,500 rpm, well up from the 804's 92 bhp, in an engine that could rev to 6,000 if needed.

In the French race the new car showed stunning speed, lapping at 88 mph and clocking 122 mph on the straight. Pietro Bordino in particular impressed, *The Motor* saying, 'Bordino was amazing on corners. His dashing driving made everyone fear for his safety.' Fiat's three entries took turns leading. But road dust and grit, inhaled by their blowers, wrecked the engines of all the Fiats.

Immediately Cavalli's team set to work on a type of blower that was less easily damaged, the twin-lobed Roots-type supercharger. Only ten days after the race, detail drawings were being made for a Roots supercharger. Like the vane-type blower it was driven from the nose of

Low at the front of its engine was the supercharger of Fiat's Type 803, winner of the 324-mile 1923 Brescia race for Voiturettes.

Pietro Bordino drove his Type 805 Fiat on the road to Tours for the 1923 French G.P, in which he and his team-mates retired.

the crankshaft through a torque-limiting multiple-disc clutch.

The change enhanced both reliability and power, the latter boosted to 150 bhp at 5,500 rpm. It also took Fiat to victory at Monza on 9 September in the 497-mile Grand Prix of Europe and Italy, making it the first to win a Grand Prix race with a supercharged car. Carlo Salamano led Nazzaro to victory in the 1923 Italian G.P. at Monza. He thus scored the first Grand Prix success for a supercharged car. In another Type 805 Pietro Bordino set the fastest lap at a whisker under 100 mph.

So successful were Fiat's innovations that they were quickly adopted by other companies, especially Italy's Alfa Romeo and England's Sunbeam. Although Bordino led early with his 805 in the 1924 French G.P, the newcomers were dominant while all the Fiats retired. With some of its drivers unwell Fiat scratched from its home Grand Prix at Monza. Although not seen as such at the time, this was a decisive act. In the future the marque would only be seen in G.P. racing as a badge on Ferraris.

In 1925 Pietro Bordino returned to America, this time driving an 805 with an intercooler between its frame's dumb irons to cool the compressed charge entering the engine. He finished ninth at Culver City in March 1925 and in April won a 25-mile sprint there with a 133-mph average. Bordino then entered the former G.P. car in the 1925 Indianapolis 500. Qualifying at 107.661 mph, he was eighth on the grid behind a solid wall of supercharged Duesenbergs and Millers. Suffering a hand injury during a pit stop, Bordino was relieved by Antoine Mourne who helped guide the Fiat to a tenth-place finish.

An enigmatic swansong for Fiat in top-line racing was heard at Monza in September 1927. Cappa and Zerbi created the Type 806, the only twelve-cylinder racing car to appear on the track under the 1.5-litre Grand Prix Formula. Two six-cylinder engines were side-by-side on a common crankcase, geared together. Producing 187 bhp at 8,500 rpm, the Roots-supercharged Fiat twelve was installed in a conventional, albeit low-profiled, chassis.

This ambitious car's only race was the rainy Milan Grand Prix of 1927, which was combined with other events at Monza. 'Others led at first in the meeting's Free Formula race', wrote Paul Sheldon, but 'the magnificent Bordino came steaming past into a lead which he held to the end, winning by no less than half a minute after just twenty minutes of racing against the cream of Italy's *Formule Libre* cars.' This was destined to be the 806's only outing. Fiat announced its definitive withdrawal from racing. With all its predecessors, the great car went to the scrapyard.

Next to a Bugatti (12) and Chiribiri (14) Bordino awaits the start of the second heat at a wet Monza in 1927 in Fiat's radical Type 806. He won.

CHAPTER 5

Alfa Romeo Arrives

**Giuseppe Merosi
8 December 1872 - 27 March 1956**

Starting in 1910 Giuseppe Merosi
headed design for Alfa and, after the
war, for Alfa Romeo.

IN 1924 Fiat technology triumphed in the French Grand Prix at Lyons – but not in a Fiat. Born in 1891 at San Giorgio Canavese 21 miles north of Turin, engineer Vittorio Jano was Piemontese through and through. He worked at Fiat for twelve years before moving to Milan's Alfa Romeo, for whom he designed a Fiat-like straight-eight racing car. This was the Alfa Romeo P2 that dominated Grand Prix racing under the 2.0-litre formula and raced again successfully at the end of the decade.

Seldom has a successful racing car been moulded from such unpromising clay. Alfa Romeo's earlier racing efforts had attracted only amiable toleration. What more could be expected from a company in Milan, far from the expert resources in Turin, that had struggled in its early years as an outpost of French car maker Darracq? Indeed, as a humble maker of taxis?

Having enjoyed success with his taxis in Paris and London, French pioneer Alexandre Darracq decided to chance his hand in the growing Italian market. Exporting built-up taxis was out of the question because they attracted high customs duties in those years when more than the high Alps blocked imports into Italy. To evade the tariff Darracq shipped his cars in dismantled form to the port of Naples where they were assembled by a company he established in February 1906. At the end of that year he set up a base for sales and service at a district called 'Portello', after a nearby gateway, on the north-west outskirts of Milan.

Alexandre Darracq's venture was ill-starred. Vehicles that coped well with the metalled roads of the benign northern capitals struggled on Italy's hills and loose surfaces. The financial crisis of 1907 was another rod for the Frenchman's back. In the autumn of 1909 Darracq declared his company's closure. Seeing possibilities in the Portello operation, a group led by the Italian company's head, Ugo Stella, obtained a half-million-lire line of credit from the Banca Agricola di Milano and prepared to make cars on their own.

At the beginning of 1910 Portello's gates opened on the Società Anonima Lombarda Fabbrica Automobili, the last four letters spelling ALFA or Alfa. To design new cars of this name the directors hired Giuseppe Merosi, just turned 37. Born not far from the Po at Piacenza, tall at more than six feet, the fashionably moustached Merosi trained at his city's technical institute. In 1905 he spent a year with Fiat in Turin, then headed design for car-maker Bianchi in Milan.

Although his degree was as a surveyor, Merosi was both able as a creative designer and adept as a draftsman, related Griff Borgeson: 'Working on a huge upright drawing board, he would lay out his key points. Then he would draw all of his horizontal lines. With these done, he would draw all of his vertical lines, zip, zip, zip – and then tie it all together.'

Merosi's first two Alfas were the 15/20 of 2.4 litres and the 20/30 with 4.1 litres, both conventional side-valve four-cylinder designs. Nevertheless the 20/30 had sporting potential that was realised after the war in its 20/30 ES Sport version, both as a limited-production model for Italy's bloods and as a mount for the company's works drivers. Sporting ambition was also shown by the Type 40/60 of 1913 with overhead valves serving its 6.1 litres. One accounted for the first appearance of an Alfa in a major race, Merosi colleague Nino Franchini's third place in the 1914 Coppa Florio behind a Scat and the winning Nazzaro. Substantially updated, in 1921 the model in racing trim was timed at 91.7 mph over a flying kilometre at Brescia.

By far Giuseppe Merosi's most ambitious pre-war effort was a pure four-cylinder racing engine for the 4.5-litre Grand Prix formula that took effect in 1914. By prevailing standards its design was very up-to-date with twin overhead camshafts, driven by a combination of gears and chains, and four valves per cylinder. Its power was moderate, however, 88 bhp at 2,950 rpm, and it was installed in a tall, antiquated-looking chassis. Worst of all the car was unready for that year's French Grand Prix and so failed to take part in the last such classic race before the war.

Though making more than 200 cars yearly by 1912 and receiving orders for military equipment, the Società Alfa was still operating on credit. The bulk of its obligations were now held by an affiliate of the Banca Italiana di Sconto, which had been set up at the end of 1914 to fund projects for the military. Effectively controlling Alfa, the bank decided to place management of the company in the hands of entrepreneur Nicola Romeo.

Short, bald and luxuriously moustached, the Neapolitan Romeo was 39 years old in 1915 when he added Alfa to his portfolio. Based in Milan since 1902, he had built up substantial companies which made equipment for mining and rail electrification. Romeo

Nicola Romeo
28 April 1876 - 15 August 1938
Immensely creative as a proprietor and executive, Nicola Romeo took Milan's Alfa into his group of companies in 1915.

A variety of sporting Alfa Romeos posed outside the plant in May 1922. Enzo Ferrari is in the second from left.

In 1921's Targa Florio Giuseppe Campari was third in this much-modified Type 40-60 Alfa Romeo.

In its racing version the 4.3-litre Type 20-30 ES Alfa Romeo was useful, Ugo Sivocci placing ninth in the 1922 Targa Florio.

swiftly converted the Portello premises to production for the military. When in 1918 he restructured his activities his Alfa car operation was subsumed into the Società Anonima Ing. Nicola Romeo & Co. The cars soon became known as Alfa Romeos.

With automobile production only one of his manifold activities, Nicola Romeo saw it primarily as a means of promoting his businesses. He asked Merosi to take the 4.5-litre Grand Prix engine out of mothballs, update it and install it in a more appropriate chassis. With such a car Giuseppe Campari was the outright winner of the 242-mile Mugello Circuit races of 1920 and 1921. Second and third respectively in the Tuscan event in 1921 were Alfa Romeo employees Enzo Ferrari and Ugo Sivocci.

Getting back into its stride as a car maker in 1922, the year in which Italy's king asked Benito Mussolini's Fascists to form a new government, Alfa Romeo began production of Giuseppe Merosi's *capolavoro*, his six-cylinder Type RL. Although its displacement of 2,916 cc had been influenced by the 3.0-litre Grand Prix limit that was in effect during its gestation, starting in 1920, the RL was not in fact raced under those rules. In Britain the RL's performance was likened to that of a 3.0-litre Bentley, which was no small compliment.

Although principally built and sold as a road car of considerable sporting style, a total of 2,640 in all versions being made to 1927, the RL also served as the basis of competition cars raced by the factory. With vertical overhead valves operated by pushrods, the six normally had four main bearings but was built in a seven-bearing version for racing with capacities up to 3.6 litres. Through 1923 these competed with oval radiator cowls much like those introduced by Ferdinand Porsche's racing Austro Daimler's in 1922. Elegant veed radiators were seen from 1924 onward.

Competing with 3.2-litre engines the Type RL's finest hour was the April 1923 Targa Florio. Ugo Sivocci won the 268-mile Sicilian race with Antonio Ascari second and Giulio Masetti fourth. Ascari should have won easily but in a bizarre incident he slid and stalled his engine almost in sight of the finish line. With push starts not allowed he lost 14 minutes rectifying his starting apparatus so that he could motor home a frustrated second ahead of Minoia's Steyr.

With only 17 starters, 'little foreign competition and a reduced average speed,' wrote W.F. Bradley, this Targa Florio 'was one of the dull races.' Nevertheless it was a triumph for Alfa in a classic event that brought the company

Pictured in October 1924 with his new Type P2, Vittorio Jano was Portello's new racing-car designer. Mechanic Giulio Ramponi is on the right.

Named after its 1923 success in Sicily, Alfa Romeo's 1924 RL Targa Florio had to settle for second in that classic race behind a Mercedes.

Drawing on his Fiat experience Vittorio Jano created this 2.0-litre straight eight for the P2. Its Roots-type blower was at the crank nose.

Introduced in 1923, the four-leaf clover identifying a works-entered racing Alfa Romeo looked good on the bonnet of the Grand Prix P2.

a wave of positive publicity. It needed this, for since 1922 Romeo's enterprises were in the hands of the Banca Nationale di Credito, a new entity created by the government to sweep up the wreckage of the Banca Italiana di Sconto, which collapsed spectacularly in 1921 while holding more than $4 million of Nicola Romeo's debts. Although the new BNC sold off several of Romeo's properties, it kept his car company going.

Convinced by the kudos gained for Alfa by the 1923 Targa success that participation in top-line racing was a Good Thing, helping to promote both his cars and his companies, Romeo approved Merosi's plan to build a new Grand Prix car to compete under the 2.0-litre formula. Gestating since the autumn of 1922, Merosi's Type P1 looked the goods with its low profile and long louvred bonnet. Under the latter, however, was a six-cylinder engine whose design seemed alarmingly agricultural with two separated three-cylinder blocks and a remotely mounted gear drive, at the rear, to its twin overhead camshafts. The P1's 93 bhp paled in comparison to the 112 claimed by Fiat for its 2.0-litre six of a year earlier.

Debut for the P1 was 1923's Italian Grand Prix in Monza's second season. Although the race was set for 9 September, practice began on 12 August. It was marred by two accidents, one killing the riding mechanic of a Fiat and the other fatally injuring Targa winner Ugo Sivocci, whose mechanic escaped death. As Austro Daimler had done the year before in similar circumstances, Alfa Romeo withdrew its team as a tribute to poor Sivocci. It is unlikely, however, that their pace would have discomfited the latest eight-cylinder supercharged Fiats. The withdrawal may have been as much strategic as respectful.

The inadequacies of Merosi's design were evident to engineer Romeo. Soon after the Monza disaster he sat with members of his racing team. Whom did they know, he asked, who could produce a successful Grand Prix car? Among them were Luigi Bazzi, recently arrived from Fiat, and Enzo Ferrari, who had recruited Bazzi. The latter sang the praises of Vittorio Jano (pronounced 'Yarno'). With Fiat since 1911 as a protégé of Carlo Cavalli, Jano had headed a design group there since 1921. Working closely with Tranquillo Zerbi, he left his fingerprints on the 501 and all the latest racing cars. An approach was made to this promising prospect.

Now 32, Jano was wedded to Fiat and Turin. His mechanical aptitude had been spotted and encouraged by his father, technical chief at the Turin arsenal. Young Jano was reluctant to leave hearth, home and Fiat's world-beating racing cars for a job in Milan, which all good Turinese disparaged as a frivolous environment. However the offer of a doubling of his salary appealed, as did the offer of accommodation and a bonus scheme. By October Vittorio Jano was at work in Portello assisted by designer Secondo Molino, another ex-Fiat engineer.

The newcomer's assignment was chiefly racing cars, with Giuseppe Merosi remaining in charge of Alfa's production models. The two men worked harmoniously, recalled mechanic Giulio Ramponi: 'They respected each other and were great friends. In terms of seriousness, meticulousness and patience, both had the same mentality.' Recognising, however, the arrival of a striking new talent – for at the end of 1924 Jano was asked to design a touring car for Alfa – Merosi resigned his post in January of 1926. In his seventies he was rehired as a troubleshooter for Alfa Romeo's industrial products, at which he proved proficient.

Jano's new regime was a dash of cold water for Portello's racers. Mechanic Giovanni Battista Guidotti told Doug Nye that under Merosi, on the test bed, they took full-power readings with a run of only thirty seconds because any longer would risk the engine. When Jano saw

ANTONIO ASCARI

Alfa's commercial director Giorgio Rimini, left, joined with Antonio Ascari, centre, and Giuseppe Campari in 1924.

One of three brothers and a sister born near Mantua, Antonio Ascari began racing seriously in 1919 at the age of 32. By 1920 he was driving the Alfa Romeos with which he would be indelibly associated. Named general agent for Milan AND Lombardy, Ascari's commercial links with Alfa helped him influence its product policy. In 1921 he inspired Alfa's launch of its 20/30 ES Sports, which not only sold well but also served as a basis for racing cars that could hold the fort until the pukka P2 designed by ex-Fiat man Vittorio Jano was ready to compete in 1924.

The breakthrough driving season for Antonio Ascari, called 'blond and bull-like' with the bold jaw of an Egyptian sphinx, was 1924. In June at Cremona he won a 200-mile race at a speed just over 100 mph with the Alfa P2 and was clocked at 121 mph over 10 kilometres – impressive for a car of only 2.0 litres. He was not, a reporter wrote, one of the 'many over-inflated balls' among the drivers of the day. Ascari represented a 'school of his own' with a style that was 'calm, safe, vigorous and valorous'. Later that year he won the Italian G.P. at Monza, then in its third year, and in 1925 he was victorious at Spa in the European Grand Prix.

The calmness and safety of Ascari's style were sometimes in dispute. Monza's officials went so far as to warn Alfa that the driver would be unwelcome there unless he moderated his 'impetuous' style and stopped cornering 'dangerously'. 'You see,' explained the driver himself, 'the difficult thing is not letting yourself – how can I say? – be tempted...charmed by speed. It's like being in a big tube. But you have to resist.'

Journalist Sandro Ferretti said at the time that Ascari's 'apparent audacity was the fruit of the methodical training that he conducted, scrupulously and zealously, over the route of every race.' He knew the road so well, in other words, that he exploited it more fully than less assiduous drivers could.

Antonio Ascari brought both an 'exceptional physique and inextinguishable passion' to his race driving, Ferretti continued, adding, 'the smile on his lips, a bit sceptical, was reflection of his profound generosity. When he spoke of his family, his broad face was illuminated by a serene and radiant glow.' He welcomed his son Alberto to the pits and the races, where he posed in his sailor's suit with his successful father.

Alberto was only five in 1923 when, on park roads in Milan, his father perched him on his thighs, presented him with the steering wheel of his RL Alfa and said, 'Now you drive'. Undaunted, already experienced with his own pedal car, the lad gripped and turned with confidence. 'He'll be an ace,' bragged his proud dad. Later at Monza after a day of testing the Alfa P2 young Alberto again perched in his father's lap to guide one of Italy's finest racing cars around its newest track.

Antonio Ascari was in search of a hat-trick third G.P. win in a row when, on a Friday, he left his family at their villa on Lago Maggiore to travel to Paris to compete in the French Grand Prix over the 7.7-mile Montlhéry track on its outskirts. The race started at 8:00 am on Sunday the 26th. With the rest of the Alfa team Ascari had already tested at Montlhéry, honing his precise knowledge of the demanding circuit. This helped him leap into an immediate and commanding lead.

After a 15th-lap pit stop for fuel and rear tyres Ascari retained the lead. A light rain began falling. Starting his 23rd lap he gestured, expressing confidence, with his right hand in front of his pit. He did not complete the lap. On a fast left-hand bend a knock-off hub of Antonio Ascari's P2 clipped a post retaining wooden palisades and went out of control, flipping several times before coming to rest upside-down in a ditch at the side of the road, carrying the driver with it. Grievously wounded, Ascari died before his ambulance had travelled a kilometre from the gates of the circuit. It was not yet afternoon. In his honour the Alfa team retired its other two cars, one of which was leading.

Restyled to resemble Alfa Romeo's later models, this Type P2 was entered for Achille Varzi in the 1930 Targa Florio.

Number 1 exemplified the status of Antonio Ascari in the Alfa Romeo P2 before the 19 October 1924 Italian Grand Prix, which he won easily.

this 'he said "No, No, No" and took the throttle and opened it wide and hung a weight on it. It was around five o'clock in the afternoon. He said, "Now, I'm going home for a bite to eat. Don't touch the throttle and call me at home about eight o'clock to tell me how it's going." We were flabber-gasted.'

Equally flabbergasting was the need to have a team of cars ready for the French Grand Prix, scheduled for 3 August 1924. 'Jano took command in Milan,' Enzo Ferrari recalled, 'established an iron military discipline and in scant months created the P2 from scratch.' Guidotti was adamant that Jano brought no Fiat drawings with him. If that were so he had a phenomenal memory, or his sidekick Molino brought the drawings, because the very detail of the new P2 engine was identical to that of Fiat's Type 805. It produced 145 bhp at 5,500 rpm.

Instead of the 805's dimensions of 60 x 87.5 mm, Jano chose 61 x 85 mm for his P2. Instead of a combination of spur gears and shafts to drive the twin camshafts, he used spur gears alone. Instead of combining the steel-jacketed cylinders in blocks of four he chose blocks of two to reduce the rate of manufacturing loss from unsatisfactory cylinder groups. Otherwise the two straight eights were virtually identical with their ten roller main bearings, finger-type cam followers, triple valve springs and front-mounted superchargers. When Fiat's Pietro Bordino first saw the cars he said to one of the Alfa drivers, 'Eh! If you need some spare parts, just come and ask us!'

The engine first ran in March 1924. So pleased was Antonio Ascari with the unpainted P2's baptismal canter around the Portello courtyard on 2 June that he urged its entry for a 200-mile race over the fast Cremona road circuit only a week later. Wielding ample authority as Alfa's Milan distributor, Ascari was listened to by Nicola Romeo. Brushing aside Jano's protests that the car was virtually untested, Ascari took it to Cremona. He won in a virtual demonstration at 98.3 mph and covered a timed ten kilometres, six miles, at 121.18 mph.

'We were all very surprised and delighted by the sudden success,' said Guidotti. 'Even Jano seemed a little surprised that his new car had gone so well and won at Cremona.' They had little time to reflect on this, because Ascari demanded an all-out effort to prepare four cars for the French classic less than two months later. 'Every engineer, technician and fitter was called in to build the team of cars,' Guidotti recalled.

The result, said Jano, was 'Alfa's birth announcement in the world of Grand Prix racing.' Although only three of the cars started the 503-mile race on the Lyon circuit, Enzo Ferrari being unwell, the P2s of Ascari and Campari took command after shrugging off an early challenge by Bordino's Fiat. Ascari retired while leading just before the finish, leaving the win to Giuseppe Campari with Louis Wagner fourth behind two V12 Delages. Alfa had achieved that most unusual feat, a victory in a great classic race for a new car on its first attempt.

Like the racing cars of 1923, the works P2s of 1924 carried a distinctive emblem on their bonnets. This was a green four-leaf clover in a white triangle, set against Alfa's characteristically deep-hued red. This attractive hallmark of a factory-entered car survived for many future decades of competition cars from Portello.

For the rest of the 2.0-litre Grand Prix formula, expiring after 1925, the Alfas dominated. Their only loss in a major race was in France in 1925, when the team was withdrawn after Antonio Ascari's fatal crash. Fortunately – if that word can be used – riding mechanics were no longer carried. Victories were tallied in Italy in 1924 and in Belgium and Italy in 1925. In that year Alfa easily annexed the new World Grand Prix Championship, in honour of which it encircled its badge with a laurel wreath.

With a new 1.5-litre G.P. formula taking effect in 1926, this was the cue of the controlling bank, the BNC, to forbid the building of new Alfa Romeo racing cars. After the new rules proved less than a smashing success, the international

racing authority, the AIACR, threw up its well-manicured hands and offered what amounted to Free Formula rules for 1928. Seizing the day, Alfa Romeo dusted off its P2 racing cars and began entering them on behalf of drivers such as Giuseppe Campari and Achille Varzi.

Many successes resulted. None was of greater impact than 26-year-old Varzi's victory in the 1930 Targa Florio after five straight years of blue Bugatti domination. By then the old cars were updated in both suspension and body shape to resemble the more current 6C 1750 Gran Sport model while their supercharging systems were modified and new alcohol-blend fuels used to bring their power to 175 bhp at 5,500 rpm. In 1930 Tazio Nuvolari was driving P2 Alfas for the Scuderia Ferrari, formed by the former racing driver Enzo Ferrari in 1929. In due course the ambitious Ferrari would have car-building ideas of his own.

On 4 May 1930 former motorcycle racer Achille Varzi roared past the start/finish crowds in his Alfa P2 to win the Targa Florio.

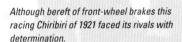

Feisty Independents

CHAPTER 6

Although bereft of front-wheel brakes this racing Chiribiri of 1921 faced its rivals with determination.

THE unique character of Italy's cars and drivers stems from their environment. The Italian peninsula is mountainous. The Alps crumple the northern terrain while the Apennines raise barriers down its spine. Adapting to these conditions, Italian cars have good brakes for their respective classes. As well, in the years before World War Two, they tended to have low intermediate gear ratios. While ideal for hilly terrain, they were not optimum for export markets where level roads allowed higher speeds.

Thanks to this topography Italy is a paradise for hill climbs. From top to toe of the Italian boot, the most glorious roads twist and turn to passes and mountain tops. In sparsely populated areas it was no great inconvenience to close a road for a few hours on a weekend to attract racing enthusiasts – and their hard cash – to compete in a hill climb. Many different classes allowed a generous allocation of trophies. The local auto club organised the event, much to the pleasure of the chamber of commerce. With competitors

fêted as well, awarded prizes and fussed over by local beauties, everybody was happy.

Some of these hill climbs have already figured in our narrative, the Sassi-Superga and Susa-Moncenisio for example. The former was held from 1902 to 1960 and the latter, west of Turin from Susa to the French border en route to the Mont Cenis pass, from 1902 to 1953. Others figuring in Italy's long history of racing are the Trento-Bondone, Aosta-Gran San Bernardo, Catania-Etna, Bolzano-Mendola, Vermicino-Rocca di Papa and Parma-Poggio di Berceto climbs. Still a vital element of Italian motor sports, hill climbs are the accessible heart and soul of the nation's racing.

Unlike Anglo-Saxons, Italians do not distinguish hill climbs from circuit races. To them a *corsa* is a *corsa* and both qualify. The Germans are similar in this respect. Hill climbs require sharp reactions and first-class judgement, competing against the clock. This is good training for a would-be racing driver. On the road circuits – of which Italy had and has many – they next learned racecraft and endurance. The latter was especially important in early events that stretched over five or six hours.

Thus it was that although they never attained the heights of the sport, the marques Chiribiri and OM had many opportunities to shine in domestic events, on

Amedeo 'Deo' Chiribiri was fastest of the team of three Chiribiris in the May 1921 Circuit of Garda, placing third behind two Bugattis.

occasion brightly. For the delightfully named Chiribiri, which styled itself the 'small aristocrat', this was in the popular 1.5-litre category in which the marque scored many hill climb and racing class successes. The hill climb wins included most of the venues above for the racing Chiribiris, which were active from 1922 through 1928.

The name came from the founder, Antonio Chiribiri, a Venetian who settled in Turin in 1910 to produce aero engines. He was inveigled into the automobile business in 1914 by an Italian noble who soon lost interest, whereupon from 1915 Chiribiri started making cars in his own name. Certainly prompted by his son Amedeo, who drove his father's cars under the nickname 'Deo', Chiribiri began racing its products after the war. Others who drove them included Turin-dwelling Englishman, Jack Scales and, in 1923 in his first car competitions, racing motorcyclist, Tazio Nuvolari.

Most competitive were the Monza-type Chiribiris, special racing cars with twin-cam four-cylinder engines introduced in 1922. They produced 72 bhp from their 1.5 litres unsupercharged and 93 bhp with the blowers – the Monza Corsa version – used later in their careers. One of the marque's most loyal, indeed, dogged, exponents was Luigi 'Gigi' Plate, who raced his Chiribiri whenever and wherever possible. In July 1925 he was rewarded by outright victory in the 162-mile Coppa Vinci at Mount Peloritani near Sicily's Messina.

In 1927 Chiribiri closed down, its works taken over by Lancia. A similar fate awaited Brescia-based OM, which stopped making passenger cars in 1930 and was absorbed by Fiat in 1933 to become part of its commercial-vehicle portfolio. Named Officine Meccaniche, simply 'Mechanical Workshops', the company that produced OM cars was the result of several mergers of firms which

In 1921's Parma-Poggio di Berceto hill climb 'Deo' Chiribiri was at the wheel of one of his company's race-prepared cars.

made railway equipment. In 1917 OM acquired the Züst car company and its plants in both Milan and Brescia.

Although the first OMs, made in 1920 to designs by an Austrian engineer, were only 1.3-litre fours, it was in the 2.0-litre category that OM came to fame on both road and track. The two-litre OMs were sixes, their engines designed by Verona's Ottavio Fuscaldo. At first glance they were banal, with simple side valves instead of the increasingly fashionable overhead valves, but closer examination revealed a rugged yet light and superbly balanced crankshaft that allowed stimulatingly smooth and high revolutions for a road car of the era, up to 4,500 rpm.

Introduced in 1923, the six-cylinder OM was Type 665, the first numeral standing for the number of cylinders and the second two for the bore diameter. Also

known as the Superba, it began to appear in Italian competitions in 1924. In 1925 OM boldly ventured abroad to compete in the third edition of the demanding 24-hour race at Le Mans. This showed great confidence in the cars from Brescia. They justified it, two OMs tying for fourth place in 1925 and finishing fourth and fifth in 1926. This won for OM and drivers Ferdinando Minoia and Jules Foresti the second edition of the Rudge-Whitworth Cup for the best performance over two successive races.

Also competing in the early 1920s was another Turin marque, FAST or Fast. Has any sporting car ever had a more appropriate name? The acronym came from Fabbrica Automobili Sport Torino, the creation in 1919 of Arturo Concaris. To designs by Alberto Orasi, who undertook a restructuring of the company after the financial crisis of 1922, Fast produced a 2.9-litre overhead-valve four.

Early auguries were good for Fast. Alberto Conelli won 1920's Aosta-Gran San Bernardo hill climb with one, company chief Concaris placing third. After the company's reorganisation Fast entered the 1924 Targa Florio with its new 2S model, capable of 75 mph, but placed only 18th and 20th overall. In the end 'fast' applied only to the company's dissolution, which took place in 1925.

In May 1926 Milan and Turin gave up the custom of driving on the left within the city limits while the rest of the

Heavy retouching doesn't obscure the effort of Jack Scales in his Type Monza Chiribiri while winning the 1.5-litre class in 1922's Aosta-Gran San Bernardo hill climb.

nation drove on the right. With 170,000 cars now on Italy's roads, traffic density made discretion the better part of valour. Nevertheless Italian cars of quality continued to have their steering wheels on the right well into the 1950s, suiting them well to racing on Europe's clockwise circuits.

Nineteen twenty-six also found a group of enthusiasts in Brescia pondering the question of what could be done to enhance Italy's prestige in the motor-sports world. Neither Fiat nor Alfa Romeo had elected to take part in the new 1.5-litre Grand Prix formula while émigré Italian Bugatti was cleaning up with his blue cars. Italian racing red needed a boost. They came up with the idea of a race from Brescia to Rome and return. Fantastic though it sounded, the Brescia quartet gained the backing of Mussolini's Fascist government, which loved the idea. They even deployed 25,000 soldiers to back up the local constabularies in policing the route.

A Brescian idea needed Brescian support, which OM provided with a team of three sixes. Although a Type RL SS Alfa Romeo led at Rome and another was running third, both retired on the final legs. This left the way clear for a one-two-three finish by the OM team. Senator Giovanni Silvestri, OM's president, posed proudly with the victors, the pairing of Ferdinando Minoia with Giuseppe Morandi. The latter was second overall the following year, when OMs dominated the 2.0-litre class. Indeed, in the 1928 Mille Miglia the first *eight* 2.0-litre finishers were OMs. The same applied in the 1930 race but in the 3.0-litre class with the OM entries bored out to 2.2 litres.

With such records, among many other successes, it is difficult to gainsay the conclusion of racing historian Edward Eves about the OMs that 'all told they were probably the most successful side-valve competition cars ever built.' Eves may have been overlooking American engines when he wrote this – or perhaps not. OM also enthusiastically embraced supercharging for its later sports and racing models.

To OM's credit it grasped the thorny nettle of a full-blown contender for 1.5-litre Grand Prix racing. This had a straight-eight engine comprising eight individual cylinder units on a crankcase full of roller bearings, topped by twin camshafts and Roots-supercharged. This Type 856's sole proper Grand Prix outing was in the very last race of the 1.5-litre era, the Italian G.P. on 4 September 1927. Over 435 rainy miles at Monza, Morandi's OM was second and Minoia's fourth. There were only four finishers in this swansong for the formula in Europe.

Although dismissed by historian Michael Sedgwick as 'the least sporting of the leading Italian makes', Milan's

Bianchi had at least a fitful career on the tracks. In his native Milan, Edoardo Bianchi established his first workshop in 1885 at the age of 20. He was soon a bicycle maker and, from 1900, a producer of motorised tricycles. Bianchi motorcycles became some of Italy's finest, attracting such eminent riders and future auto aces as Tazio Nuvolari, Achille Varzi, Dorino Serafini and Alberto Ascari.

Proper cars began leaving the Bianchi works in 1906. In 1907 the factory essayed entries in Germany's Kaiserpreis. Though unsuccessful, Bianchi had among its drivers Carlo Maserati, former head of Fiat's testing department. An entry in the 1908 Coppa Florio produced a ninth-place finish, again for Maserati.

After the war Bianchi produced a brace of its overhead-valve 2.0-litre fours kitted out as proper racing cars. Bartolomeo 'Meo' Costantini, soon to win fame at Bugatti, drove one to third place in Monza's Autumn

Far from Italy's sunshine in the 1930 Tourist Trophy at Ulster the supercharged OM of Giulio Ramponi could place no higher than 15th.

This racing version of OM's six-cylinder 2.0-litre road car was driven by Renato Balestrero to seventh in the 1926 Targa Florio.

In 1924 Captain Alistair Miller raced this Bianchi at Britain's Brooklands circuit. It lapped the banked oval at 92.2 mph.

SAN GIUSTO

Benito Mussolini's Fascist party swept convincingly to power in the elections of April 1924. In that same year, in the seaport city of Trieste, a rear-engined sports car was being produced that was as advanced in its technology as any in the world.

Dating from the Fifth century, a basilica high on the central hill of Trieste was later dedicated to Saint Justus, a Roman missionary who became the first Bishop of Rochester and the fourth Archbishop of Canterbury in the Seventh century. Called 'San Giusto' in Italian, he became the namesake of a car produced in Trieste by the San Giusto Fabbrica Automobili S.A., founded by Cesare Beltrami. The San Giusto bristled with innovative features.

Here was a small car with a rectangular-section backbone frame that carried an air-cooled four-cylinder engine mounted behind the passenger compartment and driving through an integral four-speed gearbox. Its in-line 748 cc engine was topped by a cooling chamber supplied with air by a shaft-driven axial-flow fan. Vertically finned, the engine's cylinders sat on an aluminium crankcase and had side inlet valves and overhead pushrod-operated exhaust valves.

Geometrically the San Giusto's suspension was well in advance of its epoch and more sophisticated than anything that would be produced in the next twenty years. Each 28-inch wire wheel was suspended by long, wide-spaced parallel wishbones that would have suited a Grand Prix car of the 1960s. Springing was by top-mounted transverse leaf springs.

Appearing at motor shows in Italy from 1922 through 1924, the advanced San Giustos were produced in numbers thought not to exceed the fingers on two hands. Elegant boat-tailed roadster bodies with sweeping wings were fitted to the two-seaters, whose sporty looks weren't matched by the modest 16 bhp their engines developed at only 2,200 rpm. The chassis could easily have coped with much more power. The advanced San Giusto represents a great lost opportunity for Italian motor sports.

With its backbone frame and all-independent wishbone suspension the San Giusto of 1922-24 was as advanced as any car in the world.

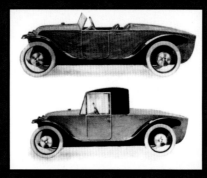

San Giusto buyers had the choice of open or closed coupé body styles.

Axial-flow cooling blower and overhung rear transaxle were advanced design features of the San Giusto.

Grand Prix over 249 miles in October 1922. Later Alfieri Maserati raced Bianchis, as did Tazio Nuvolari, Italian champion on Bianchi's motorcycles. He drove a sports Bianchi in the first Mille Miglia. On 13 April 1924, covering 139 miles on a circuit near Genoa, Tazio piloted a Bianchi when scoring his first outright victory in a four-wheeled vehicle.

At the upper end of the size scale in the 1920s was Isotta-Fraschini, renowned for its big eight-cylinder luxury carriages. Before the war, however, the Milan firm's products enjoyed a sporting presence. Its sublimely evocative name was the result of an alliance between engineer Vincenzo Fraschini and lawyer Cesare Isotta to sell Renault products in Italy. By 1902 the company was making cars in its own right, designed with the help of Fraschini's brothers Oreste and Antonio together with Ludovico Prinetti, formerly of pioneering company Prinetti & Stucchi.

After a restructuring of the company in 1904 its chief engineer in 1905 became Giustino Cattaneo, former

The third Targa Florio in May 1908 found Vincenzo Trucco the winner for Isotta-Fraschini with Alfieri Maserati his riding mechanic.

colleague of Italian pioneer Enrico Bernardi. He progressed along solid T-head-engine Mercedes lines, producing an 8.0-litre four of 70 bhp at 1,400 rpm. In the hands of Vincenzo Trucco this model took Isotta-Fraschini to victory in the 185-mile 1908 Targa Florio, defeating a factory team from Fiat. Trucco's riding mechanic was Alfieri Maserati, who had followed his brothers Carlo and Bindo to the company on Milan's Via Monterosa.

Trucco and Maserati were on the I-F strength for another 1908 event, the Grand Prix des *Voiturettes* in Dieppe. Framed to encourage speedy small cars, its rules admitted four-cylinder engines for the first time, limiting their cylinder bores to 65 mm. They would compete against single- and twin-cylindered cars perfected in previous such races. That Isotta-Fraschini would enter such a far-away contest was a sign of the interest in the company that had been taken by France's Lorraine-

Dietrich in the wake of 1907's sharp depression.

Working under Cattaneo, Giuseppe Stefanini was entrusted with the design of a team of cars for the 286-mile race on 6 July. Choosing the new four-cylinder option, he rejected the full 65 mm bore with dimensions of 61.8 x 100 mm for 1,200 cc. A vertical shaft and bevel gears at the front drove a single overhead camshaft which operated vertical valves set in pockets flanking the combustion chamber. Two ball bearings supported its crankshaft. With four speeds forward, cardan-shaft drive and delicate proportions, Stefanini's Type FE Isotta was a brilliant foreshadowing of the future potential of the small-engined sporting car.

Though winning outright was not an option against the established French contestants, Isotta-Fraschini could be proud of defeating five other four-cylinder marques to place eighth overall, best of the fours, from 47 starters. The

successful driver was Alfieri Maserati, accompanied by Girolamo Pontiroli.

Astonishingly, this superb little I-F had little commercial issue. As the Type FENC, with its engine enlarged to 1,327 cc, it was built in a batch of 100 for sale. A Milanese journalist gave it the highest praise, contrasting its agility with the stolidity of bigger cars. 'This small, swift vehicle induces a feeling of intoxication in the driver,' he wrote. 'All the pleasant sensations which the automobile normally provides are infinitely multiplied. Those who are really enthusiastic about cars must find extreme satisfaction here.'

Giuseppe Stefanini was also the architect of an Isotta-Fraschini at the other extreme, the Type KM, built, said Angelo Tito Anselmi, 'for the sheer pleasure of travelling fast, without reference to any racing formula and with no concession to mediocrity.' It was an overhead-cam four,

with four valves per cylinder, displacing a proud 10.6 litres and producing 140 horsepower. Fortunately I-F had pioneered four-wheel brakes in 1910 because the KM, of which 50 were made between 1911 and 1914, took a lot of stopping. A smaller sister of this car, the 7.2-litre Type IM, attempted Indianapolis in 1913 but without success.

The war years found former Isotta man Alfieri Maserati in Florence managing the workshops of Nagliati, which was a subcontractor to the Ceiranos' Scat in Turin in the production of Hispano-Suiza aero engines under licence. In this capacity Maserati was in frequent contact with the chief designer at Scat, Giuseppe Coda. At war's end both Maserati and Coda took up posts at Turin's Diatto, which in the early post-war years made Bugatti Brescias under licence. Diatto was the progenitor of the Maserati automotive enterprise. It is as such that we will encounter it.

Desperate conditions in 1920's Targa Florio were encountered by the Isotta-Fraschini of Veronesi, which failed to finish.

CHAPTER 7

Invitation to Greatness

AMONG his nation's auto makers, Alfa Romeo was the cynosure of Italy's leader, Benito Mussolini. Proud Fiat, based in sober Turin, preferred an arm's-length relationship with Rome. Alfa, however, was in lively Milan, the city of art and science. The Portello works was versatile, able to make aero engines and other military equipment for a resurgent Italy. It made sporting cars of quality which Mussolini admired and preferred to ride in and drive. Historian Luigi Fittipaldi credits him with ownership of 12 Alfas over the years.

In the motor shows of 1925, starting at Milan in April, Alfa Romeo displayed the chassis of a new kind of automobile that would gain for it both kudos and customers the world over. 'It is believed that the production models of this type are far from ready,' opined Britain's well-informed *Automobile Engineer*, 'the chassis exhibited bring primarily intended to maintain the interest aroused by recent racing successes.' Exploiting racing to promote the launch of a new road car is, it seems, by no means a new idea.

The new Type 6C 1500 Alfa Romeo defied convention. At a time when it was usual for 1.5-litre engines to have four cylinders and sixes to begin at 2.0-litre size, Portello's bid for a volume-production model was a six of 1,485 cc. That it was far from ready for production in 1925 was owed to 1924's all-out concentration on racing. In fact at the 1925 shows, said *Automobile Engineer*, 'little information could be obtained with regard to the internal details of the engine.'

Although Giuseppe Merosi was still Alfa Romeo's board member for engineering, Vittorio Jano was the 6C 1500's principal architect. Secondo Molino, like Jano a former Fiat man, carried out the detail drafting of its engine. Their choice of a small cylinder capacity for the new model was deliberate at a time when European car makers were paranoid about the likely impact on their markets of cheap exports from America.

'By persisting with large engines,' said a historian of the company, 'Alfa Romeo might well have failed during the world crisis of the 1930s.' Instead, he continued, 'Alfa Romeo made sure of something absolutely exclusive: it invented a type of motor car for which the world was obviously waiting.' During the second half of the 1920s Alfa's production was just over 1,000 cars per year, at a time when total yearly Italian output was around 15,000 units.

During 1926, when Jano succeeded the departing Merosi as Alfa's technical board member, the 6C 1500 was made ready for production. Jano made and tested six prototypes of the new car, for like his predecessor he 'believed in thorough and lengthy testing of any innovation.' In broad terms the new model's innovation was its lightness, through which the aim was to get brisk performance from its small engine. Although on a 114-inch-wheelbase chassis to take four-seater bodywork, the car weighed only 2,200 pounds – exceptional for its day. Although this meant light and flexible frame rails, first-rate roadholding was the result.

Its engine had a single shaft-driven camshaft above an integral iron block and head atop an aluminium crankcase with four main bearings. Valves were in line and vertical. Completely new to Alfa Romeo was valve gear that consisted of a circular mushroom tappet whose base was screwed onto a threaded valve stem, not only to attach it but also to adjust valve clearance. Locking the setting was accomplished by radial serrations between the top disc and another disc below it which was keyed to the valve stem and pressed against the upper disc by the valve springs.

Vittorio Jano's design of this valve gear was his own interpretation of a concept that had been used before by Marc Birkigt for Hispano-Suiza aero engines and by Ferdinand Porsche for many of his racing engines, starting with his 1922 'Saschas' for Austro Daimler. It was compact and light, Jano claiming for it an advantage of 1,000 rpm over heavier valve gear. Although against it was the fact that it did not isolate the valve stem and its guide from the side thrust of the cam lobe, as it wiped the tappet surface, in practice this was not a crippling defect. Jano and Jano-influenced designs would continue to use this valve gear, simplified in the 1950s, through the world-champion Grand Prix Ferraris of 1961.

Except for a staid four-door saloon for the long chassis made in the Portello works, bodies for the 1.5-litre Alfas were made by outside coachbuilders such as Castagna, Farina, Touring and Zagato. With the last, also conveniently in Milan, Vittorio Jano forged a particularly close relationship. The engineers weaned Zagato away from wood body framing toward lighter and stiffer tubular structures. Ugo Zagato's firm became the *carrozziere* of choice for the sports and racing Alfas well into the 1930s.

With its 44 bhp at 4,200 rpm the single-overhead-cam 6C 1500 was the mainstay of the new range, 806 being made of its longer 122-inch wheelbase version. With a top speed of only 68 mph, however, the new model was no threat to the Grand Prix P2. Chiribiri had a much more sporting offering while the OMs and Diattos were no poor performers. Indeed the sports version of Fiat's 501 was

In this Super Sports version Alfa Romeo's 6C 1500 won the 1928 Mille Miglia, driven by Giuseppe Campari.

Enzo Ferrari placed third in 1928's Targa Masetti at Mugello in his Alfa Romeo 6C 1500, which was easily stripped for action.

just as fast as the more costly Alfa Romeo.

Thus the pulses of Italy's sporting bloods pumped faster at the news that a twin-cam version would be launched in 1927. This had a detachable cylinder head, the easier to install its valves which were at a wide 90-degree included angle. On the shorter wheelbase and weighing only 2,115 pounds, its 54 bhp at 4,500 rpm gave lively performance to this 6C 1500 Sport model with a top speed approaching 80 mph. In 1928 and 1929 the Sport was made in a series of 171, identifiable by a radiator of smaller frontal area to suit sporting bodywork. These were snapped up by enthusiasts to whom this promised success in the 1.5-litre sports-car category.

Alfa Romeo, however, had more ambitious plans. During 1927 Jano and his team, which included engineer Luigi Fusi, developed a supercharged version of the 6C 1500 Sport. A series of 25 cars was laid down with engines set almost eight inches to the rear to make room for a Roots-type blower driven at 1.5 times engine speed from the nose of the crankshaft. Fifteen of these 6C 1500 Super Sports were unblown and the rest supercharged. Pressure induction, with the blower drawing fuel/air mixture from a Memini carburettor, brought power to 76 bhp at 4,800 rpm and top speed to 87 mph.

One such blown Alfa six was a works entry in the second Mille Miglia on 31 March and 1 April 1928. The first running of this amazing race through the north of Italy proved its merit as a phenomenal source of publicity for auto makers that Alfa Romeo could not overlook. The single supercharged 6C 1500 SS that Portello prepared for the race 'was not a pleasing-looking car,'

Accompanied by Giulio Ramponi, Giuseppe Campari won the 1929 Mille Miglia in this Alfa Romeo 6C 1750 Super Sport.

BENITO MUSSOLINI

A week and a half before the 1923 Italian Grand Prix found American racing driver Jimmy Murphy in the Monza paddock, helping assemble the engine of his Duesenberg. 'There'd been a lot of people around the garage all day,' he recalled, 'giving the rig the once-over and asking a lot of foolish questions, so I didn't pay a lot of attention to a couple of men who were standing in the doorway.' As the winner of the French Grand Prix only two years before and the 1922 winner of the Indy 500, Murphy was one of the brightest stars in racing's firmament. Interest in him was understandable.

After a while, said Murphy, one of the men 'stepped over to me and said that he wanted me to meet Mussolini. And the next thing I knew I had accepted an invitation to take lunch with Mussolini the next day.' Only the year before, as leader of the Fascist party, Benito Mussolini had been invited to form Italy's government. He was the man of the hour. 'I didn't sleep a wink that night,' Murphy related, 'worrying because I'd pick the wrong fork or something like that.'

He needn't have worried. As a great racing enthusiast, Mussolini had deep respect for Murphy, whom he treated 'cordially and courteously. He made me feel like I could have

had the whole of Italy if I'd wanted it. He certainly is one grand guy.' As a memento of the visit Il Duce gave Murphy a magnificent watch fashioned from an Italian gold coin.

Here was a man with sympathy for the world of motor sports. 'He drove fast but badly,' his chauffeur Ercole Boratto said of Mussolini, 'He adored machines, especially motor cars and parading about in them.' 'He was a daredevil driver, particularly downhill,' recalled fellow Fascist Francesco Carli. 'It was very hard to keep up. He timed his gearchanges perfectly with the engine revs and liked to drift around corners. Passengers were always scared.'

It wasn't Mussolini's style to make extravagant promises to his nation's motor industry, but he saw to it that his government took action to protect vital industries after the financial crises of the early 1920s. An active journalist and editor, Mussolini had the personality around which coalesced the forces that craved a solution to Italy's post-war problems. While the socialist left dithered, Mussolini became the focus of those on the right who thought Italy needed a more authoritarian government. This he duly delivered.

Pictured in 1934, Benito Mussolini, right, and Adolf Hitler were destined to personify the extremes of Fascism in Europe.

In August of 1932 at his Villa Torlonia, Benito Mussolini was introduced to the new P2 Type B Alfa Romeo by Nuvolari and others.

wrote W.F. Bradley, 'with its cut-off tail, its exposed petrol tank and its batteries and emergency oil tank and a single spare wheel at the rear.' Its wings were conventional complete with running boards.

Awarded the drive was Giuseppe Campari. 'Burly, swarthy, possessing a genial bonhomie,' said Bradley, 'with secret ambitions of becoming a great singer, his performance at the wheel recalled Lancia of twenty years

Driven from the crankshaft nose, the Roots-type supercharger of the Alfa 6C 1750 Super Sport delivered its mixture through a manifold finned for cooling.

earlier, for like that great Fiat driver, he handled his car as if it were a bucking bronco which must be tamed, subdued, made to comply with his will.' Blessed with a fine tenor voice, Campari foresaw a career at La Scala when his racing days were over.

Bigger-engined Bugattis led the Mille Miglia early but hit problems, allowing Campari to take the lead at Rome. Although a legend would later grow that he who leads at Rome cannot win the Mille Miglia, on this occasion the Alfa Romeo clung to its lead all the way to the finish at Brescia, shrugging off challenges from a Lancia and OM. After 19 hours of racing Campari won with an eight-minute margin over Archimede Rosa's OM. With the top ten finishers all within 1927's winning time, this was no token success for Alfa's latest creation. Second place only a minute and a half behind a 2.3-litre Bugatti followed in the Targa Florio. Bugattis still had a handling advantage over the cars from Portello.

Bad news for Alfa Romeo's rivals came in 1929 with an increase in both bore and stroke of the in-line six to bring its capacity to 1,752 cc. Although undertaken mainly to increase torque so the touring version would make fewer demands on its driver, this had its racing benefits. The result was the 6C 1750, offered as a single-cam touring car and in twin-cam form as the unblown Sport and the compressor-assisted Super Sport, the latter producing 85 bhp at 4,500 rpm.

Of 1929's 72 Mille Miglia entries, one-quarter were Alfas. A supercharged 6C 1750 with Zagato bodywork was the winner, again in the hands of the redoubtable Campari, with Giulio Ramponi accompanying him as in 1928. Numerous other hill climb and circuit successes fell to the new model.

Vittorio Jano had three more major tweaks in mind for the racing versions of this formidable family of sixes. One was a crankshaft with eight instead of five main bearings. His second tweak was a *Testa Fissa* or monobloc version

of the engine, with the head integral with the cylinders. Omitting the cylinder-head joint was an obvious aid to reliability with higher supercharging pressures, while water circulation around the engine's hottest parts was much better. Having built six such blocks for the 6C 1500, Jano made a total of twelve in 1929-30 to use in the factory's racing cars.

In a third tweak Jano replaced the small geared-up Roots-type blower with a much larger unit running at engine speed. This gave higher efficiency, as did the more direct airflow from the carburettor, which was now on the left or exhaust side of the engine so the pressure duct could flow smoothly back and up to the inlet manifold. To help cool the incoming charge, which was heated by its compression, the aluminium inlet pipes were heavily finned. Cooler, meaning denser for higher power, this design feature became an Alfa Romeo hallmark.

Deliciously sleek in its latest Zagato coachwork, enjoying chassis improvements for better braking and handling, this 102-horsepower 6C 1750 Gran Sport model showed its pace in 1930. It swept the top four places in the Mille Miglia, led by Tazio Nuvolari with Varzi second, Campari third and Pietro Ghersi fourth. 'Campari is 39 years old and looks it,' wrote W.F. Bradley. 'Nuvolari is only a few months younger and has the physical appearance of a youth of 16. But his slim frame is composed of muscles of steel – steel of the finest quality.' Winning the 1,018-mile race at a speed of 62.8 mph, he was the first to triumph at better than 100 km/h. The Nuvolari legend was shaping nicely.

Other 1930 wins for the 6C 1750 came in the Tourist Trophy – again Nuvolari – and the 24-hours of Spa in Belgium. In 1931, against stronger competition, the model could still place second at Spa and in both the Mille Miglia and Targa Florio. Successful record-breaking in the 2.0-litre class was also on this six's agenda, chiefly in 1930. The last cars of the series were built in 1933 and sold the following year.

Vittorio Jano's 6C 1750 played a role in the construction of his rival to cars that were being built for sheer speed on fast tracks, such as the 4.9-litre Type 54 Bugatti and the Type V4 Maserati, which married two eights to make a 4.0-litre sixteen. When someone said to Jano in jest that 'You should make a better car by putting two together', he responded by building a twin-engined car. He used two supercharged 6C 1750 engines, which combined to displace 3,504 cc and produce a total of 230 bhp at 5,200 rpm. Each six had its own gearbox and drive to the rear axle.

In fact only the left-hand engine resembled a standard 6C 1750, because the right-hand six was mirror-imaged so that all inlet piping would be between the engines and both exhausts on the outside. Both engines had aluminium blocks and detachable heads of the same light alloy. Each six was cooled by its half of the radiator. Completing the mirror-imaging was the positioning of the two rings and pinions in the live rear axle, which required counter-rotating engines.

Shrewdly, this layout had the added advantage of improving traction by cancelling out the torques that usually lift the right rear wheel of a live axle. With each engine driving its own wheel, a connection between them having been tried but abandoned, a differential effect was provided by giving the output shaft of each three-speed gearbox an overrunning clutch. A left-hand lever shifted both boxes though a transverse shaft.

Dubbed the Type A, this novel device made Alfa history by being its first single-seater, *monoposto*, with a centrally seated driver. Its pilot was very deeply enclosed in his cockpit to improve the A's streamlining for fast courses. The first race that met that definition was the Italian G.P. on 24 May 1931 over the full Monza road and track circuit. Two Type As suffered a tragic debut, with Luigi Arcangeli's killing him in practice and Tazio Nuvolari's breaking after only two of the race's ten hours.

On 2 August 1931 Giuseppe Campari placed his Type A fourth in the Coppa Ciano and then won the 188-mile Coppa Acerbo on the fast Pescara circuit on the 16th, averaging 81.68 mph, with Nuvolari having to settle for third after one of his sixes blew its head gasket. At the Monza G.P. in September the two twelve-cylinder Alfas (out of four made) were seen to out-corner the Type 54 Bugattis, although the French car had a speed advantage over the Alfa's 150 mph. Neither Type A finished. It was only a temporary means to an end. But Vittorio Jano's next brainstorm, his Type B, would be immortal.

Four-seated bodies were required for the Tourist Trophy races, as on this Alfa Romeo 6C 1500 Super Sports of 1929.

From left Enzo Ferrari and Achille Varzi
prepared for the 1930 Milie Migilia. In the dark
suit is Alfa Romeo's Gianferrari.

In Alfa Romeo's sports cars as well
as sports-racing cars the 6C 1750 six
generated performance out of all
proportion to its capacity.

Accompanied by
Guidotti, who
personalised this
photograph, Tazio
Nuvolari won the 1930
Mille Miglia in this Alfa
Romeo 6C 1750 Gran
Sport with monobloc
engine.

Superbly purposeful, Type 6C 1750 Gran Sport Alfa Romeos of this configuration dominated the 1930 Mille Miglia.

CHAPTER 8

Enter the Maseratis

Joviality and joy in his work shines from the visage of 32-year-old Alfieri Maserati, winner at Mugello in 1922 in his Isotta-Fraschini Special.

OF the six Maserati brothers born in Voghera in Lombardy, only Mario was not obsessed by machinery and automobiles. As an artist, however, he made an important contribution to the Maserati marque. He designed its emblem, featuring the trident wielded by Neptune in a famous statue in the heart of Bologna. In that city the Officine Alfieri Maserati was registered on 1 December 1914 to build and repair racing cars.

Only after the war did the Maseratis move from Turin – where we met them earlier – to settle in Bologna. They found premises in the Alemanni district on Bologna's eastern periphery, also known as Pontevecchio, where Alfieri was joined by brothers Ernesto, Bindo and Ettore. The eldest brother, Carlo, was felled by pneumonia when not yet 30.

At Pontevecchio, said Ernesto, 'we began with a very small shop and just a few basic machine tools. But we had very good workers, the best. Little by little we grew and our equipment improved.' As often happens with a new enterprise, not yet on its feet, its guiding spirit was still employed elsewhere. After his years with Isotta-Fraschini, which had sent him to England to look after customers, to France to race and to Argentina to explore local assembly of its products, Alfieri Maserati joined the Turin firm of Diatto after his wartime stint in Florence with Nagliati.

Tracing its origins to 1835, when Guglielmo Diatto's workshop built 15 four-wheeled carriages, Diatto expanded into railway-carriage manufacture in the 1860s. This branch of the company began co-operation with Fiat in the early 20th century and ultimately merged with Fiat in 1918. From 1905 Diatto also built automobiles, an initiative of engineer Vittorio Diatto and his brother Pietro. They got their start with a brief liaison with Clément-Bayard, whose French models were built under licence as Diatto-Cléments.

Fitful competition entries were made pre-war by Diatto, which began making cars of its own design in 1911. After its wartime duties as a supplier to the military the Turin company moved its headquarters to Rome, the better to press Italy's government for the money it was owed for its deliveries. A racing success came in 1919 when Domenico Gamboni was third in a 2.7-litre Type 4D behind a Peugeot and Itala in the Targa Florio.

With its debts satisfied at last and new management at the helm, Diatto returned to Turin in 1921. In 1922 at the Milan salon it presented its first post-war model, the Type 20. Its design had been acquired from a short-lived Turin enterprise called Veltro, meaning Greyhound, for which erstwhile Fiat and Scat engineer Giuseppe Coda had prepared an up-to-date concept.

Developed with the help of engineer Lardone, Coda's design envisioned a common chassis for models with engines of 2.0 and 3.0 litres that differed only in their cylinder dimensions. Both had vee-inclined overhead valves opened by rocker arms from an overhead camshaft driven by a vertical shaft and skew gears. Here was an ambitious engine susceptible to sporting tuning. Amenable to this was Giuseppe Coda, who was taken on as Diatto's technical board member.

After the war, at Pontevecchio in Bologna the Maserati brothers had been repairing vehicles and continuing to make the mica-insulated spark plugs that were first produced in Milan in 1916 in a joint venture with Isotta co-worker Vincenzo Trucco. These were the money-spinning activities that allowed them to conduct some projects of their own. One of these was the construction of a sprint special that raced as an 'Isotta-Fraschini'.

In 1920 Alfieri bought two war-surplus Hispano-Suiza V8 aero engines as raw material for his project. Using one cylinder block this gave a 5.9-litre overhead-camshaft twin-ignition four, for which they fabricated a steel crankcase. With suitable induction it was installed in an Isotta frame and front axle with Scat rear axle and Itala gearbox. 'It had stamina and reliability,' recalled Ernesto Maserati. 'It went very fast and, very importantly, always finished.'

Alfieri Maserati tore up the tracks with his I-F special. In the 13.7-mile Susa-Moncenisio hill climb, held in high summer, he was the outright winner in 1921 and 1922. At Mugello in 1922 Alfieri won over 242 miles at record speed, defeating some of the cars and stars of the day. Acting as excellent advertising for Maserati's talents as a car builder and driver, the Isotta special led to an invitation to take charge of Diatto's racing cars.

With the new 2.0-litre Grand Prix formula suiting his Type 20 model of the same capacity, Diatto's Giuseppe Coda prepared two racing versions to compete in 1922's Italian G.P. at the new Monza track. Engaged to drive one of them, Maserati found its front axle twisting excessively under braking in those early days of the use of front-wheel brakes. In the race this provoked a huge spin at the Lesmo bend which resulted in damage that retired Alfieri's car. The other Diatto also retired.

Committed as he and his brothers were to an independent existence, Alfieri Maserati worked as a consultant to Diatto rather than as an employee. 'Alfieri had a tremendously warm and outgoing personality,' his brother Ernesto recalled for Griff Borgeson, 'extroverted and charming. He was full of wit and charm, which attracted friends from all walks of life, from singers at La Scala to top men in government. He was a champion billiards player and a wild gambler at cards. He was not lucky, however, and quit gambling around 1922.'

Alfieri and his brothers took the 2.0-litre Diattos in hand. From Coda's raw material, which offered the benefits of hemispherical combustion chambers and a two-part cylinder block that allowed the introduction of aluminium, they fashioned the Type 20SS racing car. With the excellent output for the time of 75 bhp at 4,500 rpm, naturally aspirated, this became an effective and reliable competitor.

Noteworthy performances were achieved by the fiery Guido Meregalli in the 154-mile races on a tortuous circuit near Lake Garda. He drove Diattos to victory there in 1922, 1923 and 1924, in the last ahead of two OMs. Meregalli also scored hill climb victories with the Maserati-prepared Diatto. The high-performance four-

The roar from its 5.9-litre Isotta four added to the spectacle of the I-F Special in which Alfieri Maserati proved his building and driving skills.

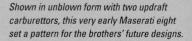

Wearing twin rear wheels, Alfieri Maserati in his I-F Special (14) faced off against Giuseppe Campari in one of the rebuilt 1914 G.P. Fiats.

Shown in unblown form with two updraft carburettors, this very early Maserati eight set a pattern for the brothers' future designs.

Built by the Maserati brothers to a scheme by Giuseppe Coda, Diatto's 1925 Grand Prix car had a twin-cam straight-eight 2.0-litre engine.

THE MONZA CIRCUITS

Road racing evolved in distinct stages. The first events were long open-road contests from city to city. Racing then moved to circuits of suitable highways. Next, shorter circuits over roads were used; indeed some like Le Mans, Monaco and Spa are still on the modern calendar, albeit using some sections modified to meet racing's needs. Evolution then led to dedicated purpose-built road-racing facilities. Italy's Monza, the first of the latter, is still in use today.

Building a dedicated circuit for racing wasn't a new idea. The steeply banked track at Brooklands in England opened in 1907 while the first races were held on a speedway at Indianapolis in America in 1909. Both, however, were circuits built for sheer speed, not for the testing of all aspects of a car's performance that helped create the versatile character of Europe's cars.

While 'Grand Prix' before World War I meant the races first organised by the Automobile Club de France, in the post-war years other nations organised events run to the international Grand Prix rules. In 1921 the first Gran Premio d'Italia was organised by the Milan Automobile Club on the Montichiari road circuit near Brescia. Looking at its financial implications, however, the club found high costs of

preparing and staffing the circuit, set against low revenue from the difficulty of adequately checking and charging spectators. Both problems could be addressed by building a permanent circuit.

Potential sites near Milan were assessed, including one at Gallarate that was later used for an airport, until the final choice fell on the park at Monza to the north of the city. Established more than 200 years earlier as a royal park, it was handsomely wooded with a hunting lodge for the King's pleasure. Portions of the park included the Bosco Bello or Beautiful Wood of several hundred years earlier. The Club's designers laid out two interrelated circuits, one a high-speed oval and the other a boomerang-shaped road course.

On 26 February 1922 work on the new track began with the cornerstone laying by two stars of Italy's racing firmament, Vincenzo Lancia and Felice Nazzaro. Only two days later, however, work was stopped under orders from the authorities responsible for protecting the landscape. Not until mid-April was their assent given to a modified plan. Work started again at the beginning of May with the aim a Grand Prix only four months away. With a workforce of 3,500, 30 trucks and three miles of light railway with two engines and 80 gondola cars, the 6.2 miles of tracks and all their ancillaries were completed in time.

With its unique setting and propinquity to Milan the future of Monza as the cynosure of Italian motor sports was secure. For its first Grand Prix in 1922 the park was thronged by almost 100,000 spectators and their 10,000 automobiles. Onlookers took advantage of the park's four restaurants and its main grandstand seating 3,000 and six others seating 1,000 each. Overpasses and subways gave them access to all parts of the track, from which they were protected by continuous fencing. An Olympic-size swimming pool and areas for camping were other amenities.

Save for the 1937 race, which was held at Leghorn, Monza was continuously the home of the Italian Grand Prix. Less steeply banked than originally planned, its fast 2.8-mile oval was used as part of the circuit for many early races. In 1939 the oval was demolished, only to be revived with high bankings in 1955. Thereafter the oval was included in the Italian G Ps in 1955, 1956, 1960 and 1061 and in the flagship 1,000-kilometre sports-car race until 1968. It was also used extensively for record breaking until it deteriorated beyond use in 1969.

In the late 1950s, in a battle with other circuits for the honour of Europe's fastest track, the road circuit was eased and shortened to 3.6 miles. In 1971 Peter Gethin's BRM was the winner of the 196-mile Grand Prix at an average speed of 150.75 mph, the fastest-ever race for a Formula 1 car. The record stood after changes were made to slow the circuit,

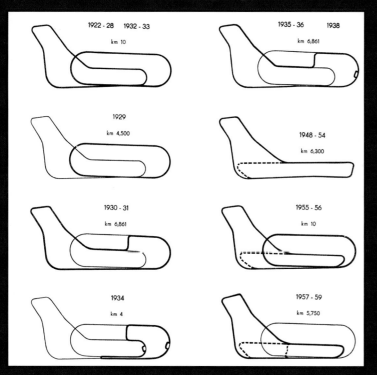

The varieties of Monza's track layouts have been added to in recent years by chicanes designed to slow the competitors.

Continued page 66

including the insertion of chicanes in 1976 and reprofiling of some corners in 1994.

Both before and after World War II Monza was in heavy use for testing, thanks to relatively clement off-season weather in Italy and its known standard as a yardstick for performance of both cars and drivers. It was not without its dangers, however. In 1933 the Monza Grand Prix (not the Italian) was run in short heats and a final on the banked track. In their heat both Giuseppe Campari and Baconin Borzacchini, on Alfa Romeo and Maserati respectively, left the south banking and

were killed. Then in the final Count Stanislas Czaykowski crashed fatally in his Bugatti.

Monza was also destined to witness crashes that took the lives of Alberto Ascari, Wolfgang von Trips, Jochen Rindt and Ronnie Peterson, to name only the great aces who succumbed to their injuries in the Royal Park. Set against that toll are the names of the men who have won at Monza, from Rosemeyer to Regazzoni, from Ascari to Andretti, from Nuvolari to Lauda, from Farina to Fittipaldi and from Fangio to Prost. Theirs is the roll of honour of racing's immortals.

After World War II a handsome grandstand was an iconic feature of the Monza track, as seen here in 1948.

cylinder engine was fitted to a sporting Diatto for the road, the Type 20S.

These successes helped mask financial problems at Diatto, which like Nicola Romeo's enterprises suffered from the 1921 collapse of the Banca Italiana di Sconto. The company limped on until November 1923, when Diatto went into receivership. New capital was found from the Musso brothers, prominent in textiles and banking, who installed Carlo Gorrini as Diatto's general manager. The firm was relaunched in May 1924 as SA Autocostruzioni Diatto.

Meanwhile the Maseratis continued flying the Diatto flag. For *Formula Libre* races, those with no engine limits,

they installed another of their 5.9-litre half-a-Hisso fours in a Diatto chassis. With this potent hybrid, Alfieri Maserati won again in 1923 at Mugello and in the Susa-Moncenisio and Aosta-Gran San Bernardo hill climbs. In 1924 he took it to a 386-mile Grand Prix at San Sebastian in Spain. It went well at first, holding third among current Grand Prix cars, but gave up after 27 of the 35 laps with drive-line problems. It was, after all, only a sprint special.

In 1925 this car was replaced by another Pontevecchio-built special for sprint events. According to historian Frank Lugg, the Maseratis built a 4.0-litre straight eight by mounting two 20SS blocks on a common crankcase and crankshaft. Offering an unsupercharged potential of at least 150 bhp, this was installed in a racing Diatto chassis. Though no clear record of its accomplishments survives, it could well have been the mount of Count Diego de Sterlich in his winning drive in a Diatto in 1925's Susa-Moncenisio. We will hear more of the enthusiastic Count.

A long chassis to suit this engine was available, because Diatto's new management had approved Giuseppe Coda's enterprising plan to build a pukka eight-cylinder Grand Prix car for the prevailing 2.0-litre formula. Coda presented his board with a fully formed plan after discussions with his racing consultants, the Maseratis, held at his Turin home. He told the team, led by Alfieri, that it was his aim to make an all-aluminium racing engine. Ambitious at a time when cast-aluminium alloys left much to be desired in both strength and integrity, this broke sharply with the current Italian practice of fabricated steel cylinder blocks.

Work began on the new engine in 1923. While its general concept was outlined by Giuseppe Coda, its detail design was the work of Alfieri Maserati. He gave it a detachable cylinder head on an aluminium block atop a crankcase of the same material. Twin overhead camshafts were gear-driven at the front while five main bearings carried its crankshaft. In another break with the status quo, plain bearings were used instead of rollers. The supercharged version had two updraft carburettors, specially made by Memini to be pressurised by a Roots blower mounted at the front of the engine.

In meetings with Coda the drawings prepared by Maserati were reviewed and approved. The first such engine was machined and assembled in the brothers' Bologna workshops. Then it was delivered to Diatto in Turin, where Coda and his colleague Vaccanina tested it and made the modifications they thought necessary before building additional engines to the final design. Theirs was the work on the chassis as well.

In the summer of 1924 an unsupercharged prototype of the new Diatto racer, fitted with four Zenith carburettors, was entered in hill climbs for Diatto test driver Onesimo Marchisio. The second of these was disastrous with Marchisio overturning fatally. Later in the year, the prototype was taken to Lake Garda, where Maserati placed fifth in the race.

Construction of the definitive G.P. cars continued at Diatto in 1925, with the first supercharged engine being bench-tested in June. Meanwhile Diatto's new management and Giuseppe Coda were not seeing eye-to-eye. Running dangerously late, the costly racing-car project was a source of controversy. Its moment of truth

had to come on 6 September 1925 with the running of the Italian Grand Prix at Monza, for this would be the last major race to be run under the 2.0-litre rules to which the car was built.

Two Diattos were presented, one for Alfieri Maserati and the other for Emilio Materassi. Only the latter's car had the definitive Roots-type supercharging. Thanks to their starting numbers both had front-row grid positions, but they soon fell behind the P2 Alfa Romeos and the fast

The first outing of a pure-bred Maserati was in the 1926 Targa Florio with Alfieri Maserati driving his Type 26.

With his bold May 1926 dedication Emilio Materassi hailed the arrival of Maserati's new Type 26.

The care taken by the Maserati brothers in their creations gleamed from the chassis of their 1927 Type 26B of 2.0 litres.

American Duesenbergs. They trailed the field for most of the race until retiring just before the finish.

This ignominious outing followed a season in which Alfieri Maserati had hitherto been banned from racing as a result of a quarrel over the declared displacement of a Diatto entered for a hill climb in Spain in 1924. The authorities threatened Diatto with a five-year ban but accepted instead a period of suspension for Maserati that was lifted, after negotiation, in time for him to drive in the Italian Grand Prix. During the hiatus Ernesto Maserati began a brief driving career which he revived at the end of the decade.

With this setback on his record, compounded by the failure of his straight eights to bring glory to Diatto, Giuseppe Coda accepted the invitation he had received from André Citroën to take charge of his new assembly plant in Milan. For its part Diatto declared an end to top-line racing. In fact, in 1927, it would cease production of passenger cars as well. The Maseratis had lost the patron whose largesse had allowed them to give up menial repair work and concentrate on building their beloved racing cars.

What next for the *fratelli* Maserati? Having been introduced to the world of Grand Prix racing by Diatto, they decided to continue. This was made possible by the wealth of Count Diego de Sterlich, whose home was at Teramo near Pescara on the Adriatic. De Sterlich was a passionate enthusiast and active competitor in Bugattis in 1923 and 1924 and Diattos from 1925 to 1927. In the latter role he came to know the Maseratis well.

Thanks to de Sterlich, the Officine Alfieri Maserati was able to take title to some of the racing hardware that it had produced for Diatto. The Count also stood ready to purchase an example of each of the new cars produced by the Maseratis – sometimes even two examples. He maintained this habit until 1930, thereby reportedly exhausting much of his family's fortune in support of the sign of the Trident.

The brothers lost no time in implementing their plan. Only three weeks after the disappointing Diatto debut at Monza the first drawing of a new Maserati was completed. A cross-section of the cylinder head, it was drawing number 1 of the Type 26. Built to compete under the new 1.5-litre Grand Prix rules for 1926, the straight-eight Type 26 appeared in the year for which it was named.

The new car's debut was in the Targa Florio on 25 April, where Alfieri drove it to ninth overall and first in its class. In both chassis and power train it took advantage of much Diatto materiel. Soon, however, the brothers were making more of their own cars and modifying their designs through experience.

Early production volumes were modest. The Officine averaged five and a half new cars a year, plus spares, over its first four years. This included 10 of the 1.5-litre Type 26 and six of the Type 26 B, a 2.0-litre version introduced in 1927 for *Formula Libre* racing. Both followed the Diatto pattern as in-line eight-cylinder engines supercharged by a Roots-type blower extending forward from the train of gears at the front that turned the twin overhead camshafts.

The Maserati proposition was novel. Hitherto Grand Prix racing had been the province of the big battalions, of car makers like Delage, Talbot, Fiat and Alfa Romeo who also built racing cars. Somewhat apart was Bugatti, which made both sports and racing cars in small volumes. In contrast, apart from a few inconclusive flirtations with cars for the road, the brothers from Voghera built only racing cars for their own use and for sale. It seemed a daring idea, but in fact this strict specialisation helped them survive Italy's sharp 1926 depression, a slump that wiped out all save the nation's strongest auto makers.

Italy's automotive press hailed the arrival of Maserati racing cars, saying that with them 'Italian automobilism would have a defender of stature able to continue the recent glories of Fiat and Alfa Romeo'. At first those glories were chiefly in Italy, for the early Maseratis seldom ventured abroad. Initially the 1.5-litre cars were those most raced but by 1928 the 2.0-litre 26 B was more to the fore. A good victory for the 'B' was Baconin Borzacchini's in Catania's 217-mile Etna Trophy race in May of 1928. Reliability, lacking at first, was gradually being achieved.

Enlarged to 2.5 litres as the 26 M, the straight-eight supercharged Maserati burst onto the international Grand Prix scene with several important successes in 1930. One was a one-two finish in the final of the Monza Grand Prix and another was Achille Varzi's victory in the season-ending 323-mile Spanish Grand Prix by the staggering margin of 22 minutes. The 26 M set a pattern for future designs from the Bologna house that would make Maserati a name to reckon with in racing in the 1930s, not only in Grand Prix competition but in other popular classes as well. As racing cars built for racers by racers, their pedigree was impeccable.

Luigi Fagioli drove the best-placed Maserati in the 1928 Targa Florio, this Type 26B in seventh place.

As this Type 26B Maserati demonstrated, in the mid-1920s racing cars had to cope with diabolical road conditions.

CHAPTER 9

Alfa Light and Shadow

Prospero Gianferrari, right with Italo Balbo, Italy's Minister of Aviation, headed Alfa Romeo from 1929.

ALFA Romeo's commercial director in the early 1920s was Giorgio Rimini, an engineer. A strong supporter of newcomer Vittorio Jano and his creations, Rimini was also a close ally of Nicola Romeo. In this role Rimini was a committed advocate of the merits of racing to generate positive publicity for cars and companies. He travelled with the team to give his enthusiastic support to its major races and events.

In 1926, however, Portello was witnessing change. The holder of its obligations, the Banca Nazionale di Credito, was less convinced about the value of competition. It had barred building racing cars for the new Grand Prix formula. At the beginning of the year Alfa's technical board member, Giuseppe Merosi, resigned, followed later by Giorgio Rimini. The last link with the original company was broken in May 1928 when Nicola Romeo was forced out of its board of directors. In 1929 Prospero Gianferrari, who had placed second in that year's Trento-Bondone hill climb with his 6C 1500 Alfa, became the company's new managing director.

These alterations were not to the immediate benefit of an Alfa Romeo insider who had been driving its cars in competitions. Racing only occasionally after 1924, Enzo

Ferrari was concentrating on his responsibilities at Portello, where he had been acting as the right arm of the now-departed Giorgio Rimini. Although his Alfa Romeo distributorship in Modena was considerable compensation, Ferrari had lost important allies in Romeo and Rimini. When the new 6C 1500 and 1750 models came out, he returned to the cockpit, the better to promote his sales of these attractive models.

But Enzo Ferrari, in his own words an 'agitator of men', had another idea. Hatched ironically at a celebratory dinner at Bologna for a Maserati driver, Ferrari's brainwave was to set up a private racing team. Backed by his Bologna dinner partners, textile-making brothers Augusto and Alfredo Caniato, he set up the Scuderia Ferrari in 1929, *Scuderia* simply meaning 'team'. At the young age of 31 Enzo Ferrari was ready to put wheels under other drivers.

As was often the case, Ferrari's timing was good. In 1929 his Scuderia was perfectly placed to take over the racing preparation and entries of Alfa Romeo's cars, the company having decided to unburden itself of this activity and to entrust it to a knowledgeable outsider. Founded in September, in December the Modena-based Scuderia Ferrari became Portello's official entrant. It received one P2, two 6C 1500 Super Sports and

70

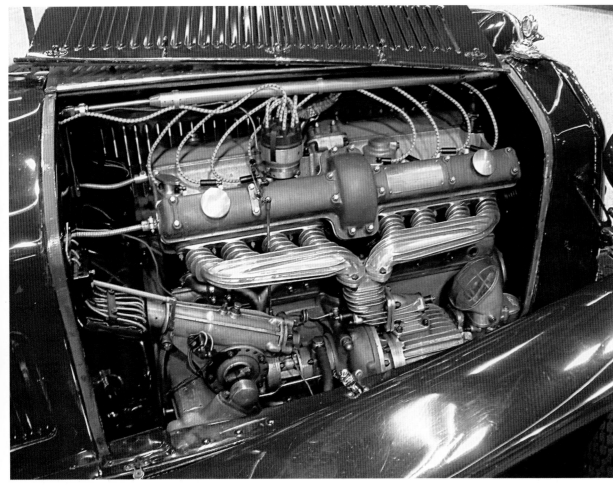

The brilliant Vittorio Jano created the straight-eight engine of the 1931 Type 8C 2300 Alfa Romeo with remarkable economy of means.

three 6C 1750 Gran Sports plus associated spares and equipment.

By the mid-1930s the Scuderia had become an engineering-racing division of Alfa Romeo, having been allocated the racing function entirely in August 1933. Ferrari could undertake design on his own while still having the support of Jano at Portello as required. With this more businesslike orientation the interests of the founding Caniatos were bought out by Count Carlo Felice Trossi, himself a driver of considerable merit. The Scuderia also prepared and entered cars for wealthy amateurs, an astonishing 50 in its first full year of 1930.

Enzo Ferrari was also able to attract such first-line talent as Campari, Nuvolari and, in 1935, French ace René Dreyfus. Wrote Dreyfus: 'With Ferrari I learned the business of racing, for there was no doubt he was a businessman. Enzo Ferrari loved racing, of that there was

no question. Still, it was more than an enthusiast's love, but one tempered by the practical realisation that this was a good way to build a nice, profitable empire.'

That Alfa Romeo was scoring outright victories in classic events was owed to the initiative of Jano and his chief Gianferrari in creating a new high-performance model that made its bow in 1931. In view of the exigencies of the time, with the depression taking its toll, they created it with an economy of means that was a tribute to Jano's ingenuity, for the 8C 2300 became an outstandingly successful racing car as well as a magnificent sporting road car.

In 1929 Jano and his team designed an eight-cylinder version of their six. Although they started with a two-litre eight using the 6C 1500's dimensions, their final engine had the 6C 1750 bore and stroke (65 x 88 mm) to give it 2,336 cc. This approach meant that they could use the six's valve gear intact, effecting a saving in cost. Its bottom end as well, using plain bearings like the sixes instead of the P2's Fiat-inherited roller bearings, would suit a less costly creation.

Whether pistons, connecting rods and bearings could be carried over to the eight depended on Jano's ingenuity. His experience with the P2's straight eight showed the need for a robust crankshaft to avoid potentially damaging harmonic vibrations, which meant bigger main bearings. To minimise the need for this, Jano recalled the layout used by Frenchman Emile Petit for Salmson's 1.1-litre eight of 1928. He laid out the engine as two fours, back-to-back, with a gear train between them to drive the camshafts. The drive to the clutch was still taken from one end of the crankshaft, but for the rest of the engine's rotating parts the advantage of a short, stiff 'four-cylinder' layout still prevailed.

While the 8C 2300's aluminium crankcase was one-piece, its heads, blocks and crankshaft were made in two pieces and bolted together. At the centre of the crankshaft were two helical gears, one to drive the magneto, on the left side, and the gear train to the camshafts, while the other larger gear drove the water and oil pumps as well as the single Roots-type blower on the right, running at 1.33 times engine speed. Unlike the sixes, all these eights were supercharged. In road cars their output was 142 bhp while for sports-car racing they were developed to 165 bhp and then to 178 bhp at 5,400 rpm for Grand Prix racing.

The new model's chassis was conventional with a solid front axle and a live rear axle guided by a torque tube. Wheelbase lengths were 122 inches for road cars and Le Mans racers, 108 inches for sports-racers, as for the Mille Miglia, and 104 inches for the 8C 2300 Monza, which had a two-seated cockpit that allowed it to race in Grands Prix as well as in the Targa Florio. Although large, brakes were still mechanical, a by-now-antiquated system that Portello persisted in using on its cars until hydraulic brakes were adopted in 1935. The first such completed chassis was driven on the road from Milan to Ferrari in Modena in December of 1930.

Although the 8C 2300 was much more sports car than racing car, in stripped short-wheelbase form it was Alfa's entry – with the twin-engined Type A – in 1931's Italian Grand Prix. Having to last ten hours, in accord with the AIACR's prevailing Grand Prix rules, the race was moved from its usual September date to midsummer on 24 May. A starting time of 8:00 a.m. promised a finish in daylight. Two 8C 2300s were the class of a mixed field, placing first and second ahead of a Bugatti with an ample 4.9 litres. The racing model's 'Monza' nickname was a benison of this brilliant success.

In their debut year of 1931 the 2.3-litre Alfas won a total of nine major events. One of these successes opened a new chapter of

Enzo Ferrari won the 14 June 1931 Bobbio-Passo del Penice hill climb in this Zagato-bodied Alfa Romeo Type 8C 2300.

Portello's golden book. Not since OM offered a challenge in the race's early years had Italian cars figured in the 24 Hours of Le Mans, by the 1930s a classic event. In 1930 Britain's Lord Howe raced a 6C 1750 at Le Mans, placing fifth. Howe returned in 1931 with a long-wheelbase 8C 2300, wearing cycle wings and the mandatory folding hood. With Tim Birkin he won the race at the record speed of 78.13 mph, becoming the first to cover more than 3,000 kilometres in the day-long race.

Thus did Alfa found a new dynasty that rivalled Bentley's of the late 1920s. With faired cycle wings an 8C 2300 won again in 1932, Raymond Sommer and Luigi Chinetti driving. Frenchman Sommer repeated in 1933 with Tazio Nuvolari sharing the drive. Remarkably the 8C 2300 won again in 1934, now with the team of Chinetti with France's Philippe Etancelin. In 1935 a 2.3-litre Alfa was 'only' second, less than a lap behind the winning Lagonda. A sports-racing car conceived as a high-performance road car turned out to be a good formula for long-distance racing success.

With its dry-sump oil tank between the front frame dumb-irons, this Alfa Romeo 8C 2300 took Tazio Nuvolari to victory in the 1931 Targa Florio.

In long-chassis guise the Type 8C 2300 Alfa Romeo was well suited to endurance racing, compiling an awesome record at Le Mans.

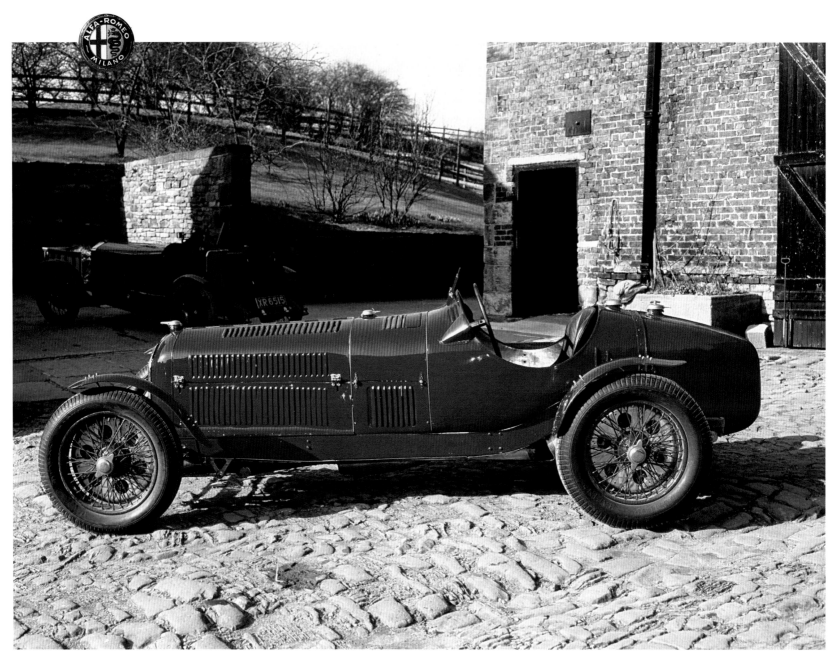

Created in 1932, the Type B Alfa Romeo was as fast as it was handsome. This one wore vestigial wings for road use.

In short-wheelbase form the 8C 2300 was well suited to Sicily's Targa Florio. Nuvolari used one to win in a wet and muddy 1931 Targa. For 1932, hoping to avoid weather problems, Vincenzo Florio planned a short cut to eliminate the highest regions. To gain the needed finance for this he arranged an audience with Benito Mussolini. 'Interviewed privately,' wrote W.F. Bradley, 'robbed of his bodyguards and officials, Mussolini lost his usual stage dignity and pomposity, showed that he had real knowledge of motoring and racing and ordered work on the new road to be undertaken immediately.' On this 'short' 44-mile circuit Nuvolari won again in 1932 while Antonio Brivio was the 1933 winner, both on 8C 2300 Alfas.

In this interim period of uncertain regulations and *Formula Libre* races the 8C 2300 Monza was also a useful

Grand Prix racer. With his private car Philippe Etancelin won several G.Ps in 1931 while Fernando Minoia placed well enough to be European champion. Competition from bigger-engined Bugattis and Maseratis was met by blocks with larger bores that raised capacity to 2.6 and later 2.7 litres, the latter producing 180 bhp in 1933. At Monaco in 1932 Nuvolari won ahead of Berlin driver Rudi Caracciola's similar 8C 2300, painted German white. In both 1932 and '33 this Alfa model won the Eifelrennen on Germany's Nürburgring.

Never satisfied with the compromised 8C 2300, which he considered 'came out too heavy, not a masterpiece,'

Vittorio Jano was working in the meantime on the design of a proper racing car. This was only possible because he had the enthusiastic support and encouragement of Prospero Gianferrari, because Il Portello was by no means isolated from the economic turbulence of the depression. The flow of orders from the government for military equipment was increasing, however, giving both men the confidence to develop a new car to contest the Grand Prix races in which *Il Duce* was clearly interested.

Dubbed simply the Type B, following the Type A with its siamesed 6C 1750 sixes, the new car first raced in 1932's Italian Grand Prix on 5 June, still in the

Magnificent symmetry was the hallmark of Vittorio Jano's engine for Alfa Romeo's Type B with its paired Roots-type superchargers.

Pride was perceptible in the presentation of Tazio Nuvolari's Type B Alfa Romeo for the 11 September 1932 Monza Grand Prix.

Alfa Romeo's Ugo Gobatto, left, and Enzo Ferrari, centre, attend Vittorio Jano's views on a 1934 Type B Alfa Romeo with aerodynamic bodywork.

the mass of the differential forward, to improve handling, while also making it easy to change overall drive ratios with the gear pairs next to the differential. As well, its driver could sit slightly lower.

Like the Type A, Alfa's B had its driver sitting centrally as was permitted by new 1932 rules and was thus a *monoposto* or single-seater. Although tall, its bodywork was slim and stylish with a well-louvred bonnet, looking the very picture of a perfect Grand Prix car. In the first batch six cars were made plus three sets of spare parts.

Between its 1932 debut and mid-1934 Alfa Romeo's Type B took part in 26 races, of which it won 22. It achieved a 92 per cent finishing record from 62 race starts in these years – an impressive achievement. The successes included three victories at Monza, one at an average speed in excess of 110 mph with a car capable of 145 mph. For the 1934 season, the first under the new 750 kilogram formula, its capacity was increased to 2.9 litres. That year the Type B – informally known as the P3 in homage to its great predecessor the P2 – won the 1934 Monaco and French Grands Prix.

These wins came after a hiatus in 1933 when a newly created Italian national entity, the Istituto per la Recostruzione Industriale or IRI, took over and effectively nationalised Alfa Romeo. This rescued Alfa from the clutches of Fiat, which had hoped to obliterate a rival while exploiting the Milan factories for truck production. Prospero Gianferrari was out and a new man, ex-Fiat engineer and production expert Ugo Gobbato, was in. Ferrari had to fight the Grand Prix wars with his Monzas. The Type Bs were withdrawn to Portello until Ferrari's pleas, helped by Nuvolari's defection to Maserati, were heeded.

Although in 1934 the developed Type B was faster than its Bugatti and Maserati rivals, it could not match the exotic new cars from Mercedes-Benz and Auto Union. Could not, that is, unless Tazio Nuvolari was at the wheel. In 1935 at the Nürburgring, the heartland of the enemy, he took the lead in the German Grand Prix on the last of 22 laps when the leading Mercedes-Benz, under heavy pressure, blew a rear tyre. It was an epic victory for both Nuvolari and Alfa.

Trying another way to beat the Germans, in 1935 the Scuderia Ferrari's Luigi Bazzi built a remarkable hybrid consisting loosely of a Type B with another engine behind the cockpit, driving forward into Jano's unique differential. Bazzi made special frames for two such cars, putting the fuel along their flanks. Allowed to compete only in *Formula Libre* races, of which there were few, these cars were capable of 200 mph but very hard on their tyres.

summertime although the race's length had been reduced to a mere five hours. For aces Nuvolari and Campari two were entered by the factory's own racing entity, Alfa Corse, while Ferrari made do with his Monzas. Against strong Maserati opposition the result was victory by a lap for Nuvolari with Campari fourth. As with the P2 it was a win for a Jano design on its first attempt.

The B's engine was akin to that of the 8C 2300 but with the longer stroke of 100 mm. Although it debuted at 2,654 cc, successive bore increases took it to 2,905 and then 3,165 cc with power moving up the scale from 200 to 265 bhp. Instead of a single blower it had two, now on the left-hand side, each feeding four cylinders and running at 1.45 times crankshaft speed. The four-cylinder blocks flanking the central gear train were now aluminium of monobloc design with integral heads.

Vittorio Jano's concentration on lightness created an engine weighing only 440 pounds in a car scaling a modest 1,680 pounds dry. While frame and springing were conventional, drive to the rear wheels was unique. Inspired by his Type A's layout, Jano put the differential behind the gearbox and from there drove each rear wheel's ring and pinion by a separate shaft. This moved

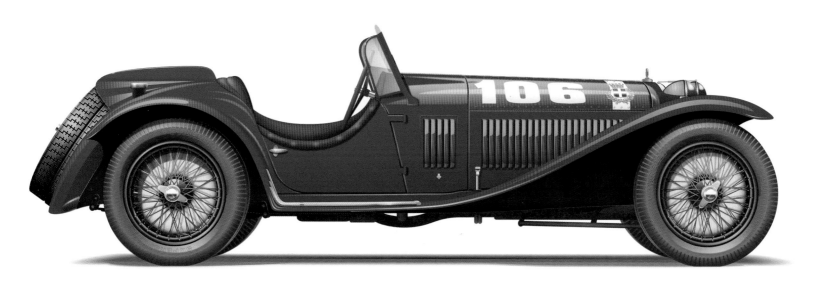

1932 Alfa Romeo Type 8C 2300

Extending his six-cylinder twin-cam concept to a supercharged eight, Vittorio Jano created this magnificent sports car, winner of the 1932 Mille Miglia with Baconin Borzacchini.

SCUDERIA FERRARI SHIELD

Savvy enough to know that he needed a distinctive symbol or emblem for his Scuderia, as a rallying point and attraction for race organisers, Enzo Ferrari had one up his sleeve. When on 25 May 1923 he won and set fastest lap with his Alfa Romeo in the inaugural Circuito del Savio at Ravenna, among those in the crowd who were impressed by the 25-year-old's form was Enrico Baracca, father of Francesco Baracca. The latter was an Italian ace of aces, responsible for 34 aircraft downed in 63 missions before he himself was killed by ground fire at Montello late in the war.

The meeting, said Ferrari, 'led to a second encounter in which I met his mother, Countess Paolina. It was she who told me one day, "Ferrari, put my son's prancing horse on your cars. It will bring you luck." The *cavallino* was black and has remained so. I added the background of canary yellow, the colour of Modena.' Although the Countess's definition of 'luck' could be in dispute, in view of her son's death in wartime, the emblem did bring the bold Baracca good fortune while his biplane was in action.

A curious twist of history is that the prancing horse is identical to that featured on Porsche's badge, which was created by Ferry Porsche from the emblem of the city of Stuttgart. Historian and author Giovanni Lurani speculated knowledgeably that the horse may have been on a German plane downed by Baracca, which the latter then, out of respect in the courtly tradition of the day, adopted for the aircraft of his squadron.

Although Lurani states that the emblem, fashioned in the form of a shield bearing the Scuderia Ferrari's initials, was first used in 1929, in fact the evidence is that its initial appearance on the team's cars was on the 8C 2300 Alfas which finished first and second in the Spa 24-hour race on 9 July 1932. The emblem's baptismal appearance as a car maker's badge was in 1935 on the Bimotore Alfa Romeo built in the Scuderia's workshops by Luigi Bazzi. As used on Ferrari cars after the war the *cavallino rampante* was in a rectangle carrying the Italian colours.

Francesco Baracca pictured next to the Spad fighter that bore his prancing-horse heraldry.

During refuelling of his Type B Alfa Romeo in the 28 July 1935 German Grand Prix Tazio Nuvolari recommended urgency.

In a race at Berlin's ultra-fast Avus track a single *Bimotore*, as it was named, beat all comers save a single Mercedes-Benz.

For the 1935 season Vittorio Jano produced an expanded version of his Type B eight with increased distances between its cylinders to permit a displacement expansion to 3.8 litres. Installed in a new chassis with a rear-mounted gearbox, swing-axle rear suspension and independent front springing, this was the Type 8C 1935. This more modern-looking car was to Nuvolari's liking. He won with it in Hungary and in the Coppa Ciano in 1936. After races early in 1937 these eights were retired in favour of a V-12-powered version of this car.

In 1936 the suspension and transmission features of the 8C 1935 *monoposto* were married with the Type B's 2.9-litre eight to create the 8C 2900 sports-racing car. Three of these readied for the 1936 Mille Miglia placed first, second and fourth, the gap being filled by a cycle-winged Type B driven by Carlo Pintacuda, the 1935 winner. Driving a developed 8C 2900 sports-racer, Pintacuda won again in 1937 and placed second in 1938, when Clemente Biondetti was the winner in another Alfa.

One of the finest of all sports cars, of which 43 chassis are thought to have been laid down, the 8C 2900 matured after Vittorio Jano left Alfa Romeo during 1937. They and their straight-eight predecessors are worthy memorials to a great engineer.

Servicing while under test in June of 1935 the Scuderia Ferrari's 'Bimotore' reveals its two Type B Alfa Romeo engines.

Frank Griswold drove this magnificent Touring-bodied long-wheelbase Type 8C 2900B Alfa Romeo to victory at Watkins Glen in 1948.

CHAPTER 10

Attack of the Trident

An ultimate creation of Alfieri Maserati and his brothers was the 16-cylinder 4.9-litre Type V5 of 1932.

HISTORIANS have described the pace of creative activity under Alfieri Maserati as 'volcanic'. The company's dynamic leader was accustomed to making quick decisions and implementing them rapidly. In this the supporting role of his brothers was vital. Belying the Italian stereotype, the Maserati brothers were calm and quiet to the point of inscrutability. Methodical and determined, they were wholly committed to the independent life that they gained by establishing their own business to make competition cars as well as the spark plugs that had long been their stock-in-trade.

Having thus constrained their scope, the Maseratis exploited every aspect of their chosen field. At the end of the 1920s their main rivals as racing-car builders were Bugatti, which was producing road cars as well,

and Mercedes-Benz, which with its S, SS and SSK models was making waves in both circuit races and hill climbs. Alfa Romeo was in a trough from which it would emerge triumphantly in 1931 with its 8C 2300.

When Grand Prix cars were still built as two-seaters it was easy enough to convert them to sports cars for the big events. Maserati did just this for the second Mille Miglia in 1928, accoutring both a 1.5-litre Type 26 and a 2.0-litre 26 B with lamps and wings. Neither did well but in 1929 Mario Umberto 'Baconin' Borzacchini led the Mille Miglia to Rome in his 26 MM. By retiring soon thereafter he contributed to the legend that the leader at Rome never wins. In fact Maserati was destined to be shut out of Mille Miglia successes in the 1930s apart from a clutch of wins in the 1.1-litre class.

By producing a small-bore version of its 1.5-litre Type 26, Maserati made its first 1.1-litre car in 1929, its 26 C. This was an ultra-small supercharged straight eight. Since the beginning of the 1920s races had been organised in Europe for small cars loosely described at first as Cyclecars and later defined as having engines of no more than 1,100 cc. This became an important sub-category for racing cars during the years when Grand Prix cars had engines of 2.0 and then 1.5 litres.

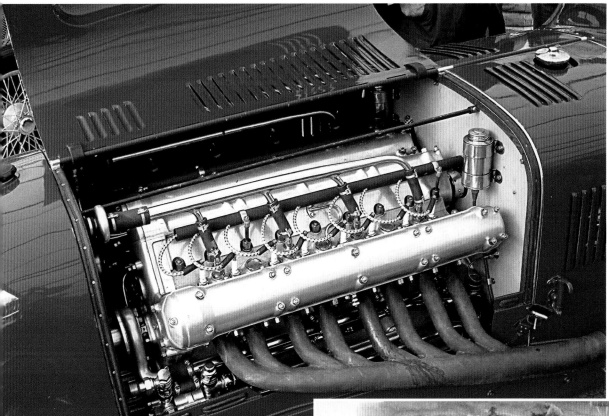

Both the Maserati V4, here, and V5 had paired in-line eight-cylinder engines on a common crankcase and geared to a central drive to the clutch.

As raced in 1931 the Type 26 M Maserati had a 2.5-litre engine of 185 bhp. This one had a silencer to race at Brooklands.

French marques Salmson and Amilcar were the stars of 1.1-litre races with interference from BNC, Austin, Sandford and Sima-Violet. Italian cars figured little, although late in the 1920s some Fiat 509s took part. It was for this category that both Bugatti and Maserati created 1.1-litre versions of their straight eights. Though heavy in relation to its 105 horsepower, the 26 C succeeded in defeating a field of Salmsons and Amilcars in the 64-mile Premo Reale di Roma in May 1930.

In the Roman race Alfieri Maserati himself was the driver in an event that turned out to be the apogee of the 26 C's career. Such was his success there, however, that it allowed the Trident to build and sell four of the new model. Its entry bought time for creation of a new twin-cam four, Maserati's first, purpose-built for the category. In sports-car trim it was the 4CS 1100 and as a *monoposto* it was the 4CM 1100. Introduced in 1931, this was the Maserati that clamped a hammerlock on the Mille Miglia's 1.1-litre class.

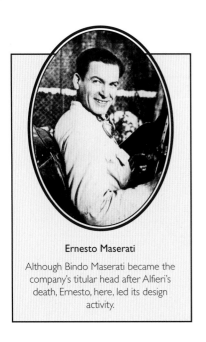

Ernesto Maserati

Although Bindo Maserati became the company's titular head after Alfieri's death, Ernesto, here, led its design activity.

Bologna grieved at the funeral of well-liked Alfieri Maserati on 5 March 1932.

Appearing in single-seater form in 1932, the 4CM 1100 triumphed in its first race, the 99-mile Coppa Ciano Junior on 31 July driven by Prince Domenico Cerami of Catania. Other privateers who campaigned the mini-Masers with success were Guido Landi, Ferdinando Barbieri, Romano Malaguti and Giuseppe Furmanik.

Meanwhile the Grand Prix races of the early 1930s were allowing cars of unlimited engine size. This too was exploited by the Maseratis and in formidable style. Aided by designer Piero Visentini, Alfieri Maserati schemed a new car with a wider frame designed to take two 2.0-litre straight eights side by side. While the left-hand unit was essentially a 26 B eight, the right-hand engine had its porting swapped so that its exhausts were on the right. Edoardo Weber, with whom the Maseratis had worked exclusively since 1928, produced special carburettors for the Roots-blown eights. They were geared together to drive a single transmission and live rear axle.

From its 3,961 cc this Type V4 – named for its quota of litres – produced 305 bhp at 5,200 rpm, the highest output of any car yet built for circuit racing. Alfieri drove it in its first outing, the Monza Grand Prix on 15 September 1929. He was just pipped in his heat by an SS Mercedes-Benz but in the final, where he had plug trouble, he matched the day's fastest lap.

A greater sensation came on 28 September when Baconin Borzacchini was timed in two directions over ten kilometres at Cremona in the Type V4 at a stunning average of 152.9 mph, a world record and 14 mph faster than the quickest Alfa. He received warm congratulations from the Duke of Bergamo. Looking back, the Maseratis would recall this as the triumph that most convincingly established their company as a serious contender in the eyes of the press, industry and public.

In the chequered race programmes of 1930 and 1931, the Type V4 enjoyed successes for both Borzacchini and Ernesto Maserati, though the powerful car made severe demands on its tyres. Stripped of its superchargers as the rules required in 1930 the V4 was entered at Indianapolis, where it fared poorly.

For 1932 the Trident unveiled an even bigger version that made use of larger bore dimensions to bring capacity of 4,905 cc. Credited with 350 bhp, this Type V5 set new lap records at several tracks but was outpaced in racing by the latest Type B Alfa Romeo, a new generation of *monoposto* racing car. Various problems beset this complicated car, reported Maserati historians Luigi Orsini and Franco Zagari: 'Due to the inefficiency of the pits they lost the Italian Grand Prix, a stupid breakage of the carburettor linkage stopped it at Avus and for banal disturbances in the steering it stopped at Miramas.'

In December 1932 Pirelli sponsored an attempt on the world one-hour record at the French banked track of Montlhéry. Early in the attack, however, lapping at 137 mph, Amedeo Ruggieri crashed fatally. This ended a year of tragedy for Maserati. Its scenario was set in May 1927 on a dusty, twisty circuit at Messina in Sicily where severe injuries were suffered by Alfieri Maserati when his car overturned. In spite of fractures and the loss of a kidney, he made a recovery. Complications with his remaining kidney were to be put right in March 1932 when, at the age of 44, the leader of the clan went under the knife. Tragically he did not survive the operation.

All Bologna turned out to mourn the loss of Alfieri Maserati, who rode to his rest in a magnificent Lancia hearse. Uniquely combining an ebullient character with skill as both driver and engineer, Alfieri had been the heart and soul of Maserati. 'Making honesty a point of honour,' wrote Orsini and Zagari, 'he had had an unlimited credit that was precious on numerous occasions of deep crisis.'

This was such an occasion. Fearing the failure of a company for which the deceased brother was the flag bearer, the Officine Alfieri Maserati's creditors pressed for immediate payment of their bills. Coping with a situation they described as 'desperate', the brothers regrouped. Having survived the economic crises of 1926 and 1929, Maserati had to continue. The eldest survivor, Bindo, left his post as chief tester at Isotta Fraschini to assume the presidency. Most outgoing of the brothers, he looked after relations with the press and customers. The youngest brother, Ernesto, stepped into the technical breach while Ettore continued his role as back-room man in charge of materials and manufacturing.

They benefited from a product range that had both symmetry and synergy. Already under development was a four-cylinder engine with dimensions of 69 x 100 mm for 1,495 cc to compete in the popular 1,500 cc *Voiturette* category. Ernesto jestingly referred to it as their '*motorino*' – a moped or scooter engine. Initially with a detachable head and later with monobloc design, from 1932 this was power for both sports and *monoposto* racers.

Also in 1932 similar components and dimensions created a new straight eight of 2,991 cc. Used initially in existing two-seater chassis, this was the 8C 3000, of which two were produced. It was the first of the Trident to win a major Grand Prix – the French race at Montlhéry in 1933 in the hands of Giuseppe Campari. During 1933 Ernesto evolved this into the single-seater 8CM, which can fairly be considered the first great road-racing

RECORD-BREAKER FURMANIK

In addition to his racing successes with Maseratis, Roman engineer Giuseppe Furmanik had a passion for record-breaking. Thanks to his design, testing, patenting and production of a successful parachute in the 1920s, Furmanik had the means to indulge his enthusiasms.

Furmanik began his record-breaking exploits at the age of 30 in 1934, when he set a flying-kilometre record of 138.34 mph on the Florence-Pistoia Autostrada in a special 4CM 1100 whose high-compression engine revved to 6,800 rpm to produce 140 bhp.

In January of 1936 the Roman engineer unveiled a version of his car with special bodywork by Turin's Viotti to a design by an aeronautical institute. It broke the flying mile record in the 1,100 cc class at 131.96 mph. Furmanik also set standing-start records for the kilometre and mile. With his new-shape Maserati Furmanik tackled records in the 1.5-litre class in 1937. His speed on the Autostrada was 148.2 mph for the kilometre.

When Ernesto and Bindo Maserati accompanied Furmanik to the Autostrada in January 1936 they brought along one of their 3.0-litre eight-cylinder racing cars. Its special preparation included an increase in compression ratio from 5.26:1 to 5.75:1. Taking it to the higher revs of 6,200 rpm for the short record distances gave it 312 bhp, a hefty increase from the normal 260 bhp at 5,600 rpm.

Giuseppe Furmanik's new speeds topped records that were already held by Maseratis, those of Whitney Straight and Laszlo Harmann. Over the kilometre he clocked 155.13 mph and 154.44 mph was his speed for the mile. Standing-start mile and kilometre records were set as well. The all-Italian success was tyred by Pirelli and fuelled by Agip.

His records added to the respect with which Furmanik was regarded in Italian motoring circles. At the end of the 1930s he was president of the Sporting Council of the Automobile Club of Italy.

Records by Furmanik on Maserati became a leitmotif of European competition in the mid-1930s.

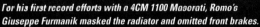

For his first record efforts with a 4CM 1100 Maserati, Rome's Giuseppe Furmanik masked the radiator and omitted front brakes.

Later in 1936 Giuseppe Furmanik unveiled a version of his record-breaking Maserati with wind-cheating bodywork by an aeronautical institute.

Maserati. It was the fastest 3.0-litre racing car of its day, as Furmanik demonstrated with more records in 1936.

In 1933-34 the 8CM was one of the mounts of Tazio Nuvolari, enjoying a glorious association with Maserati. In his first test before the July 1933 Belgian G.P, Nuvolari found the single-seater a handful, even for him. 'It was very fast and powerful,' wrote Piero Taruffi of the 8CM he raced, 'but by no means stable at speed. The frame was insufficiently rigid and the rather large amount of unsprung weight used to set up such torsional vibrations that the entire running-gear – both front and back axles – used to judder.' Nuvolari took the car to the Imperia works, located conveniently less than 20 miles from the Spa circuit, and with that company's help

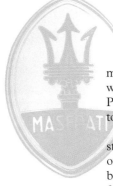

modified the 8CM. 'He changed the steering wheel to one with sprung spokes,' said Ernesto, 'installed a shorter Pitman arm and bolted some metal boxes into the frame to stiffen it.'

Arriving at Spa too late for practice, Nuvolari had to start the race from the back row. During the lap of just over nine miles he passed all the Alfas and Bugattis to lead by a gap so great – a stunning 24 seconds – that onlookers feared the rest of the field had crashed. The wiry Italian in his yellow jersey won at Spa and in his next two races at Livorno and Nice. Through 1934 the flying Mantuan drove 17 races in the 8CM Maserati. He finished second three times and suffered only four retirements for mechanical reasons.

Its 1933 successes put Maserati's 8CM in pole position among those racers who were looking to buy a car suitable for the new 1934 Grand Prix formula that imposed a maximum car weight of 750 kilograms. New 8CMs built to these rules had wider-spaced frame members to meet the formula's width requirement. But both Alfa Romeo's Type B and the new German cars of 1934 were tough competition. To meet them Ernesto

started work in 1934 on a completely new and radical design.

The result was the Type V8 RI, which on completion in 1935 looked the absolute goods with its independent suspension at all four wheels, using torsion bars in front, and rear-mounted transmission. Its V-8 engine of 4,788 cc developed more than 300 horsepower. But apart from a Pau Grand Prix victory in March 1936 by independent racer Philippe Etancelin, all this effort went for naught.

'Certain things get abandoned,' Ernesto Maserati reflected on the fate of the V8 RI. 'One knows not why.' A factor was that the driver who best mastered the new model's unusual handling, Nino Farina, defected to Alfa Romeo. Three of the four cars made went to America to compete in the 1937 Vanderbilt Cup, where one finished ninth in the hands of Wilbur Shaw. Two remained to compete at Indianapolis, where they were unsuccessful. One was acquired by Connecticut's George Weaver, for whom – as 'Poison Lil' – it dominated American *Formula Libre* road racing into the early 1950s.

With Alfa and the German cars monopolising the Grand Prix contests, the Maseratis intensified their

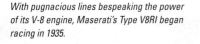

With pugnacious lines bespeaking the power of its V-8 engine, Maserati's Type V8RI began racing in 1935.

1938 MASERATI TYPE 8CTF

WHEN INDIANAPOLIS CAME IN LINE WITH THE NEW GRAND PRIX FORMULA OF 1938 WILBUR SHAW WAS QUICK TO TAKE ADVANTAGE, WINNING THE 500-MILE RACE IN 1939 AND 1940 WITH THIS MAGNIFICENT MASERATI.

The Type 6CM 1500 Maserati with its clean twin-cam six-cylinder engine was a strong Voiturette racing competitor.

Paul Pietsch electrified the Nürburgring crowd in 1939 with his third-place finish in Maserati's handsome Type 8CTF.

1936, however, Italy's war in Ethiopia siphoned off racing-car customers. In spite of the launch of the attractive 6CM the prospects for 1937 were grim. Bologna-based journalist and editor, Corrado Filippini, naturally took an interest in the fate of his home town's racing-car builders.

Filippini knew that in Modena Adolfo Orsi, a shrewd self-made businessman, was building a commercial empire. That the Maseratis had a strong and under-exploited brand name, also associated with a spark-plug business, commended them to Orsi. With Filippini as intermediary Orsi acquired a controlling majority of Maserati shares. Bindo, Ernesto and Ettore agreed to provide their services to the company for a period of ten years. They remained in Bologna until the end of 1939, when they moved their operations to Modena.

This fresh backing helped the brothers lay down a magnificent supercharged straight-eight racing car of 3.0 litres, the 8CTF, for the new Grand Prix formula commencing in 1938. Although German cars still dominated, the handsome 366-horsepower 8CTF was able to lead Grands Prix in both 1938 and 1939. In the former year, Count Carlo Trossi held pole position for the Coppa Ciano and led until brake and engine problems intervened. In 1939 German privateer, Paul Pietsch, led early laps of the German Grand Prix – Italian red ahead of German silver – and finished an excellent third.

More importantly, an 8CTF acquired by Chicago labour-union boss Mike Boyle, and tended by ace mechanic Cotton Henning, won the 500 miles of Indianapolis in 1939 and 1940, driven by 1937 winner, Wilbur Shaw. This was the first success for a foreign car in the world's richest race since a Peugeot's victory in 1919. Shaw narrowly missed another victory in 1941 when a wire wheel that was known to be suspect was fitted at the right rear in error at a pit stop. It failed when he was a lap in the lead.

In 1940 Shaw was alarmed to learn that an Argentine syndicate would field a new 3.0-litre eight-cylinder Maserati, the 8CL, with more power than his 8CTF. In fact with its four valves per cylinder and 'square' cylinder dimensions of 78 x 78 mm it was credited with 430 bhp at 6,800 rpm. Not completed in time to compete in Europe's last Grand Prix season of 1939, the two 8CLs received neither the driving nor the preparation skills needed to show well at Indianapolis either before or after the war.

The 8CL's introduction was preceded by the 1939 debut of its sister, the 1.5-litre 4CL, which had identical dimensions and valve gear in four instead of eight

Voiturette efforts. Britain's ERA had trumped Maserati's 1.5-litre fours with its sixes, to which Ernesto responded with a six of his own. The 6CM 1500 first shown in the autumn of 1935 kept the V8 RI's torsion-bar front suspension with a conventional live-axle rear end.

Uncommonly attractive, the 6CM produced as much as 175 bhp at 6,600 rpm and, in tests at Bologna, more than 200 bhp on special fuels. Winner of the Eifelrennen on its debut in June 1936 in the hands of Count Carlo Felice Trossi, the 6CM was the mainstay of the Trident's 1.5-litre offering through to 1938. Some successes in this period fell to the 4CM, which fitted a supercharged four-cylinder engine in the 6CM chassis.

Thanks to the popularity of Maserati's *Voiturettes*, 1934 and 1935 were profitable years for the company. In

cylinders. In Ernesto's ingenious design it also used the same cast-iron cylinder blocks, in unit with their heads, which held two cylinders apiece – four for the bigger engine and two for the smaller – bolted to an aluminium crankcase. Built in response to the challenge from Alfa Romeo's Type 158, the 4CL carried over the general chassis characteristics of the successful 6CL.

Supercharged to deliver 220 bhp at 6,600 rpm, the 4CL was too new in 1939 to give of its best. Three appeared in the first big race of the year for *Voiturettes* at Tripoli in May, one in fully streamlined all-enclosed bodywork with which lead driver Luigi 'Gigi' Villoresi seized pole position. It faded early in the race, however, as did its sisters, leaving a one-two victory to Mercedes-Benz in the only entry of its Type W165 in a *Voiturette* race.

Among private owners of the 4CL, Britain's Johnny Wakefield and Reggie Tongue as well as the Scuderia Automobilistica Ambrosiana's Giovanni Rocco enjoyed successes. The Ambrosiana outfit was set up in November 1936 by four Milanese racers and named after that city's patron saint, St. Ambrose or Ambroeus in Italian.

Italy's racing continued into 1940, with Gigi Villoresi winning Europe's last pre-war single-seater contest in Sicily's Palermo Park with his 4CL from an all-Maserati field on 23 May. After the war these *monoposti*, especially those from the Ambrosiana stable, would be just the ticket for the new Formula 1, which accommodated 1.5-litre supercharged cars.

Pictured in 1939, Britain's Charlie Dodson was a Maserati adherent. He finished fifth with this 6CM at Donington in 1939.

The Autostrada was used for tests of the streamlined body used by Maserati on its new Type 4CL in 1939's Tripoli Grand Prix.

Great driver in a great car: Ted Horn at Indianapolis in 1947 in Wilbur Shaw's former Maserati 8CTF; he placed third.

CHAPTER 11

Portello's Sixes and Twelves

IN 1933 Alfa Romeo was one of the first companies to be taken under the wing of IRI, the government-owned industrial holding company, after its formation that year to prop up selected enterprises in Benito Mussolini's Italy. In 1933 Alfa would make only 408 cars, but it was growing in importance as a supplier of trucks and aircraft engines to a rearming Italy. Since 1927 Vittorio Jano had overseen aviation engines as well as cars, producing successful radial designs. These as well as licence-built German trucks became the company's main activity in the mid-1930s while car production dwindled to double-digit depths.

One idea for Alfa Romeo's future was a small car. Starting in 1935 Jano's team created three prototypes of the 4C 1500 – as its name indicated, a 1.5-litre four-cylinder model. In the 6C tradition it would have offered both single- and twin-cam versions, mounted in a platform frame with all-independent suspension. After its development was dropped in 1937 the cars were used for experiments in battery-electric propulsion during the war.

By then Portello was already producing the car that was intended to be its mainstream model. Initiated when Prospero Gianferrari was running Alfa, it was first displayed at Milan's auto show in April of 1934. This was the 6C 2300, which carried its 2,309 cc in an iron block of six cylinders with a detachable aluminium cylinder head. Valves at 90 degrees were opened by twin cams driven by a chain at the front of the engine, a solution that Jano had hitherto disparaged as unsuitable for speeds over 4,000 rpm. Seven main bearings assured robustness and smoothness.

On the 6C 2300's shorter wheelbase of 115.2 inches with its conventional leaf springs Carrozzeria Touring built three fabric-roofed coupés to compete in the Targa Abruzzi run by the Pescara Automobile Club over its 15.8-mile circuit on the Adriatic. Starting at noon on 12 August, for the first time it was a 24-hour race for production cars. Overcoming problems with their knock-off wire wheels, the cars finished one-two-three. They justified their new name, 'Pescara', by taking the first two places in another 24-hour race there in 1935.

Nineteen thirty-five saw the introduction of a more modern version, the 6C 2300 B, with hydraulic brakes and four-wheel independent suspension from the pens of Ferdinand Porsche's designers. One such with sporting coupé bodywork by Touring was entered in the new National Touring category in 1937's Mille Miglia by Mussolini for his chauffeur Ercole Boratto, an Alfa test driver who had long been on loan to *Il Duce*. He was accompanied by Portello's Gianbattista Guidotti, who in fact did all the driving to win the category and placed fourth overall. With 95 bhp at 4,400 rpm the Mille Miglia model could reach 96 mph.

It was the fashion among dyed-in-the wool Alfa Romeo fanatics to disparage these 'downmarket' sixes, many of which were overbodied and underpowered. Nevertheless they had to esteem the 6C 2500 introduced in 1939. An enlarged bore brought capacity to 2,443 cc and power, in the SS Corsa competition version, to 124 bhp at 4,800 rpm with triple Weber carburettors. Married with the light and shapely bodies being made in Milan by Carrozzeria Touring, this created a sports-racer that commanded respect.

In the absence of a Mille Miglia in 1939, Marshal Italo Balbo of the Italian Protectorate of Libya arranged for his Tripoli auto club to stage the second Littoranea Libica over the nation's coast roads to and from Tobruk. Not far short of 1,000 miles, the distance was 1,500 kilometres. In a race lasting ten and a half hours the winners in a 6C 2500 SS Corsa were Ercole Boratto and Consalvo

Sanesi, the latter an Alfa tester who was having his first racing drive for Il Portello. Biondetti's similar car was second. Giuseppe 'Nino' Farina drove one to second place behind a BMW in the 1940 closed-circuit Mille Miglia.

By this time the cars were being entered by Alfa Corse in Milan, no longer by the Scuderia Ferrari. Nineteen thirty-seven was a transition year in racing for Alfa, which acquired 80 per cent of Scuderia Ferrari in March. By the end of the year it was ready to re-establish its own racing department, Alfa Corse, in new buildings in Milan. Although Enzo Ferrari was at least nominally in charge of Alfa Corse, its competition cars were no longer overseen by Vittorio Jano. After Vincenzo Lancia's death earlier in the year, partly to fill the considerable vacuum left by the founder, Jano returned to Turin and joined Lancia.

Under the IRI's ownership and Ugo Gobbato, recalled an Alfa engineer, 'the management was very hard, very severe. However good you were, whatever brilliant work you had done in the past, if you did not deliver you could be dismissed.' Since 1934 Gobbato had pared away Jano's other responsibilities, leaving him in charge of car design only. In this sphere his resources were severely

As bodied by Carrozzeria Touring the 1937 Second Series of Alfa Romeo's 6C 2300B was a purposeful 2+2 grand touring car.

Late in 1935 Alfa Romeo introduced its 8C 1935 Grand Prix car with a 3.8-litre straight eight producing 330 bhp at 5,400 rpm.

Bruno Trevisan's 4.0-litre V-12 design for Alfa Romeo was clearly of the Jano school, although with a big Roots-type blower low at the front.

circumscribed by car output that fell to 91 and then 10 units in 1935 and '36 respectively.

Instead of desperately needed money and men, wrote colleague Gioachino Colombo, his bosses motivated Jano with 'more or less authoritative messages, directives and appeals.' In the factory, he said, there was 'great confusion about roles, too many people all wanting their own way in the matter of planning. It's a matter for amazement that he managed to build a vehicle at all under those conditions.'

Nevertheless for the 1935 season Vittorio Jano managed to produce a new Grand Prix car powered by an expanded version of his Type B eight-cylinder engine, the 8C 35. The eight was a stopgap until the engine arrived for which the car was intended, an all-new V-12. On 10 May 1936, at the Tripoli Grand Prix in North Africa, it made its bow as originally planned with its V-12 engine as the 12C.

Detailing of this twelve was the work of 43-year-old Bruno Trevisan, a reserve major in Italy's

Air Force. An engine expert at Fiat, Trevisan was recruited to Il Portello by Ugo Gobbato, with whom he'd enjoyed a childhood friendship. He moved to Milan in October 1934, just in time to start work on the new twelve. Although the work was done by the major, the engine bore the unmistakable fingerprints of Jano.

The V-12 was a work of commendable purity. Its vee angle was 60 degrees, while its two valves per cylinder were angled symmetrically at the wide spread that Jano favoured, 104 degrees, using typical Jano valve gear. All the engine's main castings were in light alloy, with the crankcase cast of magnesium alloy. Pioneered for racing cars by the Maserati brothers, magnesium was used successfully in the 3.8-litre eight that powered the chassis in its original form as the 8C 1935.

Driven directly from the nose of the crank was one rotor of a Roots-type supercharger which blew upward and back into the centre of inlet manifolds that were partly integral with the blocks. Under it was the inlet ducting for two horizontal twin-throat Weber carburettors. Other gears turned the single magneto and the water pump on the right, from which two manifolds ran back along the blocks to inlets below the exhaust ports.

By Alfa Romeo's racing-car standards this was an epic engine, its most potent yet. The twelve's capacity of 4,064 cc produced 370 bhp at 5,800 rpm. 'They were confident,' wrote historian Laurence Pomeroy, Jr. 'that with the extra power available from this they would be able to take full advantage of their new independently sprung chassis and reassert in 1936 the supremacy which had been theirs only two seasons before.' Six in all were made, plus four spare engines.

The first race outing at Tripoli on 10 May 1936 showed promise. On this very fast circuit the Alfas were only two seconds slower than the Mercedes-Benzes on a lap of 3¾ minutes. At the finish, however, the three twelves were sixth, seventh and eighth and, indeed, behind an 8C Alfa in fifth, trailing the German cars.

On a more challenging track at Barcelona's Montjuich Park on 7 June Tazio Nuvolari drove the sole 12C-36 to a tremendous victory over both German teams in spite of two pit stops over 188 miles; the new car was proving hard on its tyres. Nuvolari won three more times that year in the new twelve, at Milan, Modena and – most importantly – the 300-mile race on the new Roosevelt Raceway on New York's Long Island for the George Vanderbilt Cup. Though no Germans were present, this gave both Tazio and Alfa Romeo major bragging rights over the winter.

Nevertheless 1936 had not been a good Mercedes-Benz season. Vittorio Jano knew he had to extract more power from his twelve for 1937, terminal year of the 750-kilogram formula. He and Trevisan enlarged both bore and stroke to bring the twelve to 4,495 cc. Boost pressure went up with higher supercharger efficiency thanks to the use of two smaller Roots-type blowers running at 1.5 times engine speed.

Weighing 474 pounds, the revised engine produced 430 bhp at 5,800 rpm. This was as naught, however, against the 575 horses of Mercedes-Benz and Auto Union's 520-plus. In the major races the best that Alfa could muster was Nuvolari's fourth in the German Grand Prix. In minor events, against occasional Auto Union entries, wins were achieved at Turin, Naples and Milan. Laurence Pomeroy wrote that 'during 1937 so far from narrowing the gap, Alfa Romeo fell farther behind.'

Portello nursed high expectations for a new low-chassis model that made its debut at Pescara in August. Marrying the existing power train and suspension to a narrow chassis – virtually a backbone – and a much lower profile, a quartet was put on wheels. The new model was far off the pace. Of the two entries only one started for Nuvolari, who struggled to run ninth before handing his car to Nino Farina, who retired. This catastrophic launch on home territory, said Alfa engineer Luigi Fusi, 'cost Jano his parting with Alfa Romeo.'

For 1938 Grand Prix cars could be 4.5 litres unblown and 3.0 litres supercharged. With odds strongly favouring the latter, Alfa shrank its twelve to 2,997 cc and without

greatly changing its blowers or boost pressure extracted 350 bhp at 6,500 rpm. This, in the lower chassis, was Alfa's Type 312 for 1938, for which the 35-year-old Gioachino Colombo, a close ally of Jano, had some design responsibility. Three of the new cars were built, cadging components from their predecessors.

The 312's performance in its few 1938 appearances led many to suggest that this Alfa could be a contender if its maker were inclined to back it with conviction. Problems in setting up the new Alfa Corse didn't help, nor did Alfa's dalliance with 8- and 16-cylinder engines for the new formula and its heightened interest in the 1.5-litre *Voiturette* category, for which it had the eight-cylinder Type 158 designed by Colombo and built in Ferrari's Modena workshops.

All three 312s were at Tripoli in Libya, one of Italy's African protectorates, for the first big Grand Prix of 1938 in mid-May. Two started, with the thrusting Nino Farina showing the 312's potential but crashing out – as he often did. The other twelve crashed as well, killing its unfortunate driver, Eugenio Siena. Of two cars in July's German G.P. one crashed and the other retired.

Pairs of cars competed at home in August in the Coppa Ciano and Coppa Acerbo. In both they had to give best to a Mercedes, but nevertheless took second and third places. In the Swiss Grand Prix on 21 August Nino Farina

In 1936's Italian Grand Prix at Monza Tazio Nuvolari's 12C 1936 Alfa Romeo placed second amidst the vaunted German Auto Unions.

Alfa-mounted, a begrimed Nuvolari has just finished his winning drive in 1931's 363-mile Targa Florio.

Pictured in 1934, Mantua's Tazio Nuvolari was at the peak of his legendary skills at the age of 42.

TAZIO NUVOLARI – THE FLYING MANTUAN

In all the long history of motor racing there can only be one person who stands out above all others not only for their achievements but also for their style and personality. That person is Tazio Giorgio Nuvolari. He was in his era and remains today an iconic figure representing the best in drive, determination, skill, competitiveness and fairness in combat.

Timing wasn't ideal for Nuvolari. After his birth in 1892 near Mantua – hence his sobriquet 'Il Mantovano Volante' – his racing career was interrupted at critical stages by the two world wars. The short, wiry Tazio only commenced racing at 28 in 1920 on motorcycles, encouraged by an uncle successful in that sphere. Italian champion in 1924 on Nortons and Bianchis, he rode for Bianchi in the late 1920s.

By 1927 Nuvolari was competing in a Type 35 Bugatti, whose agile handling suited his style. In cornering he took huge liberties, skiing the car around turns in slides, balancing it against the engine's power. He was distinctive with his yellow jersey and leather waistcoat, sitting high behind the wheel in total dominance, his deeply tanned visage long and sharp.

Great successes soon came Nuvolari's way. For the Scuderia Ferrari's Alfa Romeo stable he won the Mille Miglia and Tourist Trophy in 1930 and in 1931 the Targa Florio and three Grands Prix, two at Italy's temple of speed, Monza. In 1932 with the new Type B Alfa the 40-year-old Tazio swept the board, winning eight major races and the Italian and European championships. Wins at Le Mans and the Mille Miglia came in 1933.

In the years of the 750-kilogram formula, 1934 through 1937, 'Nivola' was Italy's hero, battling against the might of the German teams. First briefly with Maserati and then with Ferrari's Alfas he drove out of his skin with the products of Vittorio Jano, at only one year older an almost exact contemporary. Memorably in 1935's German Grand Prix at the challenging Nürburgring he so harassed the leading Mercedes-Benz of Manfred von Brauchitsch that the silver car failed a tyre on the last lap to give Nuvolari and Alfa one of the most dramatic and famous victories in Grand Prix annals.

In 1936 Tazio was the toast of New York after his win in Long Island's Vanderbilt Cup, posing with a trophy almost as big as he was. In 1938 he was signed by Auto Union as team leader to replace Bernd Rosemeyer, killed early in the year in a record-breaking attempt. Although Mercedes-Benz had the better cars, he won the 1938 Italian Grand Prix and both that year and in 1939 had winter bragging rights with wins in the seasons' final races.

Although he was 47 in 1939, such was Tazio Nuvolari's spirit and vitality that he could well have carried on had war not intervened. In an ultimate irony, when he returned to the tracks a lung ailment had made exhaust fumes hazardous to his health. Nevertheless his epic drive to second in the 1947 Mille Miglia with an outclassed Cisitalia was a historic achievement that held all Italy enthralled. Piero Dusio hoped he would race his Grand Prix Cisitalia but this was not to be.

Tazio raced some of the first Ferraris, leading the 1948 Mille Miglia until the hard-pressed car gave up not far from the finish at Brescia. His final races were in 1950, driving sports cars derived from the last Cisitalias for Carlo Abarth's new stable. He retired in the Giro di Sicilia but won his class in a hill climb at Palermo the following weekend, 10 April. He never competed again. He was 61 when he died at home in Mantua.

In commemoration of the great driver's career the route of the Mille Miglia was diverted through Mantua from 1954 through 1957. As well, the Nuvolari Prize was awarded for the fastest time from Cremona through Mantua to the Brescia finish. These were fine gestures, but in fact no memorial to Nuvolari was needed. His character and career were amply adequate.

was fifth behind three Mercedes and an Auto Union, albeit two laps behind the winner after 50 laps. French ace Jean-Pierre Wimille was seventh in a sister car.

Wimille and Piero Taruffi had 312s for the Italian G.P. at Monza, where both retired. No more entries of the twelve were made until the Belgian Grand Prix on 26 June 1939, where one was entrusted to Frenchman Raymond Sommer. He was fourth, twice lapped, behind the Germans in the wet race in which Britain's Richard Seaman was killed. This – just missing the podium – would be the 312's best performance in a major Grand Prix.

Nor did the Alfa V-12 star in a series for which it could have been tailor-made: the *Formula Libre* races in Argentina at the beginning of 1948. Achille Varzi, who had raced there in 1947, arranged for Alfa Romeo to build a 'special' for his next campaign. Il Portello married a pre-war chassis that had been used for a 3.0-litre V-16 with a 1937-style 4.5-litre supercharged twelve to create as formidable-looking a racing car as has ever been con-trived. Its looks flattered to deceive, however, for the best that Varzi could manage with it was a second at Mar del Plata.

In a 'waste not, want not' frame of mind, Alfa Corse itself made use of redundant 4.5-litre V-12s before the war. In 1939 it used its G.P.-car componentry to build a sports-racing car on the lines of the famous 8C 2900B Mille Miglia model but powered by

The loss of a tyre didn't dissuade Tazio Nuvolari in his 12C 1936 Alfa Romeo in 1937's Masaryk Race at Brno in Czechoslovakia; he placed fifth.

Fitting snugly in the 12C 1936 Alfa Romeo, the Jano/Trevisan V-12 was enlarged to 4.5 litres and 430 bhp for 1937.

An ultimate Alfa Romeo monoposto was the V-12-engined car built for Achille Varzi to drive in the 1948 Argentine Temporada races.

an unblown version of the big vee-twelve to compete in events where super-chargers were banned. With its super-charger deleted, the twelve had new inlet manifolding carrying three downdraft double-throat carburettors to pro-duce 220 bhp at 5,500 rpm.

Dubbed the Type 412 and bodied by Touring, two of these formidable sports-racers were ready to race over the streets of Antwerp, Belgium on 31 May 1939. They finished one-two against opposition largely

from France, where this category was very popular. They were due to meet the French again at Liége on 20 August, and were fastest in practice, but the onset of war forced the race's cancellation.

After the war the 412s were recovered from safe storage. 'Everything was covered in thick grease,' an Alfa man remembered. 'It was just a question of cleaning it all carefully and with nothing more than normal preparation we could immediately race again.' One car was sold to Felice Bonetto, who won with it in Portugal in 1950 and had it magnificently rebodied by Vignale for the 1951 Mille Miglia, in which he was sixth.

The sister 412 was acquired by Swiss sportsman Willy Daetwyler, who raced it extensively and successfully in and around his homeland. For the 1953 season he had his 412 rebodied in a lighter style. From Alfa's stores he obtained a supercharging kit which would have given it

Of quintessentially Alfa Romeo design was the cockpit of Varzi's 1948 V-12-engined special with its left-hand gear change.

power akin to that of the Varzi single-seater. Ultimately this potent machine was acquired by the Schlumpf Collection in Mulhouse.

For Alfa Corse in Milan the 1930s ended in a burst of ludicrously unproductive yet costly activity. Its sponsor and promoter was a Spanish engineer, Wifredo Ricart, who arrived in Milan in the role of a consultant in 1936 at the age of 39. His authority continued to expand until by 1938 he was originating and building completely new racing cars that were as radical and bizarre as previous Alfas had been conservative and practical.

One, for the 3.0-litre supercharged Grand Prix races of 1938 and later, was the Type 162. This had a V-16 engine with its banks at 135 degrees and four valves per cylinder. When finally tested in 1940, with two-stage supercharging, it was said to produce 490 bhp at 7,800 rpm. The car, best described as ungainly, was only briefly assessed. 'Everyone understood it was no good at all,' tester Consalvo Sanesi told historian Doug Nye. By then, of course, war had called time on Grand Prix racing.

Ricart's other brainstorm was his Type 512, a mid-engined car of 1.5 litres with a flat-twelve engine to compete in the *Voiturette* races that were seen then, correctly, as harbingers of a future Grand Prix formula. Its driver was seated far forward, ahead of its central fuel tank. Consalvo Sanesi found that this impaired his control, doubly handicapping the driver of a car whose handling was treacherous. With racing-car development continuing into 1943, Sanesi recalled, 'I did about 2,500 miles testing

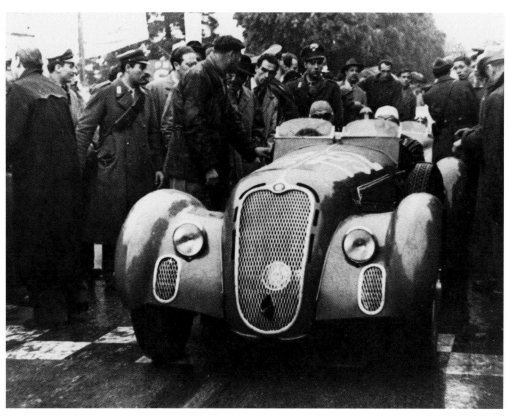

in the 512.' But it was never faster than the less powerful Type 158 Alfa of conventional design – a great car which we will meet in the next chapter.

Marrying the V-12 engine with the 8C 2900B chassis created the Type 412 Alfa of 1939. This one was competing in the 1950 Mille Miglia.

This styling mock-up was prepared for Wifredo Ricart's Type 162 Alfa Romeo Grand Prix car of 1939, with its supercharged wide-angle V-16 engine.

CHAPTER 12

Admirable Alfetta

Pictured by Rodolfo Mailander in the early 1950s, Gioachino Colombo was the architect of Alfa Romeo's Ferrari-built Type 158 Voiturette.

O N the subject of motor sports Briton John Lloyd wrote that the Italians 'had of course one less year of war than the other contestants and do not take war seriously enough to exhaust their total wealth and manpower in its following as it was necessary for us to do to secure victory.' Ruled as it was with fascist monomania by Benito Mussolini, Italy took a virulently anti-Communist line that drove it into alliances with the similarly minded European power, Hitler's Germany.

The links between Rome and Berlin were formalised with a pact to 'protect European culture and world peace from the Bolshevik menace' in November of 1936. May of 1939 found the two nations allying in what they called the 'Pact of Steel'. Knowing full well that his forces were inadequate to meet the military commitments that the pact might demand, Mussolini called it defensive rather than offensive. Nevertheless he joined the fray with a declaration of war against Britain and France on 10 June 1940.

That declaration was enough to end Italy's road racing, but as we saw at the end of the last chapter, racing-car development continued into 1943. Physical testing went underground after the beginning of September 1943 when Marshal Badoglio, successor to the deposed Mussolini, signed an armistice with the Allies. Any hope of easy success in the Italian peninsula faded when the Germans rushed troops there to oppose the Allied forces that had occupied Sicily.

Italy's racers turned their hands to the demands of the wartime economy. 'At the Milan Fair in April 1941,' wrote Luigi Orsini and Franco Zagari, Maserati was 'present under a new image with a vast assortment of machine tools, lathes, grinders and milling machines, inaugurating a new branch of activity.' For their part the Maserati brothers – daily commuters from their homes in Bologna – developed electric trucks and vans to meet wartime needs. This was the role of Bindo and Ernesto while Ettore took care of the spark plugs.

From 1944 with the help of engineer Alberto Massimino the Maseratis began work on the new unblown six-cylinder car that they foresaw as the basis of their peacetime production for both road and racing. With a rough provisional body, the prototype of this Type A6 took to the road during the war and was still circulating in 1946. As well, in a spirit of optimism Massimino suggested a magnificent 90-degree V-16 of 1,477 cc for Grand Prix racing. Penned in 1944, Massimino's ambitious design was never realised by Maserati.

For Alfa Romeo's part its Ugo Gobbato committed resources to the construction of a huge new plant at Pomigliano, near Naples, to produce aviation engines. None of his own company's designs was judged suitable, however. Opened in June 1940 by the Duke of Bergamo, the vast factory and its ancillary facilities made Daimler-Benz V-12 aero engines during the war. After the armistice, however, the Germans spent a week demolishing the plant. 'The destruction is utter and complete,' said a visitor, 'and the whole site is the most appalling bedlam and confusion imaginable.'

Far to the north, fortunately, were the best of Alfa Romeo's pre-war racing cars. They were dispersed to various locations not far from Milan, where bomb damage at Portello was severe. After Italy's Liberation Day, 25 April 1945, chief tester Consalvo Sanesi and colleagues went to retrieve them. 'It was difficult to remember where everything was!' he told Doug Nye. 'It took more than a month to find it all.' Some assembly was required, because the cars had been dismantled to make it less easy for them to be exploited if they were found by other than Portello personnel. All this took place without Ugo Gobbato. Three days after the liberation he was gunned down in the street as a reward for his enthusiastic collaboration with the Nazis.

Among the Alfa Romeos recovered were seven examples of the finest *Voiturette* of the pre-war era. This was the Type 158, named for its 1.5-litre capacity and eight cylinders in line. The Type 158 Alfa traced its beginnings to 1937, a season in which the red cars from Milan were shut out of success in front-line Grands Prix by Mercedes-Benz and Auto Union. Enzo Ferrari, responsible for racing the cars assigned to his Scuderia by Alfa, decided to build a 1.5-litre machine to run in the increasingly popular *Voiturette* events.

Although the decision was Ferrari's, credit for inspiration and encouragement was owed to Gioachino Colombo. Born 20 miles from Milan in 1903, Colombo's career at Portello dated from 1924 when he was a young member of the team creating the P2 for Vittorio Jano. The latter said that during the 1930s 'Colombo began to be my right arm,' the man who helped realise his ideas.

Colombo also had ideas of his own. His suggestion to Enzo Ferrari in the spring of 1937 was that they follow the Auto Union example by building a mid-engined 1.5-litre racer. Although this was too radical for Ferrari, he agreed to propose to Alfa that his Scuderia take on the task of creating a *Voiturette* with design help from Portello. In this, said historian Aldo Zana, he was suggesting an outsourcing of the job to him 'by a company distressed by management conflicts, erratic production programs, lack of strategic vision and badly defeated in racing.'

For Ferrari the project's *capo di tutti capi* was his technical chief Luigi Bazzi. With his astonishing Bimotore, Bazzi had proven his creativity and skill. With designer Colombo, Bazzi directed the job along lines that were conventional, although specifying an eight-cylinder engine was ambitious. It was to prove an inspired choice. So was the decision to use the relatively small bore of 58 mm so that the engine's length wouldn't be ungainly. With a 70 mm stroke its capacity was 1,480 cc.

Also with compactness in mind Bazzi and Colombo eschewed Jano's central camshaft drive and placed the gear train at the front of the engine. However the screw-adjustable tappets and wide 100-degree valve angle were authentic Jano. An advanced feature was a crankcase cast

Porsche-type front suspension was exposed by the narrow bodywork of the Type 158 Alfa Romeo as it first raced in 1938.

Nino Farina leans insouciantly on the Type 158 Alfetta that he raced so effectively in the Swiss G.P. at Bern in 1939.

In his Alfa Type 158 Nino Farina dominated proceedings in both heat and final of the 1946 G.P. des Nations at Geneva. Jean-Pierre Wimille followed here.

raced, Alfa Romeo took over Ferrari's complete organisation and hired him to run its revived in-house racing department, Alfa Corse. At its Milan base the cars were completed, the first one being ready for function testing at the end of 1937. It was a spare, trim car, simply executed by people who were well aware that they would have to service it as well as build and race it.

With Alfa's new Grand Prix cars for 1938 taking priority, early that year the 158 had had to wait. By June, however, the Alfa Corse team could address their attentions to the new *Voiturette*. Chief tester was Attilio Marinoni with Consalvo Sanesi as his deputy, also responsible for car preparation. Their trials at Monza in May and June, shared also by Enrico Nardi, showed the new car capable of competitive times, so an entry was made for the Coppa Ciano on 7 August 1938 at Livorno. In the 90-mile race for *Voiturettes* the three dark-crimson Alfas started from the front row. Shrugging off the best Maseratis, they went on to place one-two and seventh, Emilio Villoresi the winner.

This was a stunning entree for an all-new racing car, first and second on its debut. A week later, however, the Maserati brigade had its revenge on the long road course at Pescara where one Alfa left the track and retired and the other was fourth after a long stop. To gain time for reflection, entries for races at Bern and Lucca were abandoned. This delivered dividends at Monza on 11 September where another one-two finish was scored over 109 miles against a vast fleet of Maseratis. At Modena a week later, however, victory went to the home-town Trident team.

The Type 158's first appearance in 1939 was in the heat of the Italian Protectorate of Libya on Africa's north coast for the Tripoli Grand Prix on 7 May. On practice times the cars were outpaced both by Gigi Villoresi's streamlined 4CL Maserati and by the two new V-8 W165s built by Mercedes-Benz for the race. Although Alfa Corse fielded six 158s, the best they could do was third behind the two silver cars from Stuttgart.

In August 1939 Nino Farina and a 158 Alfa took on the full Grand Prix Mercedes and Auto Unions at the fast Bern course, shocking onlookers by holding second place on the first lap and finishing sixth ahead of two of the fabled silver cars. Although war erupted in Europe a month later it did not immediately involve Italy, so work on the cars continued. To improve engine cooling, inadequate in hot races, the 158's bodywork was revised to the wider shape that was to become world-famous.

The competition calendar for 1940 still offered numerous events including the Mille Miglia as well as

of ultra-light magnesium, a technique proven at Portello on the Grand Prix V-12 of 1936. Bolted to it were two four-cylinder blocks of aluminium. Into their integral hemispherical heads steel cylinders were screwed, forming a robust gasket-free unit that could take high supercharging pressures. A Roots-type blower was on the engine's left side, driven by a shaft from the front-end gearing.

Assisting Colombo were draftsman Giovanni Nasi and the versatile Alberto Massimino, who joined the team to work on the transmission and rear-suspension design. The Type 158's four-speed gearbox was under the driver's seat, in unit with the final drive. Attached to a ladder-type frame of oval tubes, suspension was independent at front and rear with transverse leafs the springing medium. Geometrically the suspension resembled Auto Union's with parallel trailing arms in front and swing axles at the rear, guided by trailing radius arms. As experience was gained, more negative camber was introduced at the rear to give improved cornering grip under power.

Early in 1938 the first four Type 158s were being assembled in Ferrari's shops in Modena. Before they were

single-seater races for 1,500 cc cars, to most of which the German teams had committed entries. Expecting another visit to Tripoli by Mercedes, Alfa Corse tested one of its revised cars extensively on the hot, sandy Mellaha road circuit. Three from a quartet of entries dominated the podium places at the finish, led by Nino Farina. His speed over the 214 miles was a fantastic 128.2 mph, 14 mph faster that that year's Indianapolis 500 and 5.3 mph faster than the winning Mercedes-Benz of the previous year. This triumphant showing was their last before being dismantled and preserved in the heavy grease that protected them during the war.

Soon after their appearance these 'little Alfas' were given the appropriate Italian nickname of '*Alfette*' or, in the Anglicised world, 'Alfetta'. This was warmly affectionate, though the cars didn't always deserve such sympathy. At Pescara in 1939 Giordano Aldrighetti crashed fatally in one, while earlier in the year Emilio Villoresi was killed at Monza during a banal commercial demonstration, a loss for which his younger brother Gigi never forgave Enzo Ferrari. In 1940, testing a 158 with experimental de Dion rear suspension, Attilio Marinoni was killed when he encountered Autostrada traffic at high speed.

Two-stage supercharging, using a large Roots blower that fed a smaller one, had been adopted by both German teams in 1939 and readied by Mercedes-Benz for its

W165 in case of a return to Tripoli in 1940. This gave higher power, partly because it was a more efficient means of delivering high boost pressures and thus absorbed less engine power to drive it. After laying out a V-12 engine and car concept for Enzo Ferrari, Gioachino Colombo returned to Alfa Romeo in November of 1945 to help design, test and fit such a system to the Type 158.

The Alfetta eight responded enthusiastically to higher boost pressures. In 1938 it initially gave 190 bhp at 6,500 rpm; as raced in 1938 205 at 7,000; and in 1939 up to 225 at 7,500 rpm, when a needle-bearing crankshaft and crankcase improvements allowed higher revs. Two-stage blowing initially gave 254 bhp at 7,500 rpm. Tested during 1946, the twin blowers were introduced on all the cars for 1947. In 1948 a new version with a larger primary blower appeared for Reims practice and in the Italian Grand Prix. This Type 158/47 delivered 310 bhp at 7,500 rpm as a rule, some engines being rated at 335 bhp at 8,000.

The first post-war race for Alfa was on 9 June 1946 in the St. Cloud district of Paris. Neither Nino Farina nor Frenchman Jean-Pierre Wimille finished. This sorry result is notable because Alfa Romeo did not lose another Grand Prix race until 14 July 1951 – and apart from a sabbatical in 1949 they entered all the big ones. In 1947 Alfettas won the four major races run to the new Formula 1 for 1.5-litre supercharged cars pitched against unblown cars

From left to right: Alfa Romeo engineers Livio Nicolis, Orazio Satta Puglia and Giuseppe Busso oversaw the Alfetta's early post-war successes.

Juan Manuel Fangio, for whom it was the dream of a lifetime to race the Alfetta, won his heat in Silverstone's 1951 International Trophy.

A good sense of his imperious style at the wheel of the Alfetta was given by Farina en route to victory in the 1950 British and European G.P.

A sore loser but happy winner, Nino Farina showing the latter side of his character in 1951.

GIUSEPPE 'NINO' FARINA

No driver is more closely associated with the scintillating career of the Type 158 Alfetta than Nino Farina. This outstanding driver, the first world champion in 1950, was born in Turin in 1906 into a family deeply involved with motor cars. His father Giovanni was proprietor of a leading coachbuilding firm where his uncle Battista, nicknamed 'Pinin' for his small stature, was also active.

Nino studied law, earning a doctorate, while active as a sportsman in riding, skiing and other pursuits. His record as a cavalryman in national service was first-class. He had been driving since the age of nine, his first car a twin-cylinder Temperino. In 1930 he and Giovanni took their Alfas to the Aosta-Gran san Bernardo hill climb. When the impetuous Nino crashed and was hospitalised with a broken clavicle his father grounded him.

By 1933 Nino Farina was back on the tracks with Alfas and Maseratis. His first major success was in 1934, a Voiturette victory in the Czech Grand Prix at Brno. In these glory years of Tazio Nuvolari the Flying Mantuan was the driver to emulate, which Farina unashamedly did, sitting well back from the wheel in an imperious stance that communicated total control. Tazio returned the compliment, tutoring the eager newcomer in the ways of the sport.

His rapid rise found Farina on the Scuderia Ferrari strength in 1936. The following year he won the Naples Grand Prix in a V-12 Alfa on his way to the Italian championship, an honour he retained through 1939. In the right place at the right time, Nino was perfectly placed to take command of the new Type 158 Voiturette being fielded by Alfa Corse.

Though not the first to win with it, still being asked by Alfa to fight the vain fight in the big league against the Germans, he joined the Alfetta effort in 1939. Farina won three of the 1.5-litre races that year and stunned the Grand Prix runners with his pace in the final of the Swiss Grand Prix. He also won the 244-mile Tripoli Grand Prix in May of 1940 at an average five miles per hour faster than the previous year's winning Mercedes.

Nino Farina's standing as Italy's premier racing motorist was sealed when he was picked to lead the Alfetta team in 1946. The first victory to fall to the Type 158 was in that year's Geneva Grand Prix, Farina leading the Alfas home. In 1947 he worked with Ferrari to perfect his new Grand Prix cars, then raced Maseratis in 1948 and '49. When Alfa Romeo returned in 1950 Farina rejoined the team with Fangio and Fagioli, creating the 'Three Fs' driver troika.

Juan Fangio had plenty of chances to watch Farina in action. 'When I followed him in the Alfa Romeo it was incredible,' he recalled; 'he drove like a madman. We used to say that he was protected by the Madonna, but even the Holy Madonna's patience has a limit and he should have considered that she could not be at his disposal all the time.' By then the veteran with the noble visage, sensitive about his thinning hair, demanded the right of way as his exclusive prerogative.

No outcome could have been more fitting in 1950 for the world of Italian racing red than a world championship for Nino Farina driving Alfa Romeo. Fangio took the honours in 1951 with Farina fourth on points behind the surging Ferraris. Although in 1952 and '53 Nino had to play second fiddle for Ferrari to the sublimely talented Alberto Ascari, he scored several worthy wins. The proud Farina continued with Ferrari into early 1955 before finally retiring.

Enzo Ferrari called Nino Farina 'a man whose courage was so great that it bordered upon the impossible. He was a great, great racer, and for that reason one was always apprehensive about him, especially at the beginning and one or two laps before the end of a race. He was like a thoroughbred at the gate who would break in the first passionate sprint away from the pack; he was also capable of madness as he neared the finish line. So he had memberships in the hospital wards.'

Active after retirement as an auto distributor and Italian Automobile Club official, Nino Farina was on his way to a meeting in Geneva in his Lotus Cortina in 1966 when an icy road caught him out. The great racer died in a banal road accident.

1951 ALFA ROMEO TYPE 159 'ALFETTA'

LIVERIED TO SHOW THE CAR THAT JUAN MANUEL FANGIO DROVE IN THE 1951 GERMAN GRAND PRIX, THE TYPE 159
ACHIEVED A PHENOMENAL RECORD OF SUCCESS FROM ITS FIRST RACES AS THE TYPE 158 IN 1938.

Seen on its left side, Alfa Romeo's masterful Type 158/159 eight had a large primary blower feeding a smaller second supercharger.

In his Alfetta with imperious ease Nino Farina won a 35.7-mile race at Goodwood in September 1951.

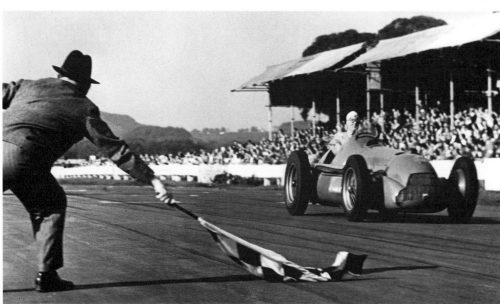

with 4.5-litre engines. They also entered four and won four in 1948, usually finishing one-two in these years and often one-two-three.

The tall Frenchman, Jean-Pierre Wimille, who led the Alfa team during those years was acknowledged as the finest driver of his day. However Wimille was killed in a racing accident in a Gordini early in 1949 and by April it became known that Alfa Romeo would not compete that year. Instead it developed the engine further to 350 horse-power, matched a stronger gearbox to it, designed bigger brakes and made enough other improvements to warrant changing the Alfetta's designation to Type 159. Cars of this design were phased in during 1950 when Alfa rejoined Grand Prix racing.

Nineteen fifty was the first year of the world championship for drivers. It was won by the proud and crash-prone Nino Farina, astride an Alfa. The team from Milan entered ten races that year and won them all, monopolising the major Grand Prix races as few have dreamed of doing before or since.

As Alfa prepared for the 1951 season, fated to be the last under the 1.5/4.5-litre Formula, major engine revisions and still more boost allowed the 159 to scream up to 10,500 revs on the test bed and register 404 horsepower – well over double its original rating. At 9,500, a more workable limit in the gears, 385 bhp were on tap. Featured were large side-mounted fuel tanks and, on some cars, de Dion rear suspension. That year, in spite of three defeats by Ferrari, they achieved enough wins and placings for Argentina's Juan Manuel Fangio to win the first of his five world championships.

Rivals though they were, Farina and Fangio both performed outstandingly well for the Alfa Romeo team, which was controlled rigidly from the pits by Gianbattista Guidotti, passenger to Tazio Nuvolari in his 1930 Mille Miglia victory. They also raced with the knowledge that a substantial organisation backed them up. It was not unusual for Alfa Romeo to arrive at a major race with two spare cars, more than two dozen mechanics, eight five-ton vans and a mobile workshop with its own generator set. At the height of their success the cars were maintained in the same unstinting style: transmission and axle gears replaced after every race, cylinder liners, pistons and roller bearings after four races, connecting rods after six races and crankshafts and superchargers after every season.

These Alfas raced in 44 completed events for cars of their engine size from 1938 through 1951 and on only five occasions were beaten when one of the 158s was still running. One of the great historians of the sport, Laurence Pomeroy, Jr. gave due credit to the fabulous record of the Type 158/159 Alfa Romeo in Volume II of his book *The Grand Prix Car*. Wrote Pomeroy:

'In this period (1947 through 1951 only) [Alfa Romeo] made 99 separate entries in 35 races. Of these they won all but four, so they had 31 victories together with 19 second places and 15 thirds. They made fastest lap in 23 of the races and suffered only 28 retirements. Taking into account retirements, the cars raced a total of 18,153 miles under Formula 1 (plus 854 miles in 1946), an average of 6,800 racing miles per car for an overall reliability factor of 81 per cent. This is a record of reliability and success without parallel in motor racing history.'

Even though a subsidy from an enthusiastic distributor had helped persuade Portello to continue in Formula 1 in 1951, the company's accountants blanched when the season's cost was totted up. Racing had cost Alfa a horrendous half a billion lire. Continuing in 1952 was out of the question, concluded the company's chairman Giuseppe Luraghi. But Luraghi had faith in the value of competition to promote the Alfa Romeo brand. Racing flames at Portello were not that easily extinguished.

Felice Bonetto arrowed his Type 159 Alfetta into the Nürburgring's Karussell in 1951's German G.P. He suffered a rare retirement.

In its most muscular final form the Alfetta took Juan Fangio to victory in 1951's Spanish G.P. and his first world championship.

CHAPTER 13

Ferrari to the Fore

Enzo Ferrari
20 February 1888-14 August 1988

The mature Enzo Ferrari of 1950, posing for Rodolfo Mailander at Monza, had skyrocketed to prominence as an auto maker.

In 1919 Enzo Ferrari was 21 when he drove a CMN in the Targa Florio – and retired. He would bring his racing experience to his car company.

THE stunning arrival of Ferrari as a force in the building and racing of cars after the war had few parallels in the world of automobiles in general and even fewer in Italy. Consider the speed of Ferrari's impact from a standing start. In 1947 his company built three cars and in 1948 five, followed by 21 in 1949. Yet in 1948 the first great victories fell to Ferrari in the Mille Miglia, in the Targa Florio, run as a lap of Sicily, and in the 12 Hours of Paris at Montlhéry. Nineteen forty-nine brought victory in the 24 Hours of Le Mans and the first win in a classic Formula 1 race at Bern for Alberto Ascari. And by 1952 that great driver was Grand Prix world champion – Ferrari-mounted.

Italy's only comparable leap to sustained motor-sporting success was that of Alfa Romeo in the early 1920s. It was no coincidence that Enzo Ferrari's ascent resembled that of Alfa. His role model in Italy's world of cars was a man ten years his senior: Antonio Ascari. Closely affiliated with the founders of Alfa Romeo, Ascari became one of the new company's first and largest dealers in Milan. He raced Alfas with vigour and success and had a significant influence on the design of its products.

Ferrari watched Ascari persuade Alfa Romeo's management to build a series of sports models based on the modified side-valve four-cylinder Type 20/30 that Ferrari drove to second place in the 1920 Targa Florio. 'If he came upon a technical problem that he couldn't crack,' Ferrari recalled of Ascari, 'he was not afraid to ask for advice or suggestions from someone who knew more than he did.' Enzo Ferrari would often – although not always – display the same trait when seeking solutions for his own technical problems.

Working at the side of Alfa's technicians and production men as he raced their cars in the 1930s from his independent Scuderia, Enzo Ferrari realised that although making automobiles is an exacting task, it was one that he could master. In fact by the end of that decade, when he oversaw the building of the Type 158 *Voiturette* for Alfa, Ferrari was knowledgeable enough to be sceptical of the technical direction that Alfa Romeo was taking – and with good reason.

Another aspect of Alfa Romeo provided a goal for Enzo Ferrari's hopes and dreams. 'I had had ambitious plans for launching out into the manufacture of high quality cars,' he wrote in his memoirs. 'I remembered that I had joined Alfa Romeo when they were endeavouring to produce a car a day, and I too had hopes of achieving this same target.' It was an objective that he approached in 1960 and surpassed in 1961 with production of 441 Ferraris.

At Alfa Corse in Milan close to the Portello factory, Ferrari had ample opportunity to observe what had become of the company with which he'd been associated for two decades. He scorned the pretensions of Spanish engineer Wifredo Ricart and his costly but impractical racing creations. He was equally at odds with the philosophy of Alfa Romeo's chief Ugo Gobbato, 'a great industrial organiser, [who] expected everything to be arranged in advance, with every last detail foreseen and worked out. He hated having to adapt to sudden changes, while for me the act of makeshift was almost part of my religion.'

On Gobbato's side there was a suspicion that Ferrari was finding ways to line his own pockets by overcharging Portello for some racing services. This was all the Alfa chief needed to dismiss Ferrari late in 1939. While his severance pay was generous, Ferrari had to agree to refrain from a direct involvement in motor racing for four years. He regrouped at the old Scuderia Ferrari building in Modena, setting up Auto-Avio Costruzioni as his business vehicle. He made good on the 'Avio' part of the name by turning the skills of his 40-strong staff toward the production of small engines for training aircraft.

The onset of war was timely for Enzo Ferrari, who could serve out his suspension from racing under its shadow. When he heard from Corrado Gatti, a Turin machine-tool dealer, that fine hydraulically controlled grinders from Jung in Germany were much in demand but difficult to get, he decided to produce them after ascertaining that their patent protection didn't apply in Italy. Here Ugo Gobbato came to his aid, having the engineering drawings made at Portello and agreeing to buy Ferrari's production. The accuracy of the grinders astonished the Germans, who disbelieved that their own workmanship could be rivalled.

In 1943, to conform with an industrial decentralisation edict, Ferrari moved his plant from Modena to a small town some ten miles to the south, Maranello, where he had some land and a small stone summer house. A friend

Tazio Nuvolari's first drive in a Ferrari, a Type 125S, brought a 1.5-litre class victory at Forli on 6 July 1947.

helped him acquire additional acreage on both sides of the main north-south highway, the Via Abetone Inferiore leading to the Abetone Pass. On the east side of the road he established a machine-tool factory of 40,000 square feet which soon was employing between 140 and 160 workers. In spite of its remote location the factory suffered air-raid damage in November 1944 and February 1945.

In 1945 – at the age of 47 – Enzo established Auto Costruzioni Ferrari, a new company with the mission of building cars and taking part in competitions. Ferrari admitted that 'the demands of mass production are contrary to my temperament, for I am mainly interested in promoting new developments. I should like to put something new into my cars every morning – an inclination that terrifies my staff. Were my wishes in this respect to be indulged, there would be no production of standard models at all, but only a succession of prototypes.'

The first of these beloved prototypes took to the road for its initial trials on 12 March 1947. It was a two-seater sports car of a type the world had never seen before, powered by a V-12 engine of only 1.5 litres. The size made sense because the popular 1½-litre category had been tipped as a likely future Formula 1, with superchargers allowed. The capacity could also be attractive for a sports car in a straitened post-war world in which big-displacement engines would – at least at first – be extravagant rarities.

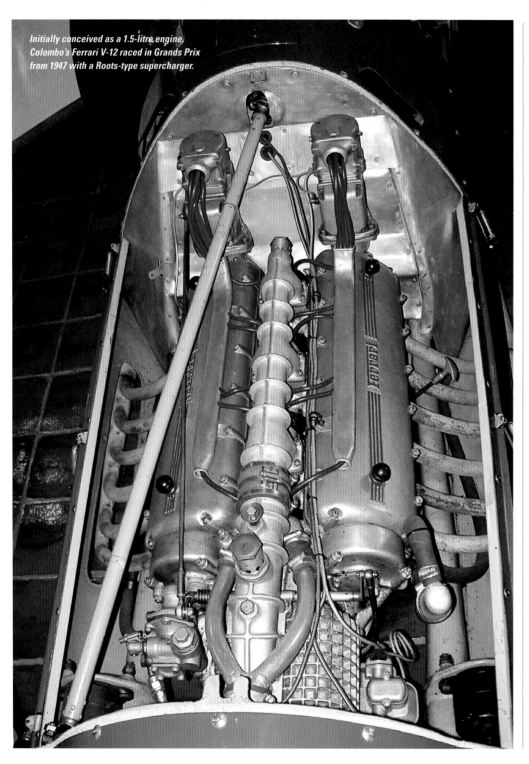

Initially conceived as a 1.5-litre engine, Colombo's Ferrari V-12 raced in Grands Prix from 1947 with a Roots-type supercharger.

The choice of a twelve was suggested by Ferrari's nominated designer, Gioachino Colombo. From June 1945 the swarthy, balding engineer was at a loose end, his avid pre-war support of Fascism having rendered him *persona non grata* at Alfa Romeo. 'Maserati has a first-class four-cylinder,' he told Ferrari at their meeting in July, 'the English have the six-cylinder ERA and Alfa Romeo has the eight-cylinder. You, in my view, should be building a twelve-cylinder!' 'My dear Colombo,' Ferrari replied, 'you've read my thoughts! For years I've been dreaming of building a twelve-cylinder. Let's get to work right away!'

Enzo Ferrari admitted that many thought him mad: 'I came in for a great deal of criticism; it was forecast that I was bringing about my own downfall, the experiment being too daring and presumptuous.' 'It was an *idee fixe* with him,' recalled racing driver Franco Cortese, 'and one for which he was heavily criticised. Several forecast, "He's a nutcase. It will eat his money and finish him." In particular the Maserati brothers were highly critical. But if he'd made a four, or a six or even an eight, Ferrari wouldn't have enjoyed the great success he's had.'

From August through November of 1945 – when Colombo was rehired by Alfa Romeo – the engineer's drawings were hand-carried from his Milan flat to Maranello, where 'Ferrari had created a small but very efficient group of designers who transformed my layouts into working drawings in their format.' An Alfa technician, Giuseppe Busso, joined Ferrari in June 1946 to oversee the new car's gestation. From September 1946 through March 1947 he had the help of an ambitious young engineer, Aurelio Lampredi.

Ferrari's V-12 first ran on 26 September 1946. Initially it was no power prodigy, with its single Weber carburettor. 'It gave 60 to 65 horsepower,' said Lampredi, 'and revved up to 5,600 – not even 6,000. The problem was the ignition, which was outdated. Nobody had done anything new since 1937-38.' Finally it was encouraged to produce 72 bhp at 5,400 rpm, the figure quoted in the first sales brochure for the 125 Sport. With triple carburetion for the 125 *Competizione* its output was 118 bhp at 6,800 rpm on a higher compression ratio that required special fuel.

In its 125 C version the twelve was capable of revving to 7,000 rpm – very fast for that time. 'You had to pay very close attention to the revs with this engine,' said Franco Cortese, the first man to race it. 'It was a somewhat different engine, one that went up to speed very quickly. If you were used to normal fours and sixes, this twelve was like an electric motor. It revved so easily that you always had to be on your guard. You had to drive with your head…and with your eye on the tachometer.' With an eye to its torque characteristics, Colombo gave the 125 a five-speed gearbox – very unusual for those days.

To open its valves Colombo used a single central chain-driven camshaft for each head, working through rocker arms, while hairpin-type springs closed them. To get the high revs the engine needed, needle-bearings were used at first in the bottom end of racing versions. Soon, however, British Vandervell bearings with lead-indium-plated copper-lead surfaces on steel backing came to the rescue. Aurelio Lampredi judged that the British bearings 'saved' Ferrari's V-12 engine.

Only two months after this new Ferrari car first ran, it was raced. 'We raced every Sunday to prove the car,' said Franco Cortese. 'Against the Maseratis, more than others. But we had an advantage. The Ferrari was a more modern machine, indeed exceptional for those days.' 'They took part in ten races,' added Colombo: 'they won six of them, were second in one and had to withdraw from three.' This was an exceptional performance for a radical new design.

Gioachino Colombo left Alfa to join Ferrari on a part-time basis from September 1947 and full-time from the beginning of 1948. By November of 1947 he had laid out a design for the Grand Prix Ferrari, the Type 125 F1. Driven from the front accessory case of the 1.5-litre V12 was a single Roots-type blower, fed by a Weber carburettor. Initially it developed 225 bhp at 7,000 rpm. In 1949 this was raised nearer to 250 bhp, which took Ascari to victory in that year's Swiss Grand Prix – helped, to be sure, by Alfa Romeo's sabbatical that season.

In September Ferrari entered Alberto Ascari in the Italian Grand Prix, this time with a completely new Colombo design, Ferrari's ambitious GP49. This added twin-camshaft cylinder heads and two-stage super-

charging, provided by twin blowers driven from the timing-gear case. Although this elaborate twelve was beset by maladies that included severe overheating and by early 1950 was abandoned, its 305 bhp at 7,500 rpm took Ascari to victory in 1949's Italian G.P. at Monza.

Giuseppe Busso was tasked with the original V12's enlargement to 2.0 litres for racing in the new Formula 2 and also for sports-car competition. 'We approached it in stages,' he said, 'first with the 159, whose engine was fired up at the end of July, and later with the 166, which gave its first sneezes at the end of November.' In their two-litre format the early Ferraris were highly successful. The Type 166 SC sports version produced 130 bhp at 7,000 rpm,

Initially cycle-winged, Ferrari's 1949 Type 166 Inter spider was later given attached wings when sports-car rules changed.

At the 1951 Turin Salon Rodolfo Mailander, Aurelio Lampredi pictured with the big new V-12 he had developed for Ferrari's road and racing cars.

One of the great designs of all time, giving Ferrari a distinctive style, Touring's Berlinetta was fitted to Ferrari chassis Types 166, 195, 212, 225 and 340.

Kleenex tycoon Jim Kimberley, who could afford to buy and drive the latest Ferraris, brought this Type 340 America to Elkhart Lake, Wisconsin in 1952.

FERRARI'S TYPE 815

After severing his links with Alfa Romeo Enzo Ferrari set up Auto-Avio Costruzioni in Modena. Although barred by his Alfa severance terms from competing in his own name for four years, this new entity could build racing cars. An attractive target was the 1940 Mille Miglia, scheduled for a fast road circuit near Brescia on 28 April.

Worthwhile rewards were on offer. The prize for a class victory was 10,000 lire. In addition, Fiat posted a prize of 5,000 lire for a win by a car that was a Fiat or at least Fiat-based. Near the end of 1939 Ferrari discussed the idea of a 1.5-litre car for this class with a wealthy Modenese marquis, Lotario Rangoni Machiavelli, and with a new driver, a successful motorcycle racer named Alberto Ascari, son of Ferrari's mentor at Portello. With only four months to go before the race, at a Christmas-Eve dinner party, Ferrari agreed to build each a car.

To qualify for the Fiat prize the two spiders were based on the chassis of the Fiat 508C Ballila with straight-eight engines made up of many Fiat parts. Their open bodies were built by Carrozzeria Touring in Milan. Designed by Alberto Massimino and tested by Enrico Nardi, the cars were created in secret by the cautious Ferrari and entered only provisionally just two weeks before the Mille Miglia. They were dubbed the Type 815, in a cheeky inversion of the numbering system used by Alfa Romeo.

After a haranguing by a Fascist-party official Ascari's 815 was flagged away at 6:21 am, a minute after Rangoni's sister car. Alberto, wearing the Nuvolari-like kit of a motorcyclist's sleeveless waistcoat over his jersey, soon overtook his team-mate and easily assumed the class lead. On his second lap one of the Fiat-made rocker arms failed and Ascari was out. Rangoni lasted longer in a car that had enjoyed more pre-race testing, but retired as well.

Enzo Ferrari admitted in his memoirs that 'the car was not a success, mainly on account of the haste with which it had been constructed.' It was anything but a total loss for Ascari, however. In February 1943 he sold his 815 for the handsome sum of 42,000 lire. Ferrari's price to him had been 20,000 lire.

Powering the Type 815 from Enzo Ferrari's Auto-Avio Costruzioni was a 1.5-litre straight eight using many Fiat components.

Before the 1940 Mille Miglia held on roads near Brescia, Alberto Ascari poses with his brand new Auto-Avio Type 815.

while the single-seater 166 C that dominated Formula 2 through 1951 delivered 160 bhp at 7,200 rpm on alcohol.

For the Type 166 MM sports car of 1948, recalled Gioachino Colombo, 'what we needed was to find suitable "clothing" for this car, to give it a characteristic Ferrari appearance – since up to this point there had been no distinctive "Ferrari look". We spent many hours in the late spring and early summer of 1948, trying to get exactly the right lines for the bodywork of the new Ferrari 166 MM.'

This was done in partnership with Milan's Carrozzeria Touring, which had developed and patented a method of body construction it called *Superleggera* or super-light. The press and public first saw the 166 MM at the opening of Turin's 31st motor show on 15 September 1948. So unusual was the 166 MM compared to previous

All Aurelio Lampredi's work, the Type 500 F2 Ferrari of 1952-53 brought Alberto Ascari two world titles in succession.

sports-car designs that it caused a considerable stir. Hitherto sports cars featured low ground clearance and body sides that sloped outward toward their sills. Instead, the 166 MM's flanks rolled under to soft, rounded forms that seemed to embrace the wheels.

In the *Gazzetta dello Sport* influential journalist Giovanni Canestrini explained his reaction to his readers. This was not an open sports car of the usual type, a spider, torpedo or skiff. Instead, he said, its 'disconcerting' shape resembled that of a small boat, a *barchetta*. Catching the spirit of the new creation, this became its nickname. The 166 MM won both the Mille Miglia and Le Mans in 1949.

In the 1950s Ferrari fully exploited the potential of his Colombo V-12. With a magnificent coupé body based on the *barchetta* shape its 2,341 cc version, the Type 195 S, won the 1950 Mille Miglia. The larger Type 212 was introduced in 1951 with 2,563 cc, scoring a sensational one-two victory in Mexico's Carrera Panamericana, while 1952 brought the 225 S of 2,715 cc, winner of that year's Monaco Grand Prix for sports cars.

The Colombo twelve reached full flower in 1952 with the 250 S of 2,953 cc, which won that year's Mille Miglia. In 1953 it matured as the 250 MM, producing 240 bhp at 7,200 rpm. These founded Ferrari's fabulous clan of 250-series engines, even though they gave away 1½ per cent of the allowable capacity in their 3.0-litre class. This Colombo-based engine also powered Ferrari's 235 bhp 250 GT road-car models, starting in 1958.

An even bigger V-12 was created when, in 1950, Aurelio Lampredi was given full responsibility for Ferrari's racing designs. With Enzo Ferrari's approval and the

The suspension of Gigi Villoresi's Type 375 F1 Ferrari was heavily depressed through the 'Ring's famous Karussell banked section in 1951. He placed fourth.

110

financial support of Pirelli he designed an engine that was similar in its valve gear but longer, for bigger bores, with steel cylinders screwed into the heads in the manner of the Alfetta. He baptised it in 3.3-litre form as the Type 275 F1 at 3,322 cc for the Belgian Grand Prix in 1950. During that year Lampredi's twelve was enlarged to 4.1 litres. With 230 bhp at 6,000 rpm this version powered the 1951 Type 340 America, Ferrari's first sports-racing car to use the long-block engine.

For the last championship race of 1950 at Monza the twelve was opened out to 4.5 litres, the largest allowable size for Grand Prix racing. As the 375 F1 it was now rated at 350 bhp at 7,000 rpm. In 1951 its power peak was raised to 7,500 rpm and its output to 380 bhp to complete what Lampredi regarded as his 'real' Formula 1 engine.

Its punch and superior fuel economy were enough to allow Ferrari to beat the Alfas at last in Britain and Germany, although not quite to seize the world championship. Although the contest went down to the final wire at Barcelona, a poor tyre choice blunted the Maranello attack.

In 1952 one single-seater evolved from this type qualified to race at Indianapolis, its output stepped up to 400 bhp, but retired with rear-hub breakage. A final evolution of the big twelve for sports-car racing increased its capacity to 5.0 litres for the Type 375 Plus, in 1954 the winner both at Le Mans and in the Mexican Road Race. In only a few short years Ferrari had raced to the fore in both Grand Prix and sports-car racing. And there was much more to come.

Aurelio Lampredi enlarged his fours to 2.5 litres for the new Formula 1 of 1954, as in this Ferrari Type 625 F1.

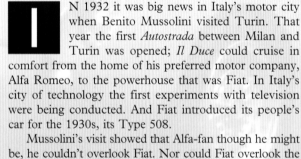

CHAPTER 14

Incredible Etceterinis

N 1932 it was big news in Italy's motor city when Benito Mussolini visited Turin. That year the first *Autostrada* between Milan and Turin was opened; *Il Duce* could cruise in comfort from the home of his preferred motor company, Alfa Romeo, to the powerhouse that was Fiat. In Italy's city of technology the first experiments with television were being conducted. And Fiat introduced its people's car for the 1930s, its Type 508.

Mussolini's visit showed that Alfa-fan though he might be, he couldn't overlook Fiat. Nor could Fiat overlook the power of Italy's Fascist corporate state. For just that reason the 508 was nicknamed 'Ballila' in honour of the state organisation for the encouragement of Fascist sentiments among Italy's youth. Founded in 1926, the Ballila movement took its inspiration from the nickname of a teenager who, according to legend, threw the first rock at Austrian forces during a rebellion in Genoa in 1746. From the age of eight to 14 boys were 'Ballila' in the organisation that swept aside all others save those for Catholic youth.

The first 508 Ballila had a side-valve four of 995 cc. In 1933 with 30 horsepower this powered the 508 S, a sports version with rakish two-seat bodywork. The following year output jumped to 36 bhp thanks to a new overhead-valve cylinder head, Fiat's first of the 1930s.

Thanks to its class-winning performance in a 1934 contest – the Coppa d'Oro dal Littorio which raced 3,535 miles around Italy's coastline in stages – this became known as the 'Coppa d'Oro' model. With its four-speed gearbox this was a serious as well as great-looking sports car that was timed by *The Autocar* at a top speed of 70.31 mph with its windscreen down.

Both affordable and available, Fiat's 508 S Ballila was a breakthrough car for enthusiasts not only in Italy but also abroad. It created what was called 'a new idiom in small sports cars' with its pleasingly high gearing, good brakes and light steering. It came to dominate the 1,100 cc sports category across Europe for several seasons, helped by such advocates as Bologna-born Amedeo Gordini, who settled in France in 1926 at the age of 27 to fettle and sell Fiats and their French equivalent, Simcas. Gallicised as Amédée, he campaigned the new Turin models with great success.

In 1937 Fiat followed up with its 508 C, the 'New Ballila', with a completely overhauled 1,089 cc four with pushrod-operated overhead valves. This marked the beginning of the legendary 'Fiat 1100' era that not only carved its own niche in motor-sports history but also provided a base on which countless tuners and enthusiasts built their own competition cars.

Shown in second-series form, competing after the war, Fiat's 1939 508 C Mille Miglia was an authentic pioneer of low-drag design.

Fiat's own effort was the 508 C Mille Miglia, a fully aerodynamic coupé built in two series in 1937 and 1939. Its post-war successor was the 1100 ES coupé with a sleek body by Savio that gave 95 mph from only 51 horsepower. In the Mille Miglias of 1948, '49 and '50 Fiats won both the 750 cc and 1,100 cc classes.

A surprising sporting entry by Fiat appeared in 1952, its 8V sports car. Under the bonnet of this futuristic coupé was a 2.0-litre V-8 with a 70-degree vee angle and pushrod overhead valves. Capable of 119 mph from its 110 bhp, an all-independently-sprung chassis gave the 8V good grip. A Zagato-bodied version was a feisty competitor, winning its class in Italy's GT championship in 1954.

The 8V's suspension and power-train components were enthusiastically embraced by car-maker Siata, on the Via Leonardo da Vinci in Turin's southern sector. One of the most fascinating and creative yet enigmatic Italian sporting companies, Siata was the acronym of the firm founded in 1926 by enthusiastic accountant Giorgio Ambrosini, Turin's superintendent of schools, to make accessories and go-faster equipment for Fiats. Siata shot to prominence in 1933 when its overhead-valve conversion and four-speed gearbox electrified the performance of 508 C Ballilas in the Mille Miglia.

In 1937, after a decade of improving Fiats, Siata began making sports-racing cars in its own right based on components of the popular 500 Topolino. Siata bodywork was by Motto and Bertone, *inter alia*, who continued to work with Siata after the war. A pre-war Siata model was the Amica, a name that was revived after the war for charming Bertone-bodied coupés and roadsters for the 750 cc class. Founder Giorgio's son Renato Ambrosini won the Italian class championship in 1948 with a cycle-winged version.

Encouraged by interest from the US market, Siata built some 50 Bertone-bodied spiders with Crosley and Fiat engines, followed by a series of roadsters and coupés using Fiat's 1400 four. This was the Daina, in both open and closed versions. Although outclassed in European racing, all these Siata models were raced enthusiastically and successfully in America.

In 1950 Rudolf Hruska, an Austrian engineer who had worked with the Porsche design office before the war, joined Siata. He came in time to assist with Siata's version of the Fiat 8V, which absorbed almost half of the 200 component sets made. The resulting 208 S was made as a coupé, with a sleekly menacing Stabilimenti Farina design, and as a spider with sublimely gorgeous Bertone coachwork. Like the smaller Siatas these were welcomed

Styled by Fabio Luigi Rapi, Fiat's 1952 Type 8V was a feisty 2.0-litre class competitor both as standard, here, and Zagato-bodied.

in the USA. In 1960 Doug Diffenderfer was the SCCA's F Production champion in a 208 S spider. These were Siata's salad days as a maker of competition cars. The company expired in 1974, coincidentally the year of its founder's death.

Survival just into the early 1990s was possible for another Turin-based sporting specialist, Moretti, because much like Siata in its later years it concentrated on bodywork conversions of Fiats. Born in 1904 in Reggio Emilia, Giovanni Moretti built a motorcycle at the age of 21 and his first car two years later.

Moretti transferred early to motor city Turin. There during World War II Fabbrica Automobili Moretti SpA designed and built electric delivery vehicles that met wartime needs. After the war Moretti converted to building a twin-cylinder small car, followed in 1948 by a 592 cc four-cylinder model that was the cornerstone of his post-war production.

Turin's Siata exploited both the 70-degree vee-eight engine of Fiat's 8V and its suspension to build its own sports-racers.

The team of Venturelli/Ceroni drove this wonderfully Siata-improved Fiat 500 in 1940's Mille Miglia held near Brescia.

Above right: Sublimely lovely lines penned by Giovanni Michelotti gave exceptional presence to the little Moretti 750 Gran Sport Berlinetta.

Giovanni Moretti made no compromise in the complete production of his cars. All elements of the 1950s Morettis – engine, transmission, suspension, chassis, body – were of his own design and manufacture. Moretti increased the size of the single-overhead-cam engine of his standard two-door sedan to 612 and then 748 cc in 1953. Based on this engine he introduced a twin-overhead-cam version that made Moretti a motor-sports contender.

The fingerprints of the peripatetic Alberto Massimino, or an acolyte, were on the engine's design. Its valves were inclined at a 90-degree included angle in a hemispherical chamber. As in the single-cam engines the main bearings – three in early engines and five later – were carried in split 'cheeses' which were inserted into the one-piece crankcase from the rear. This robust Weber-carburetted all-iron engine was credited with 71 bhp at 7,000 rpm.

Moretti's own craftsmen made the square-tube frame and aluminium body of the 750 Gran Sport Berlinetta to a brilliant design by Giovanni Michelotti that gave the taut lines of a larger coupé in miniature. Though suspension by quarter-elliptic springs and steering by a meandering linkage were less sophisticated, the little car handled well both as a coupé and in spider form.

Enjoying their best season in 1954, the twin-cam Morettis were class-winners in rallies and races. Lino Fayen, the French Moretti importer in Neuilly, was a winner at Montlhéry in a standard car while Elio Zagato, driving a Zagato-bodied 750 Gran Sport, won at Gorizia, Foggia and Monza. Meanwhile in a spider-bodied 750 the

Moretti importer Ernie McAfee was winning at Palm Springs, California.

While the modest Giovanni Moretti kept a low profile, this was not the character trait of industrialist and passionate car enthusiast Piero Dusio. Born in Piedmont in 1899, he gravitated to its capital Turin. Becoming Italy's first maker of oilcloth at the age of 27, he expanded into the fabric products of which he was the main supplier to Italy's army. Wealth thus earned allowed Dusio to enjoy his love of motor sports.

Starting at the top with a Maserati in 1929, Dusio set up the Scuderia Torino in 1938 and equipped it with four *Voiturettes* from the Trident. That same year he took part with an Alfa Romeo in the Mille Miglia, in an excellent result placing third overall behind the works cars from Portello. He also raced a Siata before the war. Gaining a jump start on rivals, in 1943 Dusio set up the mechanical-engineering company that became Cisitalia Automobili in 1945.

Piero Dusio's idea was to produce a small single-seater using some Fiat 1100 parts for private owners to race when the war was over. For the original design he engaged Fiat engineer Dante Giacosa. A friend from pre-war days, engineer-driver Piero Taruffi helped with testing and development. When Giacosa returned to Fiat, Giovanni Savonuzzi took over final proving and creation of the production design, helped by émigré Austrian Karl 'Carlo' Abarth.

Fittingly, Dusio himself won the first race in which his Cisitalias competed at Turin in September of 1946. With

PORSCHE'S TYPE 360 FOR CISITALIA

Former racing driver Piero Dusio, founder of Cisitalia in Turin, was beguiled by the image of German engineering superiority. Flush with funds after the war, Dusio decided to follow up on his 1.1-litre competition cars with a full G.P. entry. Against the advice of close associates who felt he should recruit Italian talent, Dusio engaged the isolated Porsche team in Austria's Gmünd to design a Formula 1 Grand Prix car.

Among the personalities associated with this spectacular initiative were Tazio Nuvolari, who was a link between the Porsches and Dusio, journalist Corrado Millanta, who would become Porsche's business agent in Italy, and engineers Rudolf Hruska and Carlo Abarth, who acted as liaison between Gmünd and Turin. Desperately in need of hard currency, not least to buy freedom from imprisonment in France for Ferdinand Porsche and his son-in-law Anton Piëch, the designers under Ferry Porsche and Karl Rabe made Dusio an offer he couldn't refuse.

The supercharged 1.5-litre design sent to Turin from Gmünd in mid-1947 was a masterpiece. Porsche's Type 360 bristled with such ingenious ideas as part-time four-wheel drive, a tubular space frame, a flat-twelve mid-placed engine with two vane-type blowers, synchronised progressive five-speed shifting and an advanced independent rear suspension. More to the point, these concepts were blended in a car of balance and beauty.

But it was numbingly expensive. A first estimate of 20 million lire to build it was quickly passed as Dusio ordered even more projects for sports and Formula 2 cars from the Germans – whose key people were in fact largely Austrian. Thirty million

had been spent before work even started on building the cars. In a heated meeting that he called, Dusio's own chief engineer Giovanni Savonuzzi expressed serious misgivings about the project, saying that it could easily cost Dusio 100 million lire. 'I don't care,' shot back the entrepreneur. 'I may go broke but I must have the Grand Prix car.'

This was an accurate forecast. The project broke Cisitalia. One car, looking complete at the end of 1948, was displayed on the Cisitalia stand at the Turin Salon in February 1949. Hans Stuck said he briefly tested it in Italy in the late summer of 1949; others say it never ran in Europe. In 1949 Dusio journeyed to Argentina to get financial help from the Perón regime. This resulted in the Type 360 being packed aboard a ship in December 1950 bound for Buenos Aires. There it immediately gave rise to rumours that Juan Fangio and Froilan Gonzalez would be racing for an Autoar, nee Cisitalia, team in Europe in 1951.

In 1953, under the direction of Autoar engineer Giovanni Rossi, the Type 360 was laboriously made to run. No small feat in the complete absence of the car's designers and builders and negligible technical information, this nevertheless resulted in readings of 350 bhp at 10,500 rpm from the flat-twelve. After making some track appearances, driven by Felice Bonetto and Clemar Bucci, it set a new South American speed record of 144.8 mph with cautious runs owing to piston-burning problems. Its chassis and handling received unstinting praise.

The history of Grand Prix racing is littered with many might-have-beens. Books have been written about exotic cars that never raced. None of these deserved more of a chance to strut its stuff than this brilliant and forward-looking Austro-Italian effort.

Features of the Porsche-designed Formula 1 Cisitalia were part-time four-wheel drive and side-mounted fuel tanks.

Porsche used a sophisticated parallel-arm rear suspension for the Cisitalia and placed the flat-12 engine well forward.

That Piero Dusio had serious plans for his Cisitalia company was shown by its production of 31 of these pretty single-seaters in 1946.

The agility of the little Type D46 Cisitalia was exploited by Felice Bonetto in a race at Mantua in 1948.

special aluminium cylinder heads, their Fiat engines were mounted in a novel frame made of small-diameter aircraft tubing in a truss-type design that became known as a 'space frame' for the distances between the tubes. This gave maximum strength and stiffness for a given weight. The D46, as the model was known, was Italian champion in the 1.5-litre racing-car class from 1947 through 1949, in addition to many other successes.

Pursuing a Giacosa idea, the saturnine Giovanni Savonuzzi created a two-seater version of the racing car by widening its space frame. To get maximum performance from the Type 202's 1.1-litre engine he evolved a super-streamlined coupé body in the wind tunnel of the Turin Polytechnic. In its striking realisation by Alfredo Vignale, stabilising tail fins were a prominent feature. Tests on the *Autostrada* found it capable of

125 mph from only 61 horsepower. For use on tighter circuits a roadster version was built by Turin's Garella coachworks.

Cisitalia requested and received permission to name its open model 'Nuvolari' after that great driver, now in the September of his career and chronically short of breath, worked miracles in the 1947 Mille Miglia. Leading the race at Rome, he lost 20 minutes for ignition repairs in monsoon conditions on the return leg yet finished second, 16 minutes behind the winning Alfa Romeo. Other Cisitalias were third and fourth behind Nuvolari, the moral victor.

This was a high-water mark for the racing career of the Cisitalia sports car. For a series of production versions Pinin Farina was engaged to adapt Savonuzzi's concept to a practical road sports car. He did so with consummate style, creating an iconic coupé. Hailed as an immaculate design, it broke new ground with its low bonnet and oval grille. Thus did Farina respond to Dusio's request for 'a car that is wide like my Buick, low like a Grand Prix car, comfortable like a Rolls-Royce and light like our single-seater.' Built in both coupé and convertible

1947 Cisitalia 'Nuvolari' Spider

Representing Italy's charismatic 'Etceterinis', Cisitalia's 1.1-litre spider earned its nickname with

Tazio Nuvolari's spirited drive to second place in the 1947 Mille Miglia.

From Fiat clay Carlo Abarth fashioned his brilliant Zagato-bodied 750 cc coupés, class winners on all continents.

styles, the closed version was an active road-racing competitor.

Although Cisitalia limped on until 1963, its Piero Dusio era ended early in the 1950s after his company was fatally weakened by spending on an exotic Porsche-designed Grand Prix car. Carlo Abarth picked up many of the pieces, including sports-racers nearing completion. He gave his cars the marque of a sting-tailed scorpion, his canny choice from his astrological sign of Scorpio.

Abarth carried on Cisitalia's car making, initially on a smaller scale. His breakthrough came with Fiat's introduction of the rear-engined 600 in 1955. Not only was Abarth's 750 cc version extremely popular, it also served as a superb basis for special-bodied cars that sold as Abarths in their own right.

With Zagato's distinctive double-bubble roof the cheeky Abarth coupés were soon wreaking havoc on race tracks around the world. Low-drag versions were breaking records at Monza in class after class. Soon Abarths were part of the American racing scene. Franklin Delano Roosevelt, Jr., a striking dead ringer for his father, imported them in addition to Fiats. Rampaging American circuits, the red coupés made Abarth a household name in SCCA circles.

By 1969, as we see at Mugello, Carlo Abarth was building and entering serious sports-racers like this Group 4 2.0-litre spider.

Through 1966 Abarths totted up more than 3,600 class and overall victories. Carlo Abarth and his trusted lieutenant Renzo Avidano improved their cars and built more adventurous machinery, competing well in classes up to two litres. Attempts at Formulas 1 and 2 and a big V-12 to fight the Porsches and Ferraris (see chapter 18) were a reach too far, however, for Abarth and his team. Their high costs contributed to the company's 1971 acquisition by Fiat. Under the larger firm's protection it concentrated on rallying but did produce a batch of Fiat-powered single-seaters for the one-make Formula Italia.

Turin didn't have all the fun in small-capacity racing. Fiat, however, was the force behind the creations in Modena of Vittorio Stanguellini, who was the company's main dealer in that city. Starting in 1936 with the preparation of Maseratis and Fiat Ballilas, Stanguellini was soon building Fiat-based creations of his own, one with Siata overhead valves. Several were bodied in radical all-enveloping 'tank' style, including the 1.1-litre class winner in 1940's high-speed Mille Miglia, which narrowly defeated another Stanguellini.

After the war Vittorio Stanguellini resumed building sports cars both cycle-winged and envelope-bodied, with chassis design by the inevitable Alberto Massimino. One of his body suppliers was Ala d'Oro, which had commissioned Aurelio Lampredi to design a twin-cam head for the Fiat 1100 block during an early hiatus in his work for Ferrari. When Ala d'Oro went out of business Stanguellini took over this project, which gave him an engine producing 80 bhp at 6,500 rpm. Later a special aluminium block was made to create a 750 cc version.

The result was class-winning performance for Stanguellinis of both sizes. In Italian racing they took the 1,100 cc class championship in 1947 and 1950 and the 750 cc honours in 1947, 1952, 1954, 1955 and 1956. The pretty little spiders competed abroad in SCCA racing and long-distance events.

A windfall for Vittorio Stanguellini was 1958's introduction of Formula Junior, conceived by driver and editor Giovanni 'Johnny' Lurani to base 1.1-litre single-seaters on standard-car components. Stanguellini was the champion marque in Italy in Junior's first year of 1958 and again in 1959 when the category became international. With drivers like Wolfgang von Trips and Lorenzo Bandini making their mark in Stanguellini Juniors, the new formula fulfilled Lurani's aim of making it a training ground for Grand Prix drivers. Such men too made vital contributions to the patrimony of the red racers.

Dominating its category with a scintillating twin-cam four, this Stanguellini was the 750 cc class winner at Sebring in 1957.

Sleek front-engined Stanguellinis led the field away in the Formula Junior race at Monaco in 1959.

CHAPTER 15

Racing's Red Tide: Part I

First raced in 1948, this captivating 1.1-litre Type Mt4 Osca was being warmed up to compete at Elkhart Lake in 1952.

ONLY Jaguar, Aston Martin, Mercedes-Benz and Cunningham stood in the way of complete domination of sports-car and Grand-Prix racing by Italian marques in the early 1950s. Modest interference was offered by France's Gordini and Britain's BRM, while Germany's Porsche and Borgward were tough rivals in the smaller classes. Otherwise Italy's red tide swept across the sport with an ascendancy that bordered on arrogance, recalling the palmy years of the late 1920s and early 1930s when only Bugatti stood in their way.

No small role in this competitive superiority was played by the intense rivalries among Italy's actors in the sport. Only a dozen miles apart at Modena in the Emilian plain, Ferrari and Maserati were bitter competitors.

Both aimed to attract teams and individuals around the world to buy their competition cars. The best way to do that was to demonstrate superiority on the track, which each sought to do with the best drivers, picking their events strategically.

Having had a good war, Maserati proprietor Adolfo Orsi was well placed to resume automotive activity in peacetime. When racing was revived the first important Grand Prix successes fell to Maserati, whose 4CL was tailor-made for the new Formula 1. This was galling to Enzo Ferrari, wrote journalist Brock Yates: 'Ferrari considered the Orsis interlopers on his turf and below his station. Moreover, their products were aimed at the same clientele of gentlemen drivers, which qualified them as commercial enemies of the first order.' With this as background, said Yates, the implacable rivals 'were locked in a struggle for bragging rights in Modena.'

Thus did Italy's Modena become a thriving centre of racing-car design, manufacture and development. From 1949 the city opened for testing and racing its dual-purpose Aerautodromo, an airport surrounded by a peripheral road that also served as a track. Other racing-mad locals, like Fiat dealer Vittorio Stanguellini, got in on the act. Guglielmo 'Mimo' Dei established his Scuderia

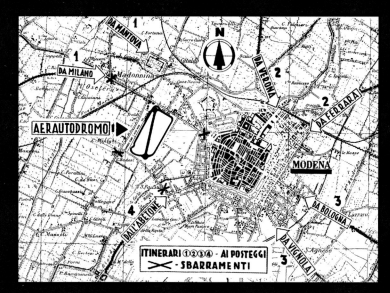

A map of Modena clearly showed the city's medieval centre, the Via Emilia from top left to bottom right and the Aerautodromo.

MODENA – EPICENTRE OF ITALIAN RED

Known to the Romans as the Via Aemilia, the die-straight Via Emilia slashes calf-high across the boot of Italy from Rimini on the Adriatic coast north-west through Forli, Faenza, Imola, Bologna, Modena, Reggio Emilia and Parma to Piacenza on the doorstep of Milan. It is a major trade artery of the region of Emilia-Romagna, which is traversed as well by the Po River and bordered on the south by the foothills of the Appenines. Mutina to the Romans, Modena is the capital of the province of the same name. It rests at an important crossroads between Verona in the north and Livorno on the Gulf of Genoa.

No stranger to conflicts, Roman colony Mutina was sacked by Attila's Huns and then, in the 13th century, became one of the arenas of battle between the Guelfs, loyal to Rome, and the Ghibellines, allied with the German emperors. Stability came in the 14th century under the Guelf-leaning Este dynasty with its base at Ferrara, north of Bologna. Modena became their stronghold in 1598. With one Napoleonic interruption, the Estensi ruled Modena until 1859, when the province became part of the kingdom of Italy. Its medieval defences are still evident in the pentagonal plan of the city's partly moated centre.

For many years the Via Emilia was an important Modenese dividing line. 'Modena in the 1950s was a very exciting place to work,' former Ferrari racing manager Romolo Tavoni told Graham Gauld, 'as there was great rivalry between Maserati and Ferrari. Indeed, the rivalry was so great that the Via Emilia, the old Roman road which runs through the centre of the city, became the boundary. The Ferrari offices and service

departments were only about 500 metres from the Maserati factory on either side of this road. If you worked on the north side of the Via Emilia, you were a Maserati man, and if you worked on the south side, you were a Ferrari man.

'At the height of the rivalry,' Tavoni continued, 'it was generally known that if you worked for Ferrari you would never be employed by Maserati and vice versa.' In fact Tavoni himself disproved this adage by switching from Maserati to Ferrari to become secretary to Enzo himself and later his racing manager. Others who crossed the Via Emilia included engineers Valerio Colotti, Vittorio Bellentani and Alberto Massimino, racing manager Nello Ugolini, coachbuilder Medardo Fantuzzi and, vividly, British racing driver John Surtees, who became the first and only man to win championship Grands Prix for both rivals in a single season.

Many of these intramural battles could be traced back to trials and contests on the 1.4-mile perimeter track of Modena's Aerautodromo. From 1949 the city's fathers made this dual-purpose facility available for testing and races. Its sweeping turn and wriggling chicane were the yardsticks of performance for the latest and best products of Ferrari, Maserati, Stanguellini, Osca and others.

From 1962 auto racing was banned at the Aerautodromo, whose safety provisions were unequal to rising car speeds. Indeed in the 1950s it took the lives of a talented Ferrari engineer, Andrea Fraschetti, and star driver Eugenio Castellotti. After the 1961 race the circuit was declared unsafe for car racing, although motorcycle races persisted to 1976. Nevertheless car testing by both Ferrari and Maserati continued on the perimeter track into the early 1970s. With the advances being made in racing cars its layout was clearly outdated; Ferrari last tested there in 1971.

Finally the Aerautodromo was closed and retired to wooded parkland with facilities for expositions. Although it was named the Parco Enzo Ferrari, which is appropriate enough, a dedication could well have been made that offered a tribute to the rivalry among Modena's racing-car builders that transfixed not only the city's passionate residents but also the world.

Pits were along the left side of the Modena Aerautodromo, which served both cars and aviation in its heyday.

An appreciative crowd saw Gigi Villoresi win the 1948 British G.P. in his 4CLT/48 'San Remo' Maserati.

With its two-stage Roots-type blowers, one above the other at the front, the Type 4CLT/48 Maserati was a favourite of private Grand Prix entrants.

Right: Raced by Juan Fangio in 1949, this 4CLT/48 Maserati carried the Argentine colours. Its shift lever was between his legs.

Centro-Sud in Modena, chiefly racing Maseratis. In 1952 Sergio Scaglietti, who had worked with Ferrari before the war, set up his own *carrozzeria* in Modena and began to clothe the Prancing Horses.

These enterprises drew upon a network of proven suppliers. Ball bearings came from Turin's RIV, a child of Agnelli's Fiat, while Britain's Vandervell supplied vital engine bearings. Magneti Marelli delivered electrical components, Fren-Do brake linings, Cogne special steels, Borrani wheels, Houdaille shock absorbers, Mondial pistons, Livia valves, Gilco frames, Regina roller chains, Rejna chassis springs and Champion spark plugs.

Farther east down the Via Emilia that was the region's lifeline, Bologna also had a role to play. The *Fratelli* Maserati never ceased dwelling in Bologna, so when its contract with Adolfo Orsi expired at the end of 1947 it established its own company, Officine Specializzate Costruzioni Automobili or 'Workshop Specialising in Automobile Construction' in that city. It was destined to gain international fame as OSCA or Osca. Orsi retained the rights to the 'Maserati' trade name.

As in the 1930s Osca's prime movers were product designer and developer Ernesto, now 51, manufacturing chief Ettore, 55 and works manager Bindo, 66. That their energy and dedication were still running at high revs was shown by the creativity that they invested in their first Oscas. They were at the extremes of the capacity scale from a 4.5-litre V-12 built with France's Gordini as a potential customer to a 1.1-litre four which, at first, had a single overhead camshaft similar to the Maserati A6G that Ernesto had been working on during the war.

The project for a big V-12 engine to compete in Formula 1 foundered when Gordini withdrew. The brothers persevered with it, installing one in a Maserati chassis for Birabongse Bhanudej Bhanubandh, Prince of Siam, who raced as 'B. Bira'. In 1951 he won a short race with it at Goodwood in Britain but its later history was chequered, as was the record of the two complete Oscas built to use the engine. Both ended their careers converted to sports-racers.

'We had spent a fortune on it,' Ernesto Maserati said of the ambitious V-12. 'We couldn't afford to go on and it just stood. There wasn't the ten million lire to do the job!' Nor were they able to do full justice to a very pretty 2.0-litre in-line six that they built to compete in Formula 2 racing. Such Oscas were bought and raced by French drivers Elie Bayol and Louis Chiron in 1952 and '53. These light live-axle single-seaters showed promise but not enough development to keep up with the Ferraris and Maseratis.

Exploiting wartime developments by the Maserati brothers, the Orsi regime produced this 2.0-litre Type A6GCS sports-racer in 1947.

Far more fruitful was their focus on small-displacement sports-racing cars. The first Oscas of 1948 were 1.1-litre cars with cycle wings so they could compete in both sports and *monoposto* events. They did so with such aces as Gigi Villoresi, Felice Bonetto, Raymond Sommer and Luigi Fagioli at their wheels, thanks to the brothers' long friendships with the greatest racers of the day.

Fagioli was the driver who put Osca on the map in the 1950 Mille Miglia. The brothers had just introduced their Type Mt4, a twin-overhead-cam version of their 1,092 cc four. Installed in a twin-tube live-axle chassis of spare simplicity made with superb craftsmanship, it produced 92 bhp at 6,600 rpm. Luigi Fagioli not only won his class with one in the Mille Miglia on 23 April, permanently displacing the formerly dominant Fiats and Cisitalias, but also placed seventh overall ahead of many much more powerful cars. Giulio Cabianca campaigned an improved version of this car with devastating success.

Most often bodied by the Morelli brothers in Ferrara, north-east of Bologna, the sports Oscas were clean-lined with vertical-barred oval grilles. Their twin-cam four proved amenable to expansion, first to 1,342 cc, then to 1,453 cc and finally to 1,491 cc with the 'square' 78 x 78 mm dimensions of the Maserati 4CL of 1939. In 1956 Osca also built an all-new 749 cc four, with the result that the 1956 Mille Miglia found Oscas winning the 750 cc,

In 1952 this Maserati A6GCS was a transitional model with integral wings and the twin-cam Formula 2 engine.

'It was powerful and well-balanced and very nimble. It was very like a Cooper in character. You could drive it as hard as you liked, slinging it sideways was no trouble, and that was a good thing because as the race progressed we found it had little or no brakes and we had to put it into a slide to slow it down.'

Into the 1960s Osca made a great variety of sports-racers, trying to cope with the rise of ultra-light concoctions from Britain's Lotus, Lola and Cooper. It also joined the Formula Junior rush, building 15 Fiat-powered single-seaters between 1959 and 1961. Fiat manufactured a 1.6-litre version of the Osca twin-cam for a sports car of its own. It allowed the Maseratis to use the same engine in their own GT models, of which 128 berlinettas were made. After 1963, when Italy's MV Agusta acquired Osca, the marque faded from the scene.

Together with Stanguellini, Bandini, Ermini and Giannini, to name those small Italian firms who were most ambitious with their Fiat-based twin-cam engine designs, Osca pitched most of its efforts below the 2.0-litre level where Ferrari and Maserati were duking it out. Both those Modena rivals had cars with engines of that size to compete in sports cars and in Formula 2, Maserati with a six and Ferrari with a V-12, initially, and from the end of 1951 with a new four-cylinder engine designed by Aurelio Lampredi.

Although superficially simple, Ferrari's new twin-cam Type 500 F2 four was in fact sophisticated with an elaborate valve gear and double-walled crankcase. In the hands of Alberto Ascari it dominated Formula 2 racing in 1952 and '53, just the years in which the world championship was decided in the junior formula because Formula 1 had run out of cars after Alfa Romeo's retirement at the end of the 1951 season. Only Ferrari had been ready to continue with its 4.5-litre cars in 1952, with BRM's supercharged 1.5-litre V-16s having proved chronic non-starters.

Maserati had been a stalwart supporter of the 1.5-litre blown category, thanks to the ready availability of its pre-war 4CLs. Before the Maseratis left in 1947 they produced an improved version with a stiffer and lighter tubular frame that also served as an oil reservoir. Dubbed the 4CLT (T for *tubolare* or tubular), it first raced at Reims in July of 1947. Another upgrade was two-stage supercharging. Used on and off in 1947, twin blowers became standard in 1948.

To respond to the revived Alfettas and to add customer appeal the Orsis hired Alberto Massimino to design yet another chassis for the sixteen-valve four-cylinder engine. He sharply lowered its profile with a new

1,100 cc and 1,500 cc classes. In the SCCA's Class H Modified, Osca power produced the champions of 1959, 1960 and 1961, and in G Modified the champions in 1954 and '55.

In the SCCA's F Modified class, American sportsman Briggs Cunningham was champion in 1954 with a 1,453 cc Type Mt4 prepared by Turin-born Alfred Momo, who had been a flight mechanic for Fiat engines in the Great War. This white spider achieved one of the great giant-killing performances in racing history. Driven by American Bill Lloyd and Briton Stirling Moss, racing in America for the first time, it outlasted Jaguar, Allard, Ferrari, Cunningham and Lancia opposition to win the 1954 12 Hours of Sebring.

'I was incredibly impressed by what turned out to be a real little thoroughbred of a car,' said Moss afterward.

tubular frame and inboard coil springs for a cleaner front suspension. Thus was created the 4CLT/48, also known as the 'San Remo', for the 1948 Grand Prix which it won on its first appearance. The San Remo rapidly became the staple machine of the many private teams that made up the bulk of the Grand Prix racing fields. In 1949 these included an Argentine team which first showcased the skills of Juan Fangio in Europe. By 1950, however, the live-axle 4CLT/48 was completely outclassed.

While Ferrari had Piero Taruffi and Nino Farina on its Formula 2 strength, as well as Ascari, Maserati fielded an all-Argentinean team of Juan Manuel Fangio, Froilan Gonzalez and Onofre Marimon. Fangio was pleased to see a newcomer to Maserati's design offices in October 1952 in the person of Gioachino Colombo. Fangio had seen the difference that Colombo made at Alfa Romeo when he returned to that team for 1951. For 1953 Colombo completely overhauled Maserati's cars, which had twin-cam sixes that had originated with the inevitable Alberto Massimino.

Although in Formula 2 Maserati couldn't cope with Ferrari and Ascari in 1953, save for a dramatic win for Fangio in the season's last race at Monza, in parallel Colombo created a sports car, the A6GCS/2000, which is

Designed with the help of Gioachino Colombo, this twin-cam six-cylinder A6GCM Maserati raced in Formula 2 in 1953.

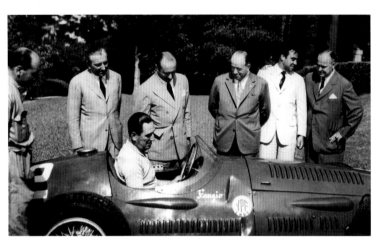

With Juan Fangio behind him and Adolfo Orsi third from right, Juan Perón inspects one of the first 250 F Maseratis in Buenos Aires in 1954.

Both fast and pretty, the Type 300 S Maserati – here at Sebring in 1957 – was a supremely versatile and driver-friendly sports-racer.

one of the great Italian classics of all time. In its first race, the 1953 Mille Miglia, it was first and second in class and sixth overall. A prominent customer for the model was Roman Luigi Musso, who marked his helmet with the sign of the Trident. After many outright hill climb victories Musso was class winner in the Giro di Sicilia and Targa Florio in 1954.

Extremely shapely with powerful brakes, the A6GCS/2000 prompted Britain's *The Autocar* to say that 'this Maserati sports car is a most desirable property, the sight – let alone sound – of which will make any enthusiast's mouth water.' Fifty-two in all were made through 1955 and sold to drivers who scored many successes with them in North and South America as well as Europe. So well-balanced and easy to handle was this

Maserati that its drivers affectionately dubbed it 'Auntie'. As late as 1959 the A6GCS/2000 was still able to place fifth in the Targa Florio, so versatile and rugged did it prove to be.

A major task for Colombo was to plan Maserati's Grand Prix car for the 1954 Formula 1, which catered to 2.5-litre unsupercharged engines. He recruited Valerio Colotti, an engineer who had been with Ferrari since 1948, to design the new car's suspension and rear-mounted transaxle. After Colombo left in October to design a Formula 1 car for Bugatti, Vittorio Bellentani took the project over. He had already worked on the car's engine, which although still a twin-cam six was entirely new.

This was the gestation of Maserati's 250 F Grand Prix car, destined to be one of the classic designs of its day. It opened its account with victory for Juan Fangio in the first two championship races of the new 1954 Formula 1 at Buenos Aires and Spa. With added points from his Mercedes-Benz successes, Fangio won his second championship in 1954. After 1955, when the Italian marques were overshadowed by Mercedes, Stirling Moss became Maserati's team leader in 1956. The Briton, who had raced a 250 F privately, won two races in 1956 and was second to Fangio in the world championship.

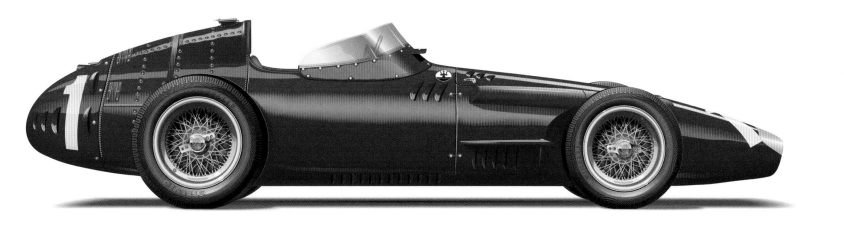

1957 MASERATI TYPE 250 F

ALTHOUGH RELATED TO THE FIRST TYPE 250 F OF 1954, 1957'S VERSION WAS VASTLY IMPROVED BY MASERATI'S GIULIO
ALFIERI. FANGIO DROVE IT TO HIS FIFTH AND FINAL WORLD CHAMPIONSHIP.

Member of a new family of four-cylinder sports-racers from Maserati, the Type 150 S of 1956 was hard-pressed to cope with Porsche's spyders.

Juan Fangio was back with Maserati in 1957, when its chief engineer Giulio Alfieri produced a completely revised 250 F. 'The car was lighter, had a bit more power and had ended up very well balanced,' said Fangio. 'You could do what you liked in that sort of car. It was nicely poised, responsive, fast and suited my driving style.' It suited him so well that he won four Grands Prix at Buenos Aires, Monaco, Rouen and the Nürburgring en route to his fifth and final world title. His thrusting drive at the Nürburgring is rated as one of his greatest, indeed one of the finest race wins of all time.

That was Maserati's last season at the coal face of Formula 1, for it was overextended financially and soon under the protection of an official receiver. During 1958 the Orsis let it be known that Maserati was withdrawing from all factory racing activity although it continued to service the cars of its customer racers.

Maserati's parlous state was owed in part to its take-no-prisoners approach to both Grand-Prix and sports-car racing during the 1957 season. Based on the components used in the 250 F, engineers Alfieri, Bellentani and Colotti created a 3.0-litre sports-racer, the 300 S. The first sports Maserati since the war to have an engine larger than 2.0 litres, it had a ready market thanks to the success of the A6GCS/2000. In all its versions through 1958 the 300 S was beautifully balanced as well as quick with handsome styling thanks to the metal-shaping skills of Medardo Fantuzzi.

The 300 S made its bow in March of 1955 at Sebring, where private entrants were third and fourth. Important wins later in the year were Monza's Supercortemaggiore 1,000 Kilometres and the Grand Prix of Venezuela. In 1956 the 300 S of Bill Lloyd was the SCCA's Class D Modified champion. 'From 1956 to 1958 I started thirteen races in 300 S Maseratis,' wrote Stirling Moss with Doug Nye, 'and I took them over after having started in a different type of Maserati on three more occasions. From that total of sixteen events the 300 S gave me nine wins, three second places, a third and a fifth and only two retirements. With a record like that, can you see why I have fond memories of these beautiful cars?'

Stirling Moss was less enthusiastic about the potent weapon that Maserati introduced for 1957, its 450 S. It was powered by the second V-8 in Maserati's history, a four-cam unit with capacity of 4,478 cc producing 400 bhp at 6,800 rpm. A big car in every way, with huge turbo-finned drum brakes, the 450 S was as brutal as it looked, 'a very powerful, big, hairy machine that wasn't

very delicate to handle' according to Moss. Although it won races at Sebring and Sweden in 1957, in others it broke and in the final championship contest in Venezuela all three V-8s crashed and retired.

With the FIA imposing a 3.0-litre limit on prototypes from 1958, the 450 S was ineligible. The picture was different in America, where the SCCA's Modified category imposed no constraints. Carroll Shelby enjoyed success in 1958 with John Edgar's 450 S while others racing the big Maseratis were Jim Hall, Walt Cline, Masten Gregory, Bill Krause and Ebb Rose.

In Vittorio Bellentani's design scheme for the 450 S V-8 its technology did double duty. One cylinder head served as the basis of a series of four-cylinder engines, the 150 S, 200 S and 250 S, their designations indicating the capacity of the sports-racers they powered. In 1960 the four was inclined and enlarged to 2.9 litres to motivate the astonishing Type 61, a great classic sports-racing car born of adversity, the difficult period in

which Maserati was recovering from corporate near-extinction.

Better known as the 'Birdcage', the Type 61 was the inspiration of chief engineer Giulio Alfieri, who conceived a radical chassis frame welded of many small chrome-molybdenum-alloy steel tubes to form the elegant and idealised structure which won the cars their nickname. Alfieri married the 2.9-litre four with the proven 250 F drive line. Disc brakes stopped a car whose exiguous bodywork was functional rather than pretty. The 22 cars made by Maserati raced to many successes in North America – including two SCCA Class D modified championships – and won the Nürburgring's 1,000-kilometre race in 1960 and 1961. Later rear-engined versions were less successful.

Although the Trident was a towering wave of racing's red tide, other Italians that swamped the competition were Lancia, Alfa Romeo and – last but not least – Ferrari.

Seen here heading a Lotus (in a modern classic race car event), and behind it a 250 F Maserati, the Type 61 'Birdcage' was the 1960 season's fastest sports-racing car.

CHAPTER 16

Racing's Red Tide: Part 2

Vincenzo Lancia last raced in 1910, driving a
Lancia like this one in a flying-mile
competition at Modena. He won his class at
70.576 mph.

THIS late in our recounting of the red-racer saga we are still encountering connections with the pioneering Ceirano brothers. Like Felice Nazzaro, Vincenzo Lancia had been an apprentice in the Ceirano workshops on Turin's Corso Vittorio Emanuele. Vincenzo's wealthy family summered at their villa in Fobello, where he was born in 1881, and spent the rest of the year in Turin in their property located, fatefully, cheek by jowl with the Ceirano factory.

Out the window went Vincenzo's father's plans for him to train as a solicitor. At school 'Censin', as he was nicknamed, was less than a success. Much more attractive were the Welleyes bicycles being produced by the Ceiranos. Before long Censin became a novice mechanic. Fascinated by engines, he succeeded in gaining his father's permission to leave school and work for the Ceiranos. Although Vincenzo was supposed to be gaining accounting experience by minding the books, he busied himself repairing engines instead.

With his colleague Nazzaro, at the age of 18 Lancia joined Fiat as a mechanic/tester when that nascent company took over the Ceirano assets. Highlights of his career behind the wheel have been recounted. A big, strapping lad when he was young, Lancia grew to become a large man with a passion for good food, drink with friends and the opera. A music buff, he was particularly fond of Wagner. In 1906 he started building cars. On 29 November of that year, together with his friend and Fiat colleague Claudio Fogolin, he founded Fabbrica Automobili Lancia in Turin.

Although one of the great innovators of the motor industry, as he proved in the 1920s with the V-4 engine, independent front suspension and self-supporting bodywork of his Lambda, Lancia didn't embrace motor sports as a means of promoting his cars. He sought an upmarket profile that differed from those of Fiat and Alfa Romeo, with their predilections to racing. Nevertheless private owners had high placings in the early Targas

Florio while Lancias won the important light-car races at Savannah, Georgia in 1908 and 1910.

Vincenzo Lancia had introduced many more attractive models to his company's portfolio when, on 15 February 1937 at the age of 55, he died after suffering a heart attack during the night. This was the exigency that drew into the company Vittorio Jano, then struggling to create racing cars to rival the Germans with the meagre resources allocated him by Alfa Romeo. At the time of Vincenzo's death his only son, Gianni, was thirteen. Control of the works was taken by Arturo Lancia, a cousin of Vincenzo. But when he died suddenly in 1948 the sole responsibility at Lancia rested with Gianni, then 24 years old.

An extrovert in his father's mould, robust of build and temperament, dead keen on car mechanics and unafraid of dirtying his hands, Gianni Lancia was the right man to break down the barriers that the indigenous technical staff presented to Jano on his arrival. Experiments during the war led to the conclusion that a V-6 was the right engine for the future. This was realised in 1950 with the introduction of the B.20 Aurelia with its 60-degree 1.8-litre V-6. All-independently sprung, it had its clutch and transaxle at the rear.

Soon evolved to 2.0 litres as the B.21 and given a fast-back coupé body that defined the genre *Gran Turismo*, the Aurelia became a formidable competition car not only in its class but overall. In 1951 Giovanni Bracco drove one to second place in the Mille Miglia while Luigi Fagioli was third in 1952, splitting two Mercedes-Benz 300SLs of half again the engine size. The 1951 Targa Florio was a B.21 benefit with Aurelias in the first three places led by Felice Bonetto.

'This was one of the two or three most outstanding production cars with sporting potential ever made,' wrote historian Mike Lawrence of the Aurelia, 'and a powerful case could be made for it being the best of all.' It enjoyed the pedigreed paternity of Vittorio Jano. He led a skilled and enthusiastic team that included Franceso De Virgilio, who had led the V-6 engine research, drive-train man Ettore Zaccone Mina, chassis designer and co-ordinator Francesco Faleo and whole-vehicle man Luigi Bosco.

In Lancia's history the Aurelia's second place in the 1951 Mille Miglia was fateful. It was an astonishing result that brought such a wave of appreciation for Lancia that Gianni Lancia decided that his company would set up a competition department for the first time and would design and build special cars for racing. His plan was not unlike that of Mercedes-Benz: a year or two of sports-car racing to get the feel of things and build up a cohesive *scuderia*, followed by a Grand Prix effort, but only when fully ready.

Above left: Franco Cortese drove this race-prepared 3.0-litre Lancia Astura to victory on Modena's city streets in 1946.

Above: Chased at Monaco in 1952 by a Frazer Nash and Ferrari, the Lancia Type B.21 Aurelia GT was adept at both racing and rallying.

Lancia had world champion Alberto Ascari to test and develop its radical D.50 Grand Prix car, an effort which took most of 1954.

Above right: Powering the Lancia Type D.50 Grand Prix car and its Ferrari successors through 1957 was this compact 2.5-litre four-cam V-8.

The new department was set up on Turin's Via Caraglio, which intersected with the Via Vincenzo Lancia.

Common to all the D-series sports-racing Lancias were 60-degree V-6 engines with twin chain-driven camshafts on each bank, using Vittorio Jano's characteristic valve gear. Like the Aurelia they had rear-mounted clutches and transaxles. Large and wide drum brakes were mounted inboard, radically at the front as well as the rear. Unusually for cars of the era, Roots-type superchargers were used for some races, such as Le Mans.

In coupé bodywork the first 3.0-litre D.20 models appeared for the 1953 Mille Miglia, in which Bonetto placed third and Biondetti eighth, with two other cars retiring. The first success came in May in the Targa Florio, won by Bracco protégé Umberto Maglioli in a D.20 after Piero Taruffi, leading in a sister car, retired. Upgraded to 3.3 litres and stripped of their roofs the cars became D.24 models for the Autodrome Grand Prix at Monza. Finishing second in both heats, Felice Bonetto was second overall.

At the end of 1953 the D.24 had a great success in the Carrera Panamericana, won by Juan Fangio with Taruffi second and a handsome newcomer, Eugenio Castellotti, third. In 1954 the Lancias suffered problems at Sebring, giving the win to the Moss/Lloyd Osca, then bounced back with wins for Taruffi in the Giro di Sicilia and Targa Florio and success also in the Mille Miglia, the

solitary victory in that great classic for Lancia and Alberto Ascari.

By 1954 Lancia racing director Attilio Pasquarelli had other concerns, because his company's D.50 Formula 1 car was beginning its tests. A magnificent cherry-red creation by the Jano team, the D.50 had four-cam V-8 power delivering 253 bhp at 8,000 rpm in an elegant tubular space frame in which the engine played a structural role. Its distinguishing feature was the use of aerodynamic fairings between the front and rear wheels that also served as fuel tanks.

In one of the great tragedies of motor racing the proving of the D.50 during 1954 was so arduous and protracted that all but one championship race went by without a Lancia for contracted driver Alberto Ascari, the reigning world champion. In the final race at Barcelona in October he showed the new car's speed but retired. In March and May of 1955 Ascari won the Grands Prix of Turin and Naples respectively in the D.50. The Naples race was his last success because Ascari, the brightest star in Italy's firmament, died at the end of May when testing a Ferrari sports-racer at Monza.

For those among Lancia's shareholders who felt that racing was a bootless extravagance at a time when Lancia wasn't prospering, the death of the team's leader – though not in a Lancia – was a final straw. The Lancia family had 49 per cent of the company's shares, of which Gianni

controlled only a portion. A majority of the directors voted to cease racing. In a touching ceremony on 26 July 1955 all Lancia's Grand Prix equipment, including six complete D.50s, was collected by representatives of the Scuderia Ferrari, which negotiated a government subsidy to support its Formula 1 campaign.

This was timely for Ferrari, which had been struggling against the might of Mercedes with its four-cylinder Grand Prix cars since the new 2.5-litre Formula 1 began in 1954. Aurelio Lampredi had produced his radical Type 553 F1 in 2.0-litre form for the Italian Grand Prix of 1953, winning Ferrari a cash bonus for an all-new car. It had ball-joint front suspension, side-mounted fuel tanks, an efficient tubular space frame and a de Dion rear suspension whose axle tube curved forward of the transaxle. When a similar design appeared on the 250 F Maserati, Enzo Ferrari accused his bitter rivals of industrial espionage.

With the Type 553 F1 handling strangely, however, Ferrari put 2.5-litre engines into his 1952-53 Formula 2 chassis as a stop-gap. A new version of the radical car, the Type 555 F1, for 1955 was no more successful.

Neither was a bizarre aberration on Lampredi's part, a twin-cylinder 2.5-litre engine with four valves per chamber. Although it produced 160 bhp at 4,800 rpm and was able to rev to 5,200, it vibrated so severely that it damaged the dynamometer. Enzo Ferrari's mortification over this fruitless freak contributed to his break with Lampredi in 1955.

Before departing Aurelio Lampredi had produced new generations of in-line engines for Ferrari's sports-racers. While the 2.0-litre four in the 1953 Mondial was not a great success, revised in the live-rear-axle Testa Rossa of 1956 it was a feisty competitor. A 3.0-litre four was developed for 1954's 750 Monza, which made America's Phil Hill the SCCA's D Modified champion in 1955. Although its handling was treacherous the Monza could win against the early 300 S Maserati. In 3.4-litre form as the 860 Monza it won at Sebring in 1956.

One of Phil Hill's early drives for Ferrari was at Le Mans in 1955 in Lampredi's formidable Type 735 LM, powered by a 4.4-litre in-line six of 330 bhp. Hill recalled Ferrari proudly showing him the new six running on the Maranello test bed. 'Here I was looking at something that

Spearhead of Ferrari's 1957 sports-racing attack was this Type 315 S V-12 of 3.8 litres, raced at Sebring by Peter Collins.

Italian racing red at its finest: the 3.0-litre Type 250 Testa Rossa of 1958, chiefly raced by Ferrari's customers in this 'pontoon'-winged form.

This Type 315 S Ferrari won the 1957 Mille Miglia for Piero Taruffi in the last year before introduction of a 3.0-litre limit for sports-racers.

to me was nothing but a big Jaguar engine instead of the wonderful Ferrari V-12s I had so long raced and respected,' Phil recalled. 'And he was so proud of it!' In fact Ferrari soon went back to his twelves, with which he had won at Le Mans in 1954 in a generous 5.0-litre size.

With the Lancias, Ferrari also acquired the prodigiously experienced Vittorio Jano as a consultant. New four-cam racing V-12s of 3.5, 3.8 and 4.0 litres for 1957 had his hallmark in their valve gear, producing up to 390 bhp and seizing sports-racing championship honours from Maserati's 450 S V-8. During 1957 Ferrari hired a new chief engineer in former Alfa Romeo man

Carlo Chiti. For the new 1958 sports-racing rules, which limited engine size to 3.0 litres, Chiti further developed the veteran Colombo V-12 to power a new Testa Rossa. Cars of this type brought world championships to Maranello in 1958, 1960 and 1961.

Concentration on best performance from the 3.0-litre V-12 also paid off in the racing versions of Ferrari's 250 GT road car. The sleek Berlinetta created for it by Scaglietti in 1958 did so well in the Tour de France that this became its unofficial name. The short-wheelbase model introduced in 1959 brought disc brakes to Ferrari's road cars and in 1960 continued the 250 GT's run of successes. In 1962 shifting the engine back and down

created the 250 GTO, the quintessential front-engined
GT Ferrari. It contributed to Maranello's grand touring
championships in 1962 through 1964.

With the rise of British-green rivals some of these
years were unproductive for Ferrari in Formula 1. Further
development of the Lancia D.50, moving its fuel tankage
to the rear and modifying its suspension, brought Juan
Fangio his fourth Grand Prix world championship in
1956. For the new 1.5-litre Formula 2 of 1957 Vittorio
Jano led the way to the creation of a four-cam V-6 with a
65-degree vee. It was named to memorialise Enzo
Ferrari's son Alfredo 'Dino', who died in 1956 at the age
of only 24.

In 1958 this Dino 156 F2 and the light, compact car
it powered became the 2.4-litre Dino 246 F1 with which
Britain's bow-tied Mike Hawthorn became world
champion. The V-6 also facilitated Ferrari's transition to
rear-mounted engines, which Carlo Chiti began in 1960
and completed in 1961. To help Ferrari race in a new
1.6-litre Formula 2 based on road-car engines, Fiat
produced a version of the V-6 that powered the 2.0-litre
Fiat Dino sports cars introduced in 1966 and '67. Ferrari's

design was adapted to Fiat's needs by none other than
Aurelio Lampredi, then a leading engine designer at the
Turin firm.

Ferrari's new bright spark, Carlo Chiti, was a questing,
demanding character who had honed his automotive skills
at Alfa Romeo. A cultured Tuscan born in 1924,
bespectacled, balding Chiti had a passion for
aerodynamics, which he had studied at university.
Entering Portello's gates in 1952, Chiti found himself
working on an exciting Alfa sports-racer in 1953.

Creation of the cars that became world-famous as the
'*Disco Volante*' or 'Flying Disc' Alfas began in near-
clandestine fashion in 1951. Thinking about a new
2.0-litre sports-racer from Portello to compete with the
resurgent Lancia Aurelias, Alfa's Gioachino Colombo
huddled with Carlo Felice Bianchi Anderloni of Milan's
Carrozzeria Touring to evolve a completely new shape.
The conspirators were the same men who 'disconcerted'
the world with their audacious *Barchetta* body for the
166 MM Ferrari in 1948.

Using Alfa 1900 components in a tubular structure they
created a form with semi-enclosed wheels which, said

Pictured at Goodwood next to a contemporary Fiat 8V, Alfa Romeo's 1953 Type 6C 3000 CM was more functional than handsome.

ALFA ROMEO TYPE 160

Attack boats used by the Italian Navy in World War II helped to inspire the radical design of an Alfa Romeo intended to compete under the new 2.5-litre Formula 1 starting in 1954. Designed by Guido Cattaneo, they had cockpits at the extreme stern from which their crew could 'aim' the whole of their boat toward a target. During that war the car's designer, Giuseppe Busso, had worked on aviation engines for Portello. In the 1947-48 period he was at Ferrari before returning to Alfa Romeo, where he was in charge of the project centre under design chief Orazio Satta Puglia.

Mulling the idea of a successor to the magnificent Type 158/159 Alfetta, Busso drew conclusions from the problems that testers had in controlling the Type 512, Wifredo Ricart's rear-engined Grand Prix car with an extremely forward driver position. This, he felt, 'prevented the driver from being able to "sense" in time the behaviour of the rear part of the car and control it properly.'

Giuseppe Busso decided 'to plan an experiment that should go all the way to the opposite extreme, the placing of the driver's seat behind the rear axle,' the terrestrial equivalent of the attack-boat design. In the summer of 1952 he obtained Satta's approval for his experiment, which was the modification of a Type 158 to have just such a location for the driver. In tests that October with a car that was the least good available, with extremely provisional steering arrangements and no windscreen, Consalvo Sanesi lapped Monza in an extremely respectable time. The experienced Sanesi was 'greatly elated' about the layout's potential.

Having also sounded out Juan Fangio and gained his approval, Busso and his team began designing their Type 160. Removing the driver from the centre of the machine meant that a fuel tank could take his place, wrapped around a large-diameter steel tube that joined the front-mounted engine to the rear transaxle. The front of the engine carried a differential casting, for Busso planned driver-selectable four-wheel drive like that of the Porsche design for Cisitalia.

Hugely ambitious, the Type 160 had a roller-bearing flat-twelve engine whose geared cam drives and output were at the centre, making it the equivalent of two flat sixes back to back. While coil-sprung de Dion rear suspension was used, at the front wide-based parallel wishbones and torsion cars were specified. Extremely wide drum brakes with helical finning were to be inboard-mounted at both front and rear. The driver sat with his legs over the rear axle and astride the transmission. Here was an amazing conception whose driver position anticipated that of the first 'slingshot' dragster by several years. It used both engine and transaxle as part of the car's structure, another forward-looking idea. Getting it built, however, was no easy matter at a time when the new Giulietta was consuming all the company's development resources. Ultimately only the engine was completed although never tested. In its technical fantasies a worthy rival to the bizarre creations of Wifredo Ricart, Alfa's Type 160 remained a secret until its revelation by Giovanni Lurani and Busso in 1967.

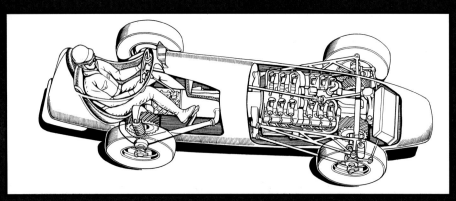

A schematic shows Giuseppe Busso's radical concept for the Type 160 Grand Prix car for Alfa Romeo with its driver well to the rear.

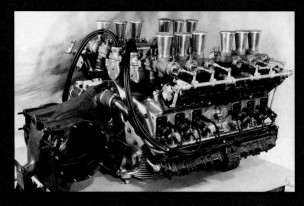

Attached to the front of the Type 160 Alfa's flat-12 engine was the housing for the front differential of its four-wheel-drive system.

Bianchi Anderloni, was 'vaguely elliptical' in its cross section and 'in longitudinal section it was similar to an aeroplane'. Bold fairings for its wheels emerged from the upper surfaces of its disc-like body. In 1952 both a roadster and a coupé were built to this style, plus a third flatter-sided spider which greatly influenced the A6GCS/2000 body that Colombo created for Maserati in 1953.

With noses whose shapes perfectly suited the Alfa Romeo grille, these audacious cars made headlines the world over. A 3.0-litre open version was built as well, using a twin-cam in-line six being developed for a possible big-car range. With the backing of Alfa president Pasquale Gallo the decision was made to build a team of 3.5-litre racing coupés for the 1953 season. These had a new multi-tube backbone chassis designed by Giuseppe Busso and coupé bodies by Colli that eschewed the 'Disco' shape. They were magnificently muscular-looking with a profusion of scoops, trap doors, deflectors, filler caps and rivets.

In their only active season, 1953, these splendid 275-horsepower cars were too new and untested to do justice to their superb chassis. Fangio finished second with one in the Mille Miglia only 11 minutes behind the winner in spite of a broken steering-box mounting that obliged him to drive with even more precision than usual. At Le Mans all three retired before 12 of the 24 hours.

The model's only victory was in September of 1953 at Merano in the Southern Tyrol. In a minor event, 15 laps of an 11-mile road course, the opposition was major: Lancia's entire sports-racing team. They suffered breakdowns that allowed Fangio to win with an open-bodied version of the Alfa.

Attending the car there was engineer Carlo Chiti, who enjoyed working with a champion of Fangio's calibre. Chiti helped to design competition versions of Alfa's 2000 and Giulietta, including the Type 750 of 1956. This was a Boano-bodied 1.5-litre spider on a steel platform frame made by Abarth which Portello elected neither to race nor produce. In the autumn of 1957 Chiti departed Milan for Maranello and Ferrari. There he found challenge aplenty.

Given coachwork by Boano as a gift from Alfa Romeo to Argentina's Juan Perón, this 6C 3000 CM was later rebodied as a 1953 competition car.

CHAPTER 17

Grand Prix Ferraris

Seen at Reims in 1957 with Maurice Trintignant, Ferrari's Dino V-6 made its debut at 1.5-litre capacity in a front-engined monoposto.

IN the crucial transition period at Maranello between the end of the 1950s and beginning of the 1960s an important passing of the baton occurred between veteran engineer Vittorio Jano and the new generation as represented by Carlo Chiti, who arrived at Ferrari in 1957, and his successor in 1962, Mauro Forghieri.

Before his death in 1965, at the age of 75, Jano generously imparted his wealth of knowledge and experience as a consultant to Ferrari. Calling Jano 'a superlative master,' Forghieri said that 'everything I know about racing engines I learned from him.' Even making allowances for hyperbole this was a compelling tribute to a great pioneer whose contributions are laced through these pages like a strand of pearls.

These years found Ferrari struggling against the British with their odd spider-like Grand Prix cars powered by rear-mounted Coventry Climax four-cylinder engines. The crucial year of transition was 1958, when Formula 1 rules mandated aviation-quality petrol instead of the exotic blends previously allowed. Also from 1958 new rules curtailed championship Grand Prix races to 300 kilometres or two hours against the previous 500 kilometres or three hours. Both changes favoured the production of smaller, lighter cars which would be easier on their tyres.

After his decades of racing the superb Alfa Romeos and his own long-nosed Ferraris, Enzo Ferrari was reluctant to conclude that the Coopers and Lotuses represented anything other than a fleeting phenomenon. He was supported in this view by others in his organisation, including engineer Giotto Bizzarrini. For Enzo a decisive constraint was the front-engined configuration of his road cars. He was deeply reluctant to build racing cars that suggested that this was anything but ideal.

'We argued a lot and we discussed it a lot,' said Carlo Chiti. For 1959 he adopted such characteristics of the British camp as disc brakes, Dunlop tyres and coil-spring rear suspension. This brought a meagre yield of two victories on the fast tracks of Reims and the Avus where higher power was decisive. Both wins went to Tony Brooks who was in close contention for the driver's title to the last race, finally placing second.

Trying to make the best of the cards dealt him by Enzo Ferrari, for 1960 Chiti produced a new front-mid-

140

During 1958 Ferrari raced its Dinos in 1.5-litre Formula 2 size – here Wolfgang von Trips at Monaco – and as 2.4-litre Grand Prix cars.

In the wet British G.P. at Liverpool's Aintree in 1961 Richie Ginther placed third in his 'Sharknose' Dino 156 F1 Ferrari.

Ferrari's new rear-engined designs worked in sports-racing too as shown by this Dino 246 SP in 1962's Targa Florio.

engined G.P. car. To gain the more concentrated central mass distribution of the rear-mid-engined car he shifted the 2.4-litre V-6 rearward within the wheelbase and placed the main fuel tanks at the sides instead of at the rear. Independent rear suspension replaced the long-serving de Dion axle. This car won only one race in 1960, however, an Italian G.P. at Monza which the British teams boycotted because the banked track, now car-breakingly bumpy, was used as part of the circuit. It was destined to be the last championship Grand Prix victory by a front-engined car.

In parallel Carlo Chiti developed a mid-engined Ferrari. 'Facts proved its effectiveness and the drivers themselves wanted to have mid-engined cars,' he said. 'There was nothing much we could really do when ugly ducklings like the 210-bhp Coopers (our cars developed 280 bhp) left us well behind.' Moreover arch-rival Maserati was tweaking Ferrari's nose by supplying 2.5-litre fours to private teams racing Coopers. Driven by Britain's Roy Salvadori, a Cooper-Maserati was eighth fastest on the grid at Monaco in 1959. Late in the race he had risen to third place, splitting the Ferraris of Tony Brooks and Phil Hill, when his gearbox failed. Salvadori pushed his Trident-engined Cooper over the line to place sixth.

A role in the drama was played by another team fielding Cooper-Maseratis, the Modena-based Scuderia Centro-Sud run by Guglielmo 'Mimo' Dei. The wily Dei recouped some of his costs by selling a spare Cooper

Driving to fourth place at Monaco in 1963 in Ferrari's Dino 156 F1/63, John Surtees would win the world championship in red cars in 1964.

Liveried to warn others to step aside, this 4.0-litre Ferrari Type 330 P was raced at Sebring in 1965 by Bob Grossman and Skip Hudson.

chassis to Enzo Ferrari. It was given close scrutiny at Maranello before being allocated to the Scuderia Eugenio Castellotti, set up in tribute to the Ferrari driver killed during testing at Modena in March 1957. It was powered by a 1955-vintage Type 555 four with 'Eugenio' on its blue-crackle-painted cam covers. Although two such cars competed in 1960 without distinction, Ferrari had subtly acknowledged the new trend.

During 1960 Carlo Chiti produced V-6-powered mid-engined Ferraris in both 2.5- and 1.5-litre sizes for Formulae 1 and 2 respectively. While the former was a modest success at Monaco in May the latter won at Germany's Solitude in July, significantly beating a phalanx of Porsches from nearby Stuttgart. As evolved by Chiti

into the Dino 156 F1 of 1961, this became the star of the 1961 season, the first under new Formula 1 rules which slashed allowable engine size to 1.5 litres.

Urged by coachbuilder Medardo Fantuzzi to investigate the merits of a split-nostril nose he'd used on some Maseratis in 1959, Carlo Chiti found reduced drag in his small wind tunnel that resulted in the 'Sharknose' look of the 1961 G.P. Ferrari. This won five of the seven Grands Prix that Ferrari contested that year, taking America's Phil Hill to the world championship.

Crucial to the new Ferrari's sparkling performance was an engine that Enzo had expressly ordered Chiti not to use: a 120-degree version of its Dino V-6. Against the weight of the 65-degree 1.5-litre engine at 320 pounds, the new six, designed strictly as a 1,500 cc engine, scaled only 265 pounds. Its wide vee angle also placed more of that weight nearer the ground. While the conception was Chiti's and the execution by Ferrari veteran Franco Rocchi, the valve gear remained Vittorio Jano's. Peak power was 190 bhp at 9,500 rpm.

Such a successful season put Ferrari in pole position for the new Formula 1. Astonishingly, however, between September of 1961 and August of 1964 Ferrari would win only a single solitary championship Grand Prix race, and that when Jim Clark's Lotus faltered. There were several reasons for this. Continuity was lost when a cadre of personnel including technical chief Chiti left Maranello at the end of 1961. Development was interrupted in 1962 by a rash of strikes by metalworkers. And the British caught up, trumping Ferrari's vee-six with vee-eights from BRM and Coventry Climax.

At the age of only 27 university-trained engineer Mauro Forghieri took charge of racing-car design at Maranello in 1962. The son of Ferrari's foundry master Reclus Forghieri, he had been with the company since 1959. Although Chiti had done his best to advance the state of the art, Forghieri found the chassis cupboard bare. 'Because we had been making cars with front engines,' he related, 'our technology was unsuitable – or perhaps inadequate – at that stage for the design and production of suitable chassis for mid-engined cars.'

For that reason Forghieri put his initial emphasis on advancing Ferrari's chassis design. The result, at the end of 1963, was replacement of space-frame tubes by a stressed-skin monocoque known as the 'Aero' frame for its similarity to an aeroplane's structure. Although this raced initially with the fuel-injected V-6 engine, the frame was designed to mate with new engines, a V-8 and flat-12, that were designed to serve as part of the car's structure. Both these pathbreaking designs were introduced in 1964,

1962 FERRARI TYPE 250 GTO

GIOTTO BIZZARRINI HELPED CREATE THE ICONIC 250 GTO FERRARI, A FRONT-MID-ENGINED GT COUPÉ. THIS ONE WAS
SECOND OVERALL AT LE MANS IN 1962 DRIVEN BY ENTRANT PIERRE NOBLET WITH JEAN GUICHET.

In Italy's Grand Prix in 1966 Mike Parkes, shown, took pole position and placed second in Ferrari's gorgeous Type 312 F1.

the V-8 Type 158 early enough to take thrusting British ex-motorcyclist John Surtees to a world championship.

Frustrating to Surtees was the broad palette across which Ferrari thinly spread the talents of his team to take part in many spheres of racing for economic reasons. Following on the success of his front-engined Testa Rossas and GTOs, a transition to mid-engined sports-racers was made by Chiti with the V-6-powered Dino 246 SP of 1961. Famously, early-1961 tests at Monza with this car led to the discovery of the value of a tail spoiler in giving stability to a low-drag shape. Ferrari's men did their best to conceal their discovery by saying that the prominent spoiler was a deflector to keep petrol away from the exhaust pipes.

In 1962 Ferrari's successful sports-racer, the 250 P, had a 3.0-litre V-12 engine in the back. This was a forerunner of the 250 LM of 1963, which introduced a twelve to a mid-engined closed GT car and won Le Mans in 1965. In that year Ferrari introduced the first twin-overhead-cam power units for its mid-engined sports-racers, using Jano-type valve gear like that of its 1957 cars. In an ultimately fruitless effort to meet the

Le Mans challenge from Ford, this line of development culminated in the magnificent 4.0-litre 330 P4, winner of the 24 Hours of Daytona in 1967.

These adventures plus chopping and changing of their high-tech equipment kept Ferrari and Surtees from realising their potential in 1965, the last year of the 1.5-litre Formula 1. Nor did 1966 start well, Ferrari having decided to use a modified sports-car V-12 to power its entry in the new 3.0-litre Formula 1. Only after Le Mans did the new car's development pick up steam, bringing a win for hawk-nosed Ludovico 'Lulu' Scarfiotti in the all-important Italian Grand Prix. We recall his eponymous forebear chairing the newly created Fiat at the turn of the century.

Starting in 1967, the surge to success of the Cosworth-built Ford V-8 in Lotus and other chassis left Ferrari's V-12 in its wake. To its credit in 1968 Ferrari was the first to use a high-mounted wing to generate downforce on a Formula 1 car, and also the first to make a Grand Prix wing driver-adjustable. However only one Grand Prix win in 1968 was followed by none in 1969. In the latter year, however, Ferrari gained stability from a compact that

LORENZO BANDINI

Much has been written about the pressures experienced by the Scuderia's drivers in the Enzo Ferrari era. What is certain is that drivers were often scapegoats for the faults of the cars. Only when a driver of unquestioned stature – an Ascari, Fangio or Prost in Enzo's era and later Schumacher – was in the cockpit and not achieving success would Ferrari and its fans concede that there might be something wrong with the cars. In these circumstances the pressure on a driver to perform was considerable.

The pressure was intensified if the red car's driver was Italian. Italian success in a Ferrari was a reason for national celebration. The failure of an Italian driver to make the most of this most glorious of all possible opportunities was cause for national despair and opprobrium. Into this maelstrom of conflicting priorities in 1962 stepped one of the most likeable men ever to drive for Ferrari, Lorenzo Bandini.

Darkly handsome in the Italian mould, Bandini was born four days before Christmas 1935 of a family that had been lured to the Italian protectorate of Libya by the riches supposedly on offer there. Disillusioned, they returned to Italy when Lorenzo was only three. At the age of only 15 Lorenzo moved to Milan to seek his fortune. He was lucky to find work at the garage of Goliardo Freddi, who not only encouraged the young man but also loaned him the Fiat in which he first raced in 1956. Seven years later he married Freddi's daughter Margherita.

Climbing the motor-sports ladder, in 1959 Lorenzo Bandini was racing a Volpini Formula Junior with results that won him a works Stanguellini drive in 1960. The following year he had his first Formula 1 outings in a Cooper-Maserati of Mimo Dei's Scuderia Centro Sud, his best result an eighth in the Italian G.P. In 1962 Bandini had three drives for Ferrari, starting out superbly with a third place at Monaco, but Maranello's equipment was sub-standard that year and next, when the best Lorenzo could do was a pair of fifth places in America and South Africa.

In 1964 and '65 Bandini was developing the flat-12 Type 1512 Ferrari, with which he was third in Mexico in 1964, John Surtees's championship year for Ferrari. That same year Lorenzo won with a Dino V-6 at Zeltweg in Austria, scoring his first championship Grand Prix victory. Piloting a bigger Dino V-6 in 1966 Bandini was second at Monaco and third in Belgium.

When Surtees left the Scuderia in mid-season of 1966 Bandini became its main man. He rose to the challenge, putting his V-12 on pole for the French G.P. at Reims and easily leading the race until his throttle cable broke. After sixths at Zandvoort and the Nürburgring he retired early at Monza. He then led at Watkins Glen only to have his engine fail.

John Surtees, left, and Lorenzo Bandini were Ferrari's lead drivers before Surtees left in mid-1966 after a disagreement over strategy at Le Mans.

Meanwhile Lorenzo Bandini was flying the sports-car flag for Ferrari. He was co-winner at Le Mans in 1963, in the Targa Florio in 1965 and, with team newcomer Chris Amon, the Daytona 24 Hours – a famous triumph over Ford – and the Monza 1,000 Kilometres in 1967 with the magnificent 330 P4. By now he was an authentic star of Italian racing, kitted out with appropriate style.

'His will, faith and deep attachment to the others on the team all made me very fond of him,' recalled Enzo Ferrari, who saw in him 'a potential Peter Collins,' the British driver to whom he'd been very close. Nevertheless Bandini had a chip on his shoulder in the glamorous world of motor sports, a readiness to take offence that reflected the inadequacies he perceived in his modest upbringing. He felt especially strongly the contrast with the wealthy Ludovico Scarfiotti, winner for Ferrari at Monza in 1966 and the other Italian on the Maranello strength.

In Formula 1 Ferrari skipped the South African race at the start of the year. It sent a team to the non-championship Race of Champions at Brands Hatch in March, where Bandini bounced back from a poor grid position in the final to finish less than a second behind the Eagle of Dan Gurney. With Ferrari's 312/67 F1 now in its stride, 1967 was shaping up as a good year for Lorenzo. At Monaco in May he qualified on the front row and led the first lap. Always amongst the leaders, he was running second until the 81st of 100 laps when he clipped the waterfront chicane and rolled over, his car bursting into flames. Grievously injured, Bandini died after 70 hours in hospital. He was 31.

Continued on page 146

Not long before Lorenzo's death, the Bandinis had bought farmland at Brisighella, near Imola, where the family had lived after its return from Libya. Driving the tractor himself, Lorenzo had been supervising the planting of crops and vines. Twenty-five years later, remembering the career of this son of their land, the good people of Brisighella founded the Trofeo Lorenzo Bandini as a tribute to the personality judged the most exciting new talent on the racing scene.

Among the Italians who have received the Bandini Trophy are Ivan Capelli, Giancarlo Fisichella and Jarno Trulli. Luca di Montezemolo received it in 1997 for his revival of Ferrari. With the last Italian having been recognised in 2000, the nation's enthusiasts are looking forward to the emergence of a new native talent who will deserve the 'Bandini'.

Left: In 1967 the coast was clear for the genial Lorenzo Bandini to lead Ferrari to Formula 1 success. Fate was to decree otherwise.

saw Fiat take a majority stake in the Maranello company in a deal that left racing under Enzo Ferrari's control.

A bright spot in 1969 was the performance of a hill climbing sports-racer, the 212 E, which dominated the sport in the hands of Swiss driver Peter Schetty. It was powered by a new four-valve-per-cylinder version of the Grand Prix flat-12, enlarged to 2.0 litres. This was a step toward a completely new 3.0-litre flat-opposed twelve conceived by Mauro Forghieri while on a semi-sabbatical

Luigi Chinetti's North American Racing Team entered the lone Ferrari 312 F1 for Pedro Rodriguez in the 1969 American G.P. at Watkins Glen.

from day-to-day racing responsibilities in 1969. He envisioned it as an integral part of a new car, the Type 312 B, whose monocoque frame extended above the ultra-flat engine to the rear suspension.

With only four main bearings for minimum friction and quick response, the 312 B engine had a troubled gestation which prompted talented New Zealander Chris Amon to leave the team in frustration. It gradually came good, however. In fact the low-profile twelve was destined to power Formula 1 Ferraris for a full decade and win three drivers' and four constructors' championships. Its first success, victory at Monza in September 1970 for Swiss driver Clay Regazzoni, was a liberating catharsis for the team.

The years of struggle weren't yet over. With Forghieri still in semi-exile, experiments with aerodynamics, suspensions and structures, including British-built monocoques, gave little satisfaction in the early 1970s. The only bright spots were a win in the German Grand Prix in 1972 for on-form Belgian driver Jacky Ickx and a makes' championship, that same year, for the 312 P, the sports-prototype version of the 312 B. This exceptionally handsome and effective sports-racer was also successful in 1973.

The 1973 season witnessed an agonising reappraisal of Ferrari's Formula 1 efforts. Enzo Ferrari called a mid-season halt to Grand Prix racing and brought Mauro Forghieri back into the front lines. To concentrate on

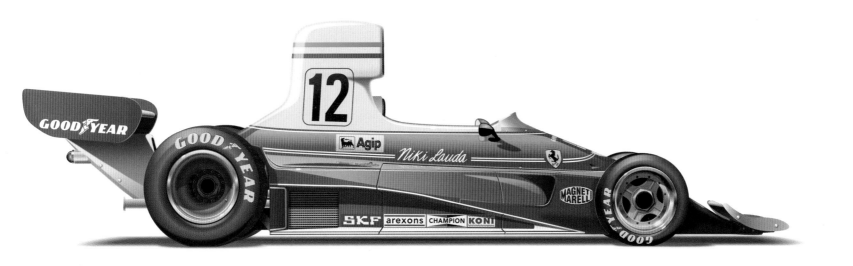

1975 FERRARI TYPE 312 T

NIKI LAUDA WAS SO SUCCESSFUL IN 1975 WITH THE TYPE 312 T FERRARI THAT HE CLAIMED, 'WE CREATED A NEW FERRARI

CRISIS BECAUSE IT COULD NEVER BE BETTERED. THE TREMENDOUS SUCCESSES BROUGHT NEW PROBLEMS.'

As raced to victory in 1970's Canadian G.P. by Jacky Ickx, Ferrari's Type 312 B was a brilliant new design by Mauro Forghieri.

Fully exploiting ground effects for the first time, Ferrari's 312 T4 took South African Jody Scheckter to the 1979 Formula 1 world championship.

races I started nine in pole position, won five times and with almost twenty points' lead was world champion. It was the reward for all our work for the last eighteen months; we got back what we gave in money, headaches and work. At the same time we created a Ferrari crisis because it could never be bettered. The tremendous successes brought new problems with them.'

Indeed, under the pressure of great expectations – always exaggerated in Italy – 1976 was a year of crisis for Lauda above all. Driving the 312 T2 he lost the championship by a single point after a dramatic season in which he crashed at the Nürburgring, staged an amazing recovery from life-threatening injuries and then voluntarily withdrew from a rain-soaked race in Japan, effectively relinquishing a title that was in his grasp. Nonetheless the constructors' cup went to Ferrari.

Still driving the 312 T2, now teamed with dour Argentinean Carlos Reutemann, Niki Lauda bounced back to win the world title again in 1977. Leaving the team early to join Brabham, Lauda abstained from the last two races and was replaced by a 27-year-old Canadian named Gilles Villeneuve. After taking a win for Reutemann early in 1978 the 312 T2 was retired after five pole positions, eight wins and twelve second places in 31 world championship races.

In a year of transition for both cars and drivers – 1978 – the revised 312 T3 was developed to make the best use of Michelin's radial-ply tyres. Adopted at the express desire of Enzo Ferrari, these had first been tested by the Scuderia as long ago as 1971. Experiments began with new body shapes to generate underbody suction, the newly discovered 'ground effects' first exploited by Lotus that used skirts along the car's flanks to channel air under the body.

The Pininfarina wind tunnel played an important role in shaping the 1979 312 T4, designed from scratch to exploit underbody effects. Styling in the Pininfarina manner also began to play a role in the looks of Ferraris during these years. Hinted at in 1974 and confirmed in 1975 was the first major departure from all-red colour for a racing Ferrari. Instead of red the tall airbox of the 312 T was white with horizontal striping in the green, white and red of the Italian flag. Areas of white continued to be featured through the 1970s, giving way again to the all-red look early in the 1980s.

Ingeniously planned and integrated, built with aerospace levels of technology, the 312 T4 was a magnificent conception. It was one of the outstanding Formula 1 Ferraris of all time. In 1979 its 515 horsepower took Villeneuve and newcomer Jody Scheckter, a curly-

Formula 1 he renounced further participation in endurance racing. A change from Firestone to Goodyear tyres was validated on Ferrari's new 1.9-mile test track at Fiorano, which was inaugurated in the autumn of 1973. More than 12,000 miles of testing over the 1973-74 winter proved the latest version of the 312 B3, which was raced under the direction of a new team manager from Rome, urbane 27-year-old Luca Cordero di Montezemolo.

The result was a transformation in Ferrari's fortunes. Three wins in 1974 brought Clay Regazzoni the runner-up spot in the drivers' championship. Calculating Austrian team-mate Niki Lauda was ready to pounce, however, which he did in 1975 to bring both titles to Maranello driving the new 312 T. Its designation came from the use of a transverse gearbox, which had the aim of concentrating more of the car's masses within its wheelbase to make it more responsive to the latest tyres.

'Great things came with a rush,' recalled unapologetically buck-toothed Lauda. 'In the unbelievable year 1975 we and the Ferrari 312 T held the entire racing world in our grasp. Out of eleven

haired South African, to three wins apiece. Placing in the points in 12 of the season's 15 races, Scheckter became world champion. Another makes' championship was Maranello's as well.

This was prelude to a disastrous 1980, in which Villeneuve and Scheckter compiled a paltry six points between them driving the 312 T5, the last car to use the flat-twelve engine. A warmed-over T4, it suffered from the increased attention that tyre supplier Michelin was giving to home customer Renault, whose turbocharged V-6 was at last showing promise.

Renault had been the first to exploit a neglected provision of the Formula 1 rules which admitted 1.5-litre supercharged engines. It was clear that with exhaust-driven turbo-superchargers they could produce much more than the 500-odd horses of unblown 3.0-litre engines, but controlling them was problematic at best.

For racing from 1981 through 1988 Ferrari created two generations of twin-turbocharged V-6 engines, the first with a vee angle of 120 degrees and the second, from 1987, with a 90-degree vee to gain better underbody suction. With competition intense, success was hard to come by. Turbocharged Ferraris scored two wins in 1981, three in 1982, four in 1983, one in 1984, two in 1985, none in 1986, two in 1987 and one for Austrian Gerhard Berger at Monza in 1988 – last year for the blown engines – the month after the death of Enzo Ferrari on

Belying perceived wisdom that turbocharged cars didn't work on twisty tracks, Gilles Villeneuve won at Monaco in 1981 in Ferrari's Type 126 CK.

14 August. Before his departure from this earth Ferrari knew well that an impressive new Grand Prix Ferrari was in the works – in England of all places.

His take-no-prisoners drives in Ferrari's turbocharged 126 CK in 1981, as here at Silverstone, won the hearts of the many fans of Canadian Gilles Villeneuve.

CHAPTER 18

Italian Endurance

With V-12 engines sized up to 6.9 litres, Ferrari's Type 612 P competed in the 1969 Can-Am series in the hands of New Zealander Chris Amon.

IN the early 1960s the balance of power in endurance racing was upset by the incursion of America's Ford. Flying its 'Total Performance' banner, Ford launched challenges in rallying, in the GT championship and in the classic long-distance races from Sebring to Le Mans. To Enzo Ferrari it was evident that meeting Ford's challenge would demand the best in men and money – especially money. He began sounding out Fiat on the possibility of support.

Little remains secret for long in Turin's automobile circles. In 1965 Carlo Abarth was firmly back in the Fiat camp after a flirtation with France's Simca. In addition to his mainstream products, modified Fiat 500s, 600s and 850s, he was making open and closed sports-racers with engines of up to 1.9 litres. Abarth continued to tot up class wins and championships in the smaller categories. But he saw no reason why he and his engineers Renzo Avidano and Mario Colucci shouldn't also build a larger racer to help Italy combat the menace from America.

Hearing that Fiat money was likely to go to Ferrari to help it make bigger-engined racers, Austrian-born Abarth's pride was pricked. He feared that Fiat would dismiss his home-town potential, saying, 'Oh, Abarth can't build such a car.' He resolved to prove them wrong. By 1965 Abarth was preparing the design of a big-engined sports-racing coupé called the T-140.

Luciano Fochi, who as a callow youth had helped detail Colombo's design for the first Ferrari V-12, designed a new 6.0-litre V-12 for the T-140. He gave it the wide vee angle of 120 degrees, the same angle used successfully in the Ferrari Formula 1 V-6 of 1961. Relying as it did on sheer displacement to make its point, Fochi's twelve had single overhead cams and in-line valves along each bank. In a Jano-like touch its camshafts were driven from the centre of the engine.

In 1966 the T-140 was taking shape in the Abarth workshops, where it was known as the 'big secret'. Carlo Abarth waited until his T-140 was virtually complete before he invited the Fiat brass to his well-equipped manufactory at Corso Marche 38 on the west side of Turin. With justifiable pride he presented the results of his team's efforts, a car that had cost them five times as much as the most expensive automobile they'd ever made. He was dismayed by their reaction. 'You don't need to

A spunky lightweight that brought fresh laurels to Alfa Romeo, its 1963 Giulia TZ was a winner in its 1.6-litre G.T class.

do that, Carlo,' he was told. 'Ferrari will build the big-engined cars,.' There'd be no funding from Fiat to make the T-140 a running reality.

Although ultimately Ferrari had to fight Ford's might on its own, conceding Le Mans victories in both 1966 and '67, by 1969 it had confirmed a deal with Fiat that gave the larger company 90-per cent control of its production-car operations with Enzo Ferrari having the same majority command of racing. The latter included a brand new 6.2-litre V-12 with four valves per cylinder that had already been initiated by Mauro Forghieri. While the engine was the detailed work of veteran Franco Rocchi, Giancarlo Bussi oversaw its development.

Initially credited with 620 bhp at 7,000 rpm, the big twelve was installed in an open spider, the 612 P, for New Zealander Chris Amon to drive in a Can-Am race at Las Vegas in 1968. Its engine sound was 'a heavy mechanical rasp overlaying a frantic animal moan'. Having no chance to show what it could do in 1968, the 612 P returned late in the 1969 Can-Am series. Raced on a shoestring as a private venture by Chris Amon, Ferrari's 612 P kept the dominant Chevrolet-powered McLarens honest in 1969 with two third places and one second.

When in the spring of 1969 design work began at Maranello on the Type 512 S, a sports-racing coupé to compete with Porsche's 917 in the World Endurance Championship, this 48-valve V-12 was the chosen power source, reduced to 5.0 litres to suit the regulations.

In order to qualify to race as a Group 4 sports car, 25 had to be manufactured. In January 1970 the FIA certified that all 25 512 Ss had been produced, even if eight of them still had to be assembled.

Ferrari's Type 512 S, of which 25 were made to compete in the 1970 season, pictured in the mist at Modena's Aerautodromo.

In the best Portello tradition both style and function were married in the shape of the successful 2.0-litre Type 33B/2 of 1968. This Alfa Romeo became known as the 'Daytona' after its success in that 24-hour race.

Moving up to the 3.0-litre category with its V-8-powered Type 33/3 spider, Alfa Romeo enjoyed three wins by this model in 1971.

In March of 1970 the 512 S scored its first success in the 12 Hours of Sebring, storming to a sensational victory with a final-hour sprint by Italian-American Mario Andretti. Porsche's new 917 was tough competition, however. During 1970 work began on a 512 M for 'Modificata' with revised cylinder heads that raised output to 620 bhp at 8,750 rpm. Victory came at Kyalami in November 1970 and in a round of Europe's version of the Can-Am, the Interserie, at Imola in 1971, but otherwise this ambitious vee-twelve Ferrari had to give best to the Porsche 917. The rules under which it could be raced expired after 1971.

Ferrari turned its attention instead to the prototype category, in which it first fielded the open 312 P in 1969. While that had a detuned Formula 1 V-12 of 3.0 litres, a 1971 successor was powered by the Type 312 B's flat-opposed twelve. In 1972 this exceptional racing car was the winner of the sports-car constructors' world championship. Placing second in points, with V-8-powered 3.0-litre spiders, was none other than Alfa Romeo, ahead of third-ranked Porsche.

Since its '*Disco Volante*' adventures Alfa had maintained a sporting profile in GT categories with cars based on production models, its 1.3-litre Giulietta and 1.6-litre Giulia. The latter reached its apotheosis in 1963 with the introduction of the TZ, standing for Tubolare Zagato in recognition of its tubular space frame and the maker of its body. With all-independent suspension the 124 TZs produced were immensely successful in their 1.6-litre GT class.

From 1965 racing Giulias were available with a twin-ignition version of their twin-cam 1.6-litre four and, in the GTA version, with aluminium bodywork. Racing preparation was by a new independent entity, Autodelta, at Settimo Milanese on the northern outskirts of Milan. A predecessor company, Delta Automobile, owned by brothers Lodovico and Gianni Chizzola had in fact built the TZ chassis under contract to Alfa Romeo.

In technical authority at Autodelta since 1964 was none other than the now-even-more-rotund Carlo Chiti. He was returning after seven years to the orbit of Alfa Romeo, where his contributions were viewed positively. After leaving Ferrari in 1962 Chiti became chief engineer of

Automobili Turismo e Sport (ATS) of Bologna. He designed two V-8s for them, a 1.5-litre four-cam G.P. engine and a 2.5-litre two-cam sports-car unit. Both powered rear-engined cars that failed to produce race results of any distinction. With him Chiti brought Teodoro Zeccoli, a driver who had been a tester and racer for ATS.

With the support of Alfa's chief Giuseppe Luraghi, its engineering head Orazio Satta and the latter's assistant Giuseppe Busso made plans for the building by Autodelta of a 2.0-litre sports-prototype that would take the fight both to Porsche and to Ferrari's racing Dino 206 P. In January of 1966 the first such car, Alfa's Type 33/2, took the track at Monza and Balocco. The latter was Alfa Romeo's own test track west of Milan. The press was shown the Type 33/2 in full detail, in the form of three completed cars, at Balocco on 6 March.

A 90-degree V-8 was the choice for the 33/2's 2.0-litre engine, joined to a six-speed transaxle. Drawing on Chiti's experience at ATS, whose foundry made the engine's main castings, the eight had chain-driven twin overhead cams on each bank and two valves per cylinder. The car's racing-style independent suspension was attached to an unique frame conceived by Satta and Busso. It was the ultimate in ladder-style big-tube frames with aluminium side members 200 mm in diameter, joined by a tube of the same size just behind the seats and ahead of the engine. A rubberised interior coating allowed the H-shaped frame to serve as the car's fuel tank.

In its open 1967 form, the 33/2 had glass-fibre bodywork of amorphous roundness with whisker-type air deflectors flanking its nose. A tall air scoop for the V-8 led to its 'Periscopo' or 'Periscope' nickname. Competing in only three major endurance races in 1967 they had little success, but in a handsome new coupé version for 1968 the Type 33B/2 brought laurels to Alfa. At Daytona, Le Mans, the Targa Florio and the 'Ring 1,000 Kilometres this 'Daytona' model won the 2.0-litre class, at Le Mans finishing an impressive 4th, 5th and 6th overall. Three more category wins came in 1969.

During 1969 Autodelta phased in a completely new sports-racer to compete for outright glory in the world championship for makes, powered by a 3.0-litre V-8. This was the 33/3, initially with a steel monocoque and in 1970 with a space frame of aluminium. Three outright wins were achieved in 1971, one in the demanding Targa Florio. Then in 1973 Alfa's maroon sports-racer became the 33 TT 12 when powered by a new flat-12 from Giuseppe Busso's drawing board.

By 1974 this new car was mature enough to win the 1,000 Kilometres of Monza with the team Mario Andretti/

Under the aerodynamic skin of Alfa Romeo's 1975 Type 33 TT 12 was a flat-12 engine giving 500 bhp at 11,000 rpm.

Arturo Merzario. In 1975 the 33 TT 12 won the world championship of makes for Alfa Romeo. For 1977 Autodelta built a new chassis, the 33 SC 12, with an aluminium monocoque frame. This was fastest qualifier and winner of all eight rounds of the makes world championship against modest opposition. As related in the next chapter, its engine also had a Formula 1 career.

Erratic though its performance had been, the Alfa/Autodelta alliance brought welcome Italian glamour to the endurance-racing scene. Fortunately for a sport that needed more than dour Porsches and functional Lolas, another Italian squad stepped into the lists in 1979. After rally successes with its front-drive Fulvias, in 1973 Turin's Lancia built its first special competition car since the D.50 of 1954-55: the mid-engined Stratos. While the Stratos met team chief Cesare Fiorio's expectations as a rally

In the Varano workshop of Gian Paolo Dallara the Lancia Beta Monte Carlo was transformed into an endurance racer with a tubular rear structure.

THE FORD-FERRARI FLIRTATION

One of the most extraordinary episodes in the history of Italian racing machinery took place during the summer of 1963. Craving an upscale marque that he could pair with the Ford brand, the Ford Division's chief Lee Iacocca fixed on Ferrari. When in March of 1963 he sent an overture to Ferrari through Ford's office in Rome, he received a positive response. Unbeknownst to Iacocca, 65-year-old Enzo Ferrari had in fact been thinking about security and succession. He desired an alliance with a mainstream auto maker.

With both sides interested in a deal, negotiations moved quickly. In May the paperwork was ready for Ford to take a majority interest in Ferrari for $10 million. However the more he saw of Ford's legalistic approach to business management, the less Ferrari liked it. He finally waved off the men from Dearborn, Michigan.

In that same summer of 1963 Ford was in the early throes of its 'Total Performance' campaign with the Ford-powered Shelby Cobras that would soon menace Ferrari in international Grand Touring competition. Participation in rallies and at Indianapolis was gearing up as well. Nevertheless this wasn't the motivation for Ford's approach to Ferrari, which was focused more on the glamour of its production cars.

Although Enzo Ferrari would send Ford another feeler in 1966, his focus thereafter was Giannni Agnelli's Fiat as a potential partner and saviour. This bore fruit in 1969. That Ford was a serious challenger for the sports-racing honours coveted by Maranello became obvious with the appearance of its GT40 on European tracks in 1964. Ford also challenged Ferrari on the road with its DeTomaso Pantera, designed at its Ghia subsidiary in Turin and built at its Vignale factory. His Italian heritage exercised a powerful pull on Lido 'Lee' Iacocca.

Ford's Lee Iacocca (left) wanted the glamour of Ferrari for his Fords…

…but Enzo Ferrari (right) feared the hot breath of Ford's bean counters.

Drivers Riccardo Patrese, left, and Walter Röhrl behind the Lancia Beta Monte Carlo Turbo at its launch in Pininfarina's wind tunnel.

winner, its forays into circuit racing were less successful. Something more suitable was needed.

An in-house basis was available, the Lancia Beta Montecarlo (Scorpion in America) introduced in 1975. Developed in parallel with Fiat's X1/9, this Pininfarina-styled sports coupé had its 2.0-litre four placed transversely at the rear. It could be the basis of a competitor in Group 5, the so-called 'silhouette' category that required entries to retain the main elements and profiles of their series-built equivalents. With the Montecarlo needing a marketplace push, Fiorio succeeded in getting the approval of Lancia – since 1969 owned by Fiat – for a racing car based on the Montecarlo.

Inspiration for the project came from a prototype that former Ferrari and Lamborghini engineer Gian Paolo Dallara showed in Paris, a Group 5 version of the Fiat X1/9 with a supercharged engine. Lancia's veteran racing engineer Gianni Tonti decided to take the same approach to extract more power from the Montecarlo's four, using four valves per cylinder as Dallara had and a single

turbocharger. To compete in the 2.0-litre class he set its displacement at 1,426 cc to take into account the FIA's multiplication factor of 1.4 for supercharged engines; the calculated capacity was thus 1,996 cc.

Building the cars – eleven in all – was the first major project for Gian Paolo Dallara at his workshops in Varano near Parma. 'They supplied the body and we constructed everything else,' said the bespectacled engineer, who also designed the chassis, 'giving back to them an entire car at the end.' The Montecarlo's central tub was given new front and rear structures and modified strut-type suspension. Psychedelically swirling red and black graphics set off the finished car with a bold Lancia logo on its front deck.

Although 1979 was planned as a season of test entries, with Italian Riccardo Patrese and German Walter Röhrl behind the wheel, Lancia in fact tallied enough points to win the 2.0-litre category of the world makes championship. It did the same in 1980 with complete domination, winning its class in every race it started and scoring outright wins at Mugello and Brands Hatch. This gave the Turin entries the overall makes' championship with more points than Porsche had amassed in its larger parallel category.

The last major event in 1980 was the Giro d'Italia, a series of speed tests and rally stages across Italy. For this

1982 Lancia Type LC1 'Barchetta'

Sponsor Martini's livery looked splendid on the spiders built by Dallara for Lancia to race as Group 6 cars during a change of rules in 1982. They put the wind up more conventional Group C entrants.

Lancia enlivened the Group C racing scene in the early 1980s with its Martini-backed LC2, here in 1983 when it won at Imola in Italy.

the cars appeared in the new livery of Martini Racing, the promotional tool of Martini & Rossi vermouth's Grigorio Rossi, a great racing enthusiast. They were white with Martini's bold striping in red flanked by two-tone blue. They were also fast, placing one-two in the Giro d'Italia. In 1981 the makes' championship was Lancia's again, albeit with a wafer-thin margin over Porsche.

It was all change for 1982, when the FIA introduced new endurance-racing rules for Group C cars. Though engine sizes were unlimited, they ran to a fuel-consumption limit imposed by the number of refills allowed during the race for a mandatory 100-litre tank. In this year of transition, however, Group 6 cars of up to 2.0 litres were allowed to compete for the new drivers' championship, but not for the makes' title. This provision was intended to help existing cars make up the numbers.

Spotting the potential of the Group 6 option, Cesare Fiorio and his team pulled off one of the most audacious coups in the history of motor racing. With Dallara's new monocoque chassis and Tonti's 500-horsepower turbocharged four, now longitudinal, they built four low, sleek open cars that although officially the

LC1, justified the nickname 'Barchetta'. With enclosed rear wheels aiding underbody ground effects, the cheeky Lancias looked sensational in their Martini striping.

The LC1s were tremendously fast as well, especially in the hands of Grand Prix driver Riccardo Patrese. This was fortunate, for they were cars built to compete in a single season only. During 1982 they won three races outright at Silverstone, Mugello and the Nürburgring. Thanks to the might of Porsche and its new 956 Jacky Ickx was the champion driver, but in a battle that went down to the last race Lancia's Patrese was a close second.

Using a twin-turbocharged 2.6-litre V-8 based on Ferrari's 308 engine, Dallara built the LC2 coupé for Lancia, its pukka Group C car for 1983. Great-looking machine though it was, the high-strung LC2 retired frequently and won one race each year in 1983 through 1985 before being withdrawn after an inconclusive 1986. By then its capacity was 3.0 litres and its output 800 bhp at 8,200 rpm. 'We should have won more often,' Gian Paolo Dallara reflected. 'The car was lovely – but the Porsche was better.'

A decade later Dallara's expertise was behind another long-distance racer. Responding to the requests of private teams, among which Momo accessory maker Giampiero Moretti was in the van, Ferrari introduced its F333 SP in 1993. The first pure sports-racing Ferrari for two decades, it was built thanks to the favourable intervention of Piero Lardi Ferrari, Enzo's son. Conceived as an open car to the rules of America's IMSA championship, the F333 SP was designed by Mauro Rioli with the assistance of British expert Tony Southgate and insights from the Dallara wind tunnel.

Based on a Formula 1 design from Maranello, the F333 SP's 65-degree-vee V-12 was sized to suit the 4.0-litre class of IMSA's World Sports Car racing series. After the first four cars were made by Ferrari, the next ten were produced at Varano by Dallara. Another 25 were built by Ferrari tuner Michelotto.

The F333 SP proved an extremely useful and long-lived racing car. Its first IMSA championships came in 1995, winning the titles for both Ferrari and driver Fermin Velez. Among its individual laurels were victories in the 12 Hours of Sebring in 1995 and 1997 and wins at Atlanta, Lime Rock and Watkins Glen in 1996. In 1998 the Ferraris were ranked first and second in the International Sports-Racing Series.

Poetic justice saw to it that when the Momo team's Michelotto-built F333 SP won at both Daytona and Sebring at the beginning of 1998, Giampiero Moretti had stints behind its wheel together with Mauro Baldi and Didier Theys. Moretti's initiative and financial commitment to the F333 SP paid off in large measure. After these successes he hung up his helmet. But the F333 SP kept on winning into the 21st century.

In 2004 Maserati introduced its 624-horsepower Type MC12, which went on to success in the FIA's GT championship.

Red-Racer Challenge

CHAPTER 19

Piers Courage in the cockpit of the de Tomaso-Ford Formula 1 car in 1970 at its Modena launch, with Alessandro de Tomaso looking on.

NO example of success begetting disaster can surpass that of the end of Ferrari's 1961 season. The Scuderia had triumphed overwhelmingly in both Formula 1 and endurance racing. Ferrari's Phil Hill was the new world champion. Production was a record 441 cars and rising.

But some signs were unsettling. For example although Phil Hill's success was a gift to Ferrari sales in the important American market, Enzo declined to send Hill and his team to the final race at Watkins Glen. Too costly, he said. He was being henpecked on expenses by his wife Laura. Convinced that spending was profligate, she was intervening in company affairs to an unprecedented degree. And when Ferrari discouraged his executives from attending the funeral of Wolfgang von Trips at Cologne, after his death in the Dino 156 F1 at Monza, they were baffled and perturbed.

Tensions between Ferrari and members of his staff escalated during September and October, with the result that eight key managers left the company effective the end of November. Defectors included engineers Carlo Chiti, Giotto Bizzarrini, Fausto Galazzi and Federico Giberti and sporting director Romolo Tavoni. Among these the most senior, Chiti, had not hesitated to cross the boss. He had taken three cars with his new 120-degree-vee engine to the Dutch Grand Prix against Ferrari's express desires, threatening resignation to get his way.

Carlo Chiti and Romolo Tavoni were caught up in the ambitions of a clutch of wealthy enthusiasts to build sports and Grand Prix cars at a new works at Pontecchio Marconi on the southern periphery of Bologna. In jig time Chiti created both a 2.5-litre V-8 mid-engined sports car for them as well as a Grand Prix car. The latter, hailed by the press as a creative synthesis of the latest light-weight British chassis ideas with Italian drive-train concepts, had a 1.5-litre four-cam V-8 engine coupled to a transaxle made by former Ferrari and Maserati man Valerio Colotti, who had set up on his own as an engineering entrepreneur.

GIOTTO BIZZARRINI

From the gaggle of Ferrari defectors at the end of 1961, Giotto Bizzarrini carved an interesting career. His activity at Maranello from 1957 had been as an engineer/tester specialising in sports and GT car development. His final achievement there was single-handed creation of the 'ugly duckling' prototype that became the successful 250 GTO of 1962.

After a brief period with Carlo Chiti at ATS, Bizzarrini joined another budding project, the ASA effort to build a small GT car using a 1.0-litre four-cylinder engine originally created at Ferrari. The resulting ASAs made a contribution in a minor key to Italian racing history. Next the versatile Giotto received a contract from tractor maker Ferruccio Lamborghini to design a new engine for his planned GT car. The result was a magnificent four-camshaft 3.5-litre V-12.

From 1960 Bizzarrini served as a design consultant for the Chevrolet-powered GT cars of Iso Rivolta. Starting with a racing prototype, the Iso Grifo A3/C, which he built while with Rivolta, he struck out on his own to build Bizzarrini automobiles with their Chevy V-8s set well back in the wheelbase in an even more extreme version of the 250 GTO. By 1964 he was in business at Livorno as Prototipi Bizzarrini, making striking Corvette-engined GT Strada coupés for road and track.

An effort to access a less expensive market segment with the Opel-powered Europa GT 1900 failed when its backers proved unreliable. To Bizzarrini's rescue came American Motors in 1969 with its mid-engined AMX/3 sports-car project. However this venture failed to attain take-off speed, a great regret to Bizzarrini as he considered it his most fully developed design. In his later years this creative engineer concentrated on one-off prototypes at his studio near the Mugello circuit. Regrettably a planned Formula 1 entry in the late 1980s came to naught.

Visibly a man of action as well as analysis, Giotto Bizzarrini had a fascinating but chequered career as an innovator in Italy's competition-car industry.

Tracing its origins to a design for Iso Rivolta, the Corvette-engined Bizzarrini GT Strada was a noteworthy mid-1960s sports car.

At the end of 1962 the ATS Grand Prix car was unveiled. A coup for Carlo Chiti was his engagement of 1961 champion Phil Hill – disillusioned by the state of things at Ferrari – to drive in 1963. However Chiti later admitted that 'I was certain we were headed for disaster because we weren't ready. We really made a huge balls-up, plagued by thousands of problems.' In five 1963 Grands Prix the cars either retired or finished far off the pace. One ATS, revived in 1964 as the 'Derrington-Francis' for a Portuguese driver, retired in its only race.

Equally ephemeral were the Formula 1 adventures of wily Argentinean Alejandro de Tomaso. From his workshops in Modena he produced a variety of mid-engined single-seaters in the early 1960s, one a Grand Prix car with a 1.5-litre flat-eight from the pen of the peripatetic Alberto Massimino. Neither it nor others with Alfa Romeo, Osca and Maserati engines succeeded in making an impact.

In 1970, flush with his deal with Ford to build the mid-engined Pantera sports car, de Tomaso introduced a Modena-built Formula 1 car powered by the ubiquitous 3.0-litre Ford-Cosworth V-8. Its design was by Gian Paolo Dallara, who had left Lamborghini, disillusioned when that company eschewed any commitment to

Although not the most gainly-looking Formula 1 car the 1972 Tecno was ambitious with its flat-twelve engine.

In 1981 Arturo 'Art' Merzario was still driving a car of his own manufacture in Formula 2 racing.

competition. A work-manlike design from Dallara, the de Tomaso-Ford was campaigned by the team of Britain's Frank Williams. Racing only in 1970, its reputation is chiefly as the car in which rising star Piers Courage, one of the most likeable of the new British breed, was killed in a flaming accident during the Dutch Grand Prix.

Meanwhile in Bologna the Pederzani brothers, Luciano and Gianfranco, were climbing the motor-sports ladder from their Tecno go-karts to single-seaters for the smaller Formula 3 and 2. For the 1972 season they won the backing of Martini & Rossi for an extremely ambitious undertaking: building an all-new Formula 1 car with a 3.0-litre flat-12 engine on the lines of Ferrari's 312 B. The Emilian rumour mill buzzed with reports that designer Gianfranco Pederzani had sight of drawings of Mauro Forghieri's engine,

though he used seven main bearings instead of the Ferrari's four.

Unlike the Ferrari, the Tecno's twelve was a fully stressed part of the rear of the car's structure, which used a monocoque and conventional suspension. After 1972's few entries were unsuccessful, Martini's British racing manager David Yorke succeeded in attracting brilliant New Zealander Chris Amon to the team, fresh from two seasons with France's Matra. Concentrating on Chris in 1973, Tecno commissioned two different wedge-shaped chassis from British designers. Bright red with Martini's striping, the Tecno's best result was sixth in the 1973 Belgian Grand Prix. When no working engines were available for the Austrian Grand Prix, Amon left the team, triggering its collapse.

In the wake of Tecno rose Merzario. Jockey-sized and prone to sporting a big straw hat, Como's Arturo Merzario enjoyed sports-car successes in the early 1970s with both Ferrari and Alfa Romeo. After forming his own team in 1977 to race British March-Fords in Formula 1 he decided to become a constructor in his own right in 1978. In spite of his use of Ford-Cosworth power this met with a lamentable lack of success. With cars described as 'appalling' Merzario entered 30 world championship races in 1978-79. In 20 of these he failed to qualify and in the rest he retired.

Much more successful in the 1970s was an alliance between the British Brabham team, owned by entrepreneur and former racer Bernie Ecclestone, and Alfa Romeo. Looking for an unfair advantage, Ecclestone negotiated successfully with Alfa to gain the exclusive use of their flat-12 3.0-litre engine for his team in 1976. In 1975, the year when Ferrari's flat-12 powered Niki Lauda to a Formula 1 world championship, the Portello twelve's peak output was a very impressive 526 bhp at 12,000 rpm.

In designing Brabhams to suit the Autodelta-built engines, Gordon Murray was challenged by the twelve's size, weight and fuel consumption. Its Formula 1 version weighed a hefty 385 pounds. It was also wide, wider than the flat-12 engine fielded by Ferrari. Previously white, the Brabhams turned red in 1976 to suit the source of their engines. Characteristic striping identified their major sponsor, Martini, bravely taking a flyer on another Italian flat-twelve in Formula 1.

Brabham used Alfa's engine from 1976 through 1979. The first year was difficult, the second less so and in the third a number of good placings were achieved plus two victories for Niki Lauda at Sweden's Andersdorp and Italy's Monza, taking Parmalat-sponsored Brabham-Alfa to third in the constructors' ranking. 'It feels a bit like a

Left: In 1976, its first year with flat-12 Alfa power, the Brabham BT45 was seen at the Dutch G.P. with Carlos Reutemann.

In discussion with Brazilian driver Carlos Pace at Monaco in 1976, Carlo Chiti was the engineer behind Autodelta and Alfa's racing efforts.

Designer Gordon Murray's ambitious idea of surface cooling for the Alfa Romeo engine in his 1976 Brabham BT46 failed to function well.

Right: In 1980, Alfa Romeo's second season with a Grand Prix car of its own, talented Frenchman Patrick Depailler raced this T179 at Monaco.

For this Brabham BT48 of 1979 Carlo Chiti produced a twelve with a 60-degree vee. Nelson Piquet is driving at Monaco.

With its novel swept-forward wings this T179 Alfa Romeo was raced by Bruno Giacomelli in the 1980 season.

diesel,' said Australian driver Larry Perkins of the flat-twelve in 1976. 'When you back off it all goes off and you find it takes a moment to come back when you put your foot down again.'

In reaching their deal with Brabham the Alfa Romeo men envisioned a scouting expedition to see how well their engine would perform in a new racing environment. Finding it promising, they designed and built a Grand Prix car of their own. By 1977 work on this car, the Type 177, was under way and by 1978 Vittorio Brambilla was testing it at Alfa's Balocco proving grounds. This car, which made several race sorties in 1979 in the hands of Bruno Giacomelli, was superseded late that year by the Type 179.

Like the Brabham of 1979, the Type 179 Alfa Romeo of the same year was powered by a version of Autodelta's twelve with a vee of 60 instead of 180 degrees. This was created to make more room for the ground-effects venturis that were just coming into use. In neither installation, however, was the narrow-angle version of the twelve successful. Although proudly wearing the white and red colours of sponsor Marlboro, in 1980 Alfa was a mortifying 11th and last in constructors' points. While Alfa chairman Ettore Massachesi was keen to see Alfa in the lists, he was unwilling to spend money over and above Marlboro's subsidy to see it do well.

In 1981 the talents of Mario Andretti were attracted to the team, as were those of Frenchman Gerard Ducarouge as chief designer, but Mario's only finish in the points was a fourth at Long Beach. From 1983 a turbocharged 1.5-litre V-8 was used but in 1984 and '85 – Alfa's last in championship Formula 1 racing – retirements were rife and the only joy Riccardo Patrese's third place in the 1984 Italian Grand Prix. 'Sadly,' wrote David Hodges of the Alfa campaign, 'through the 1980s achievements had not remotely lived up to the marque's illustrious past.' A victim of politics and no admirer of Alfa chief Massachesi, Carlo Chiti resigned from Autodelta in mid-1984.

Problematic though its own efforts were, Autodelta began supplying the little Osella Squadra Corse team with engines in 1983. Based at Volpiano north-east of Turin, Enzo Osella had run Abarth's sports-racing team in the 1960s. When under Fiat's aegis Abarth concentrated on rallying, Enzo struck out on his own with cars of the Osella marque. He started entering single-seaters with Formula 2 in 1974. His first Formula 1 Osella raced in 1980, using the Ford-Cosworth DFV V-8.

Osella worked variously with designers Antonio Tomani, Giorgio Valentini, Giuseppe Petrotta and Giorgio Sirano on the chassis designs of his Grand Prix

cars. Not until 1982 did an Osella-Ford finish in the points, driven by Frenchman Jean-Pierre 'Jumper' Jarier at Imola. For the new cars needed to carry the Alfa V-12 in 1983 Tony Southgate provided the designs, but the robin's-egg-blue cars collected no points whatsoever. When the Osella-Alfa twelve succeeded in qualifying, its best finish was tenth in Austria.

Osella began using Alfa's turbocharged 1.5-litre V-8, said to offer 670 bhp, from 1984. That season was the best in the marque's Formula 1 history with a total of four constructors' points. Osella soldiered on through the decade, switching to unblown 3.5-litre Cosworth DFR engines in 1989. That year sponsor Gabriele Rumi, maker of Fondmetal wheels, bought a majority of Osella's team and renamed its cars as Fomet in 1991 and Fondmetal in 1992. A new design by Sergio Rinland for the latter season used the Cosworth HB V-8, but it was the last – and no more successful – for Fondmetal née Osella.

In parallel with Osella's efforts another Italian team tried to make a go of Formula 1 at a time when entrants were so numerous that pre-qualifying sessions had to be staged to winnow the field down to the 26 who would actually qualify for the race. Omission from the 26 was the frequent fate of the cars fielded by Enzo Coloni, who had been Italian Formula 3 champion. His first Coloni, the

His slimmed-down Type T182 Alfa Romeo took Andrea de Cesaris to third place at Monaco in 1982.

Seen here at Britain's Brands Hatch, Jean-Pierre Jarier scored Osella's only 1982 points with a fourth place at San Marino.

Lucchini. In the first years Cosworth V-8s were used, while a British Judd V-10 in 1991 was followed by Ferrari V-12s in 1992, the last season for Dallara. Over those five years Dallaras were entered in 78 Grands Prix, in which they collected a total of 15 championship points.

A surprise arrival in the Grand Prix arena was a company that had hitherto spurned sporting activity, Lamborghini. In April 1987 Lamborghini was bought by the Chrysler Corporation. One year later it held a press conference in Modena to show two samples of its new Formula 1 V-12. Present were managing director Emile Novaro, racing director Daniele Audetto and the engine's designer, former Ferrari engineer Mauro Forghieri.

Forghieri's presence was crucial to the credibility of the initiative. Here was the handsome, bespectacled, egotistical and mercurial creative force behind Ferrari's racing cars and engines from the mid-1960s to mid-1980s. He and the tall, patrician Audetto – also a former Ferrari man – were the prime movers in the establishment of Lamborghini Engineering as a separate entity to build engines and, ultimately, cars as well. The new company set up shop in an industrial estate in Modena, at the very heart of Italy's legendary racing know-how.

Lamborghini's first customer for its 80-degree-vee twelve was the French Larrousse Calmels team, which used Lola-built chassis. 'Customer' was the correct term because Chrysler insisted that Lamborghini Engineering charge for the use of its engines; this was not to be a factory-backed engine-supply effort. *Ergo*, said Mauro Forghieri, 'we were serving teams of the fourth category. The teams of the highest standing get their engines free, but we weren't allowed to provide free engines.'

In 1989 and '90 the team run by former race and rally driver Gérard Larrousse had modest success once the V-12 got over its initial teething troubles. Additional customers were Britain's Team Lotus in 1990 and France's Ligier, founded by former driver Guy Ligier, in 1991.

Mauro Forghieri's ambition to run a complete car of his design was realised in 1991, when Lamborghini

work of former Dallara man Maurizio Ori, made its bow for the 1987 Italian Grand Prix.

Although often pretty cars, using the Cosworth V-8, the Colonis never menaced the established teams. A flirtation with the Big Time came in 1990, when a Subaru-badged flat-twelve was supplied to the team by Motori Moderni, the company set up by Carlo Chiti to build racing engines after his departure from Autodelta. This was a flop, however. In 1992 Coloni's team was taken over by Andrea Sassetti to be branded after his Andrea Moda range of shoes, perhaps inspired by Benetton's increasing involvement in Formula 1. This was an embarrassing fiasco with drivers coming and going – mostly going. Before the end of the 1992 season Andrea Moda was banned from the championship for bringing the sport into disrepute.

Also entering the Grand Prix field in the late 1980s was Gian Paolo Dallara with cars of his own marque from his Varano factory. After his 1970 design for de Tomaso, Dallara avoided Formula 1 until 1988, when he built cars for the Scuderia Italia backed by industrialist 'Beppe'

Engineering gained the backing of industrialist Carlo Patrucco for the racing of a car it had completed in 1990 under other auspices. Although the Lambo 291 showed flashes of promise, running as high as fifth in the San Marino G.P. at Imola before a last-lap retirement, it was unable to score points and the team lasted only one season. At the end of 1993 Lamborghini Engineering ceased supplying Formula 1 engines and was soon wound up.

Best known among the Italian independents to modern Formula 1 followers is the team set up in the 1970s by Giancarlo Minardi. Motor-sports enthusiasm was in the Minardi DNA; father Giovanni had raced saloons and sports cars. Their family Fiat car and truck sales and distribution business was at Faenza on the Via Emilia, Italy's lifeline for racing-car manufacture, and next door to Imola and its Circuit Dino e Enzo Ferrari.

Beginning in the 1970s with entries in Formula 2, Minardi took the step to Formula 1 in 1985 with a car designed by Giacomo Caliri, a former Ferrari engineer/aerodynamicist and a shareholder in the team. Thanks to the involvement in both entities of a Tuscan industrialist, Piero Mancini, Carlo Chiti's Motori Moderni at Novara was commissioned to make a turbocharged V-6 for Minardi. This was used in the early years.

At the urging of Fiat chairman Gianni Agnelli, who admired several good finishes by Minardi's team, Ferrari supplied 3.5-litre engines to Minardi in 1991. Later Lamborghini, Hart and Cosworth engines powered Minardis.

Although never enjoying a podium finish, Minardi had some moments of brightness especially when its first driver Pierluigi Martini was at the wheel. During the 1990s both Scuderia Italia and Fondmetal's Gabriele Rumi brought their support to much-liked minnow Minardi, which kept the flag flying for Italy's independent teams. In 2001 Australian businessman Paul Stoddart bought struggling Minardi, which he sold on in 2005 to the Austrian Red Bull company. Renamed Toro Rosso, the team was again for sale in 2008.

In one important respect Minardi was an important asset to Formula 1. It nurtured the careers of great drivers. Among them were Australian Mark Webber and Spain's double world champion Fernando Alonso. Most importantly, however, Minardi was true to its Italian roots with the opportunities it offered to Alessandro Nannini, Giancarlo Fisichella, Jarno Trulli, Alex Zanardi and Luca Badoer. If Italian drivers have failed to scale the heights of Formula 1 in the 21st century, it wasn't Minardi's fault.

Before its 1985 Formula 1 entry Minardi competed in Formula 2, here in 1981 with up-and-coming driver Michele Alboreto.

165

CHAPTER 20

Forza Ferrari

Triple world champion Alain Prost joined Ferrari in 1990 to drive its Barnard-designed Type 641.

IN 1984, a season that saw the TAG V-6-powered McLaren MP4/2 win 12 of 16 Formula 1 races, Mauro Forghieri fielded his last Grand Prix design for Ferrari, the 126 C4. At Belgium's Zolder in April it delivered a gratifying victory for Michele Alboreto, the first Italian to win a championship Grand Prix for Ferrari since Lulu Scarfiotti at Monza in 1966. At the same circuit, two years earlier, the coruscating career of Gilles Villeneuve had ended in a fatal crash during qualifying.

Forghieri, whose complete capability as a designer of racing cars rivalled that of his mentor Vittorio Jano, was right to resent uninformed criticism of Ferrari's chassis expertise: 'Maranello has been a mine of magnificent engines,' he said, 'but it has also been a mine of magnificent mechanical assemblies. You can't win a Targa Florio, you can't perform brilliantly at Zandvoort or the Nürburgring, where we have always excelled, unless you race cars that have good roadholding. When we won, however, it was said that we owed our win mainly to the engine.'

If anything, chassis development did lag the extraction of engine power. Enzo Ferrari never denied that he placed high priority on the power of his cars. 'Perhaps I underestimated the importance of the chassis,' he wrote. 'I have always given great importance to the engine and much less to the chassis, endeavouring to squeeze out as much power as possible in the conviction that it is engine power which is – not 50 per cent but 80 per cent – responsible for success on the track.'

Near the end of his life, however, Enzo Ferrari more than made up for his earlier reluctance to embrace the importance of chassis design. During 1984 Mauro Forghieri moved to another post at Ferrari and experienced Briton Harvey Postlethwaite came to Maranello to create a new chassis for the turbocharged 1.5-litre V-6, which was giving 780 bhp at 11,000 rpm. With decisive success still elusive, for what was called 'an enormous sum of money' Enzo Ferrari engaged the services of Englishman John Barnard, who had designed the successful McLarens.

Joining Ferrari from the summer of 1986, Barnard built a base in Britain where he would not only design but also fabricate chassis to carry the engines and trans missions made in Maranello. As the Guildford Technical Office it had the evocative acronym of 'GTO'. While Barnard began the team's reorganisation he relied on Postlethwaite in Maranello as well as Gustav Brunner, who created the last turbo-powered Ferraris of 1987 and '88.

Ferrari began planning a new unblown vee-twelve when, in 1986, word came that such engines would be allowed to displace 3½ litres from 1987. There was little doubt that with Ferrari's traditions the new unblown engine would be a V-12, and in this Barnard was in agreement: 'We needed to go for the ultimate power option. I was telling them to give me the power and I would package the unit in the best possible way.'

Maranello's studies identified the V-12 as the optimum where power was concerned. For the eight, ten and twelve they estimated 600, 625 and 645 bhp respectively, all other factors being equal. They were aware of advantages in mid-range power for engines of fewer cylinders, but they expected to compensate for this with a completely new semi-automatic seven-speed transmission that would help the driver keep the twelve in its narrower power band.

Work on the new twelve, Type 035, began at the end of 1986 with Giorgio Quattrini as its principal designer and former Renault engineer Jean-Jacques His overseeing development. First thoughts of a 60-degree vee gave way to a 65-degree angle to give more room for induction and to allow an oil/water heat exchanger to nestle in the vee of a cylinder block cast by Fiat's Teksid specialists of a nodular-iron alloy. With five valves per cylinder its output began at 600 bhp – matching the best specific power achieved by the 3.0-litre flat-twelve – and speeds of up to 13,000 rpm were explored.

The plan was to begin racing the engine during 1988, which would have followed a Ferrari tradition. Enzo Ferrari was adept at planning ahead in the power department, as he'd shown with his successful fours and vee-sixes. However, early race entries were ruled out for several reasons. One was that John Barnard's new car was late; the first tests of its initial version, the Type 639, at Ferrari's own Fiorano track weren't until July of 1988. Another was that the then-current turbo V-6 still needed to be brought up to scratch. Yet another reason was that Enzo Ferrari was unwell. The twelve's first race would not be until 1989.

Starting with the new Formula 1 in 1989, Ferrari remained true to its V-12 traditions through 1995, a total of seven seasons. In the six years of the 3½-litre formula, Ferrari's was almost but not quite the most successful twelve. It clocked up a total of 10 wins and six pole positions against Honda's tally of 13 wins and 11 poles, achieved in just two years. In the first year of the 3.0-litre formula, 1995, Ferrari added one pole and two more wins to its vee-twelve account.

Aiding and abetting the high-speed running of the V-12 was Ferrari's innovative semi-automatic transmission. Ferrari had developed such a transmission in the 1979-80 period and installed it for testing in the 312 T4. Push-buttons on the steering wheel triggered its ratio changes electrically. On Ferrari's Fiorano test track Gilles Villeneuve covered 100 faultless laps, pressing steering-wheel buttons to shift up and down. 'Despite this successful outcome,' recalled Mauro Forghieri, 'he wasn't convinced. Gilles said to me, "A steel shift linkage will always be more reliable than electronics." The project was temporarily set aside. Mr. Ferrari always accepted requests from Gilles.'

At John Barnard's request the concept was resurrected in the post-turbo era. One of the most awkward aspects of his job, working from England, was the insertion of a shift linkage and its needed holes and brackets into the tub he was designing. As well, contrary to the Villeneuve view the long linkage with its universal joints was an inevitable source of failures, especially if damage to the car occurred during a race. Eliminating it would be beneficial.

An overhead view of Nigel Mansell at Monaco in 1989 showed the elegantly aerodynamic lines of the Type 640 Ferrari.

Champion the previous year with Benetton-Ford, Michael Schumacher brought number 1 to Ferrari in 1996, his first season with them.

An overhead view of a pit stop in 1997 captures the narrow nose of Michael Schumacher's F310B Ferrari.

At the end of 1987 they had their first prototype, an adaptation of the existing transaxle. It worked so well, completing fully automatic upshifts with ease, that the decision was confirmed to use such a transmission in the future. Indeed, John Barnard's designs for future Formula 1 Ferraris permitted no other solution. They had to make the remote control work.

The seven-speed transmission was tested and developed on the 1988 Type 639 Ferrari, of which two were built. This was the never-raced prototype of the Type 640, the definitive 3½-litre Ferrari Formula 1 car for 1989. Improvements introduced for 1990 included better reliability and new programming that allowed the driver to skip gears when shifting down, entering a corner. Upshifting could be fully automatic.

The first Ferrari semi-automatic gearbox used longitudinal shafts for its gears. During the 1992 season Ferrari introduced a transverse-shaft gearbox for Formula 1 which carried over the automated shifting system. This was used until 1998, when new Formula 1 regulations put constraints on the cars' track widths, narrowing the space available at the rear for downforce-generating diffusers. Maranello's response was a new slimmer longitudinal transmission whose gears were between the engine and the final drive.

In the Barnard regime the coil springs introduced at the front by Aurelio Lampredi and at the rear by Carlo Chiti were replaced by compact compound torsion bars. At the front they were operated directly by the pivots of the bell cranks that drove both the anti-roll bar and the dampers. Barnard also changed from pullrods to pushrods to operate the car's springing elements. In the crowded conditions of the 640's nose, above the driver's legs, the

Another incentive for change, recalled engineer Amedeo Visconti, was that 'it was thought that the naturally aspirated engine would need to reach much higher revolutions than the turbo, which gained its power from boost. An unblown engine has to be tuned for best power in a narrow range of revs. With this narrow power window you need a lot of gears so the driver needs to shift much more often. How could we help the driver?' As well, with steering-wheel shift control the driver could more easily change gear in a corner if necessary.

MICHELE ALBORETO

In 1998 Michele Alboreto, who loved his racing, was still competing in the FIA GT championship as a member of Porsche's team.

'It was a pleasure to have a driver with whom we could at last speak in Italian.' This was the reaction of Enzo Ferrari's secretary and sometime team manager Franco Gozzi to the engagement of Michele Alboreto as a driver for the 1984 season. In fact Gozzi had been the one to tap Alboreto's shoulder late in 1983 at a motor-sports gathering in Milan, his native city, to ask him to join the Scuderia. The driver was just about to turn 27.

The rise and rise of the curly-haired Alboreto had a sense of inevitability. The son of a kindergarten teacher, he had been keen on motor sports from an early age. In 1978 he won the Fiat Abarth championship, raced with special one-make single-seaters produced by Abarth as just such a stepping stone for new drivers. After moving up to Formula 3 he won the European title in 1980 and was picked by Giancarlo Minardi to race his cars in Formula 2.

The 1981 season also saw Alboreto in the Ford-powered Grand Prix cars of Britain's Ken Tyrrell, renowned for his talent-spotting skills. Though fighting with 3.0 naturally aspirated litres against the more powerful 1.5-litre turbocharged cars, Alboreto put the Tyrrell among the leaders in 1982. At Imola he was on the podium with a third place and at the end of the season, in a bizarre parking-lot Grand Prix at Las Vegas, he won. In 1983 he won again on the streets of Detroit, the last victory for both Tyrrell and that generation of Cosworth V-8.

On the television in his office at the Fiorano track, Enzo Ferrari had been watching. 'This young man drives well and makes few errors,' he noted. 'He is also fast and has a fine style, gifts that remind me of Wolfgang von Trips, whom Alboreto also resembles in his serious and polite demeanour. With a competitive car he won't miss the chance to become a champion.' Against these merits Ferrari had to weigh the risk he was taking in engaging an Italian driver. He'd been censured as a 'Gorgon' for the deaths of Eugenio Castellotti, Luigi Musso and Lorenzo Bandini in his cars. He decided the risk was worth it.

'With a competitive car' was the operative phrase. These were years in which Maranello chopped and changed its technical staff, looking for the winning combination to exploit the new 1.5-litre turbocharged era. Early signs were good.

Wearing the sacred number 27 made famous by Gilles Villeneuve, Alboreto won the Belgian Grand Prix at Zolder from pole position in April of 1984, becoming the first Italian driver to win for the prancing horse since 1966. The rest of the season Ferrari had to give way to McLaren with its Porsche-designed TAG engines.

Hard work over the winter prepared the Type 156-85 F1 for the 1985 season. In the first two races Alboreto was second, a place he took again at Monaco. With a win in Canada he moved into the driver points lead. He consolidated this with a second in Detroit and another win at the new Nürburgring. Not until 25 August at Zandvoort was Michele demoted from the top of the points by a resurgent Alain Prost on McLaren-TAG. The man from Milan had to be happy with second place in 1985.

This was the apogee of Michele Alboreto's Ferrari career. He enjoyed no more wins. In his last season with the Scuderia, 1988, he was on the podium three times and fifth in the world championship. After spells with other teams he returned to Italian squads with Ferrari-powered BMS Scuderia Italia in 1993 – an unmitigated disaster – and in 1994 Minardi, with whom he had one point-scoring finish at Monaco. Thereafter he retired from Formula 1 with 194 starts to his credit.

'It was an unforgettable experience,' Alboreto reflected on his Scuderia seasons. 'I spent five years with Ferrari and have no regrets. My relationship with Enzo Ferrari was extraordinary. I learned a lot in human and personal terms. He had taken a risk and I tried to repay him with commitment and hard work. He taught me that I was appreciated not only for any driving skills I had but also as a person.'

In the late 1990s he revived a Maranello link with some IMSA drives in an F333 SP Ferrari. Alboreto's friends at Maranello quietly celebrated when he was on the driving team that won Le Mans in 1997, albeit with a Porsche. And they sorrowed when in 2001, during a pre-Le Mans test at Germany's Lausitzring, a tyre failure wrecked his Audi R8 and took Michele's life at the age of 44.

Alboreto, right, posing with Piero Lardi Ferrari, Enzo's son, and the 1983 Type 126C3 F1 Ferrari to herald his 1984 season with the Scuderia.

Ferrari's F2004 brought Michael Schumacher his seventh world championship in 2004, a record-shattering five in a row.

With Ferrari's F2005 for the 2005 season were, from left, tester Marc Gené, Rubens Barrichello, tester Luca Badoer and Michael Schumacher.

compact torsion bars usefully saved space. After a brief hiatus with the Type 642 during which Belleville washers on the damper shafts served as springs, torsion bars were reintroduced on the Type 643 in mid-1991.

These were some of the many highlights of the Type 640, which officially raced as the F1/89. Its aerodynamic design was of extraordinary purity with flat upper surfaces and side pods that were richly curved in plan view. Its driver cadre were Gerhard Berger, in his third Ferrari season, and the last driver personally engaged by Enzo Ferrari, Britain's infuriatingly exigent Nigel Mansell.

In spite of a pit stop to change his steering wheel, and in spite of the fact that the exotic new transmission had never completed a race distance during testing, Mansell astoundingly won the first race of 1989 in Brazil. This presented a daunting challenge to Cesare Fiorio, the permatanned former Lancia sporting chief who had just taken over that role at Ferrari. He had nowhere to go but down. Overcoming the inevitable teething troubles, late in the season came two more wins, one for each driver.

Developed to the Type F1 641, the new car had a barn-burner of a year in 1990. Replacing Berger was brilliant Frenchman Alain Prost, the crooked-nosed champion of 1985, 1986 and 1989. His engagement put

Ferrari in a no-excuses situation. If wins didn't come, it had to be the fault of the car, not the driver. And the wins did come. Prost scored five with two second places and two thirds to take the championship challenge to Ayrton Senna's McLaren-Honda. His win in the French Grand Prix was Ferrari's 100th in a championship Grand Prix. But by deliberately crashing his McLaren into Prost's Ferrari in Japan the über-competitive Senna assured himself of the 1990 championship.

During 1990 both Barnard and Postlethwaite left Ferrari, creating revolving doors through which various journeyman engineers came and went. Cesare Fiorio was out as well, while Alain Prost's public criticisms of the state of things at Maranello triggered his sacking before 1991's final race. The Frenchman's last victory had been in September 1990 in Spain. Three years and ten months would pass before a Ferrari driver, the rehired Gerhard Berger, would again stand at the top of the podium in Germany in July 1994. Rightly enough this was called 'the most disastrous period in Ferrari's F1 racing history'.

The turnaround did come. It was courtesy of Luca di Montezemolo, whom Fiat chose in 1992 to head Automobili Ferrari. As an interim measure he re-engaged John Barnard, who set up a new engineering facility at

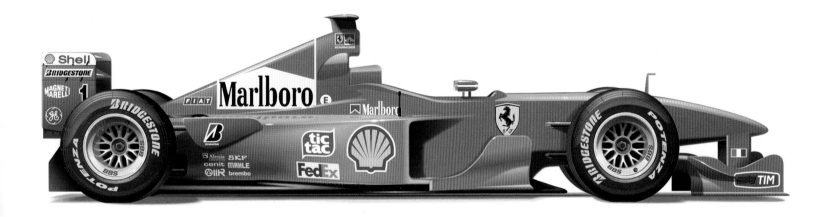

2000 FERRARI TYPE F1

RICH REWARD FOR THE EFFORTS OF FERRARI'S GESTIONE SPORTIVA UNDER JEAN TODT, ROSS BRAWN, RORY BYRNE AND
PAOLO MARTINELLI WAS THE OVERWHELMING SUCCESS OF THEIR GRAND PRIX CAR IN 2000.

In 1996 Ferrari abandoned its V-12 tradition with a switch to V-10 engines. This was the Type 51 ten of 2002.

Shelford called Ferrari Design Development. Di Monte-zemolo's key appointment in 1993 was that of Jean Todt, Peugeot's sporting director, to take charge of the racing team. 'The Scuderia is a castle,' found the petite but pragmatic Frenchman, 'but a castle in ruins!'

Todt's refurbishment of the castle included hiring Michael Schumacher for 1996, following his world championships with Benetton in 1994 and '95. As with the engagement of Prost, and indeed before him Fangio, any failure to win had perforce to be the fault of the car. Nineteen ninety-six also saw the historic change to a vee-ten engine. This was the work of Ferrari's own team headed by Paolo Martinelli, although at one stage – clearly in desperation – they had weighed adapting a British Brian Hart V-10 to their cars. This was also the year of Ferrari's innovation of warning lights on the steering wheel instead of the car's dash panel.

A final stage in the castle's renovation was the luring of Britain's Ross Brawn in 1997 to replicate his successful Benetton partnership with Schumacher as Ferrari's technical director. He was partnered by South African Rory Byrne, who designed the Type F300 for 1998. This followed a season in which the last Barnard design, the F310 B, had come close to winning the world title for Schumacher. A broken leg in a Silverstone crash in 1999 ended the German's hopes with the F399 that year. Nevertheless points gained by Ulsterman Eddie Ervine brought Maranello the constructors' champion-ship, its first in 16 years.

The promise shown was fully realised in 2000 with Byrne's more adventurous Type F1 2000. He was now fully exploiting Maranello's spectacular new wind tunnel, built to designs by Renzo Piano and opened in 1997. Above its moving ground plane

At Imola in 2006 Michael Schumacher powered his V-8-powered 248 F1 Ferrari over the kerbs to victory from pole position.

it was capable of testing models two-thirds the size of a car at speeds of up to 155 mph. Its throat could also be adjusted to accept a full-size car facing winds of up to 90 mph. It proved the value of such features as the upper-surface exhaust pipes that Ferrari pioneered in 1998.

The 2000 season was stunning validation of the Ferrari team's efforts. Michael Schumacher started from pole ten times and won nine races with the F1 2000. He dominated the race for the drivers' title and, backed by Brazilian Rubens Barrichello, brought Ferrari another constructors' championship. Such was the advantage he enjoyed with the following season's F2001, a car to prove well suited to all circuits, that Schumacher clinched his fourth world title with four races still to be run.

The red cars' dominance was even greater in 2002 when they won an astonishing 14 races with the F2002, which the team called 'one of the most innovative and sophisticated cars in the history of Ferrari.' In nine races they enjoyed one-two finishes, rolling up a total of 221 constructors' points against 92 for runners-up Williams. If as it was judged in some circles an annihilation of the world championship, this was only fair compensation for many years in the doldrums.

'We are trying to develop strong technical partnerships with our key suppliers,' said Italian Aldo Costa, who gradually took over the role of Rory Byrne as chief designer at Ferrari's Gestione Sportiva, as the racing department became known. 'We have regular discussions with them about problems and challenges.' From such a discussion with Germany's ZF Sachs came an innovation introduced on Maranello's 2003 Grand Prix car. This was the F2003-GA whose name honoured the memory of the deceased Gianni Agnelli, who had always been a stalwart supporter of Ferrari's efforts.

Instead of the ubiquitous tubular dampers, the 2003 car had a pair of rotary dampers on the same axes as the torsion-bar springs. These nestled neatly atop the gearbox. 'With the back end of the car having to be very slim,' Costa explained, 'these allowed a much better package.' It was a package which, when unwrapped, brought Schumacher and Ferrari the two major titles again although not with the dominance that had so impressed in 2002. Schumacher's margin of success was a scanty two points.

Under a regime that technical chief Ross Brawn called 'dynamic stability' the Gestione Sportiva pulled up its figurative socks for 2004. Considering that its overwhelming superiority in 2002 may have contributed to a more conservative approach in 2003, Ferrari made a major effort on all fronts with its F2004. The result was 15 wins from 12 pole positions, 14 fastest laps and eight 1-2 finishes for Schumacher and Barrichello, who were comfortably one-two in the drivers' title race. It was the record seventh world championship for the phenomenal Schumacher.

In Michael Schumacher's last two seasons, 2005 and 2006, he had to give best to the Renault team, née Benetton, and thrusting Spaniard Fernando Alonso. In fact in 2005 he lagged at third in the rankings behind Kimi Räikkönen of McLaren-Mercedes, driving an F2005 which, although not a bad Ferrari, rode on Bridgestone tyres that were not well adapted to new rules that required the tyres to last for the full race. Once an advantage, Ferrari's role as the only top team running Bridgestones had become a handicap that relegated Maranello to third in the makes' table as well.

The return of tyre changes in 2006 helped the race pace of Ferrari's 248 F1, now powered by a 2.4-litre V-8 in accord with a change of rules. In his final season Michael Schumacher had a new team-mate in baby-faced Felipe Massa, like his predecessor a Brazilian. They brought Ferrari 201 constructors' points; but Renault had 206. Alonso was again driving champion with 134 points to Schumacher's 121 while Massa was third with 80.

For 2007 it was all change at Maranello with Schumacher's retirement and replacement by monosyllabic Finn, Kimi Räikkönen. Ross Brawn, rightly credited with the long strategic view that had brought the 21st-century wave of titles, took a sabbatical. First among the equals who succeeded him was the untested Stefano Domenicali as team manager. Mario Almondo was technical director and Frenchman Gilles Simon in charge of engines.

Rivals' hopes that the new alignment would be unequal to the task were misplaced. With all teams now on Bridgestones, the tyre factor was nullified. Newcomer Räikkönen needed half the season to acclimatise fully to the Maranello set-up. From the eighth race in France onward he was on the podium save for only one retirement, scoring five wins. Only in the 17th and last race in Brazil did his victory secure the world championship by a single point ahead of McLaren-Mercedes' prodigy Lewis Hamilton and Renault's Fernando Alonso.

A great result in the company's 60th-anniversary year, this brought Ferrari the constructors' cup as well after all McLaren's makes' points were expunged when a 780-page dossier of Ferrari secrets was found in the hands of one of its engineers. The 2008 season, the last before a major rules change, showed both Räikkönen and Massa capable of winning for Ferrari, their main rivals the German squads BMW-Sauber and McLaren-Mercedes.

Still proudly liveried in the red of Italy, Ferrari is unalterably committed to Formula 1 racing as a vital and irreplaceable strand of its DNA. Throughout its factory pictorial evidence of the racing, the engines and the hero drivers of the past and present bespeak its dedication. Ferrari has so thoroughly integrated the spirit of racing with its road-car activities that the two are inseparable. Thus for Ferrari in the 21st century Grand Prix racing, at the very apogee of world-wide competition, is as irrevocably an integral part of the company's activities as the beating heart of a racing driver.

Sophisticated aerodynamic refinement was rife in the opulent forms of Ferrari's F1 2008 for the 2008 season.

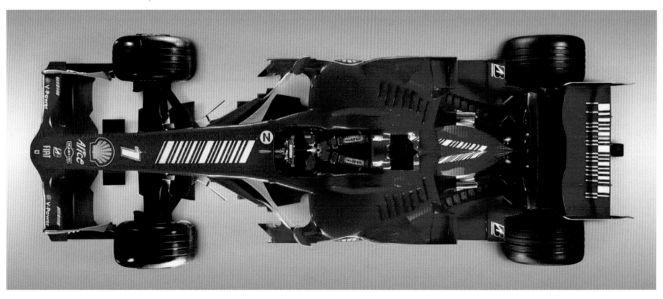

Bibliography

Amari, Giancarlo & Barberis, Matilde, *Marche Italiane Scomparse*, Museo dell'Automobile, Turin, 1972.

Anderloni, C. F. Bianchi, *Alfa Romeo Disco Volante*, Automobilia, Milan, 1993.

Anselmi, Angelo Tito, *Alfa Romeo 6C 2500*, Editoriale Domus, Milan, 1993.

___, *Catalogo Bolaffi Delle Fiat 1899-1970*, Bolaffi, Turin, 1970.

Balestra, Nino & De Agostini, Cesare, *Cisitalia*, Automobilia, Milan, 1980.

Benatti, Giancarlo and Pedroni, Piero, *Il Romanzo dei Bolidi Rossi*, Edizioni Il Fiorino, Modena, 1996.

Bertett, Luigi, *Monza Yearbook 1960, 1961, 1962, 1963, 1964, 1965, 1966*, SIAS, Milan, 1960, 1961, 1962, 1963, 1964, 1965, 1966.

Borgeson, Griffith, *The Alfa Romeo Tradition*, Foulis, Sparkford, 1990.

Bradley, W. F., *Targa Florio*, Foulis, London, 1955.

Cancellieri, Gianni, *Maserati–Catalogue raisonné 1926-1990*, Automobilia, Milan, 1990.

___, and De Agostini, Cesare, *Polvere e Gloria, La Coppa d'Oro delle Dolomiti 1947-1956*, Giorgio Nada, Milan, 2000.

Canestrini, Giovanni, *Mille Miglia*, L'Editrice dell'Automobile, Milan, 1967.

Carli, Emanuele Alberto, *Settant'anni di gare automobilistiche in Italia*, L'Editrice dell'Automobile, Milan, 1967.

Casucci, Piero, *Chiti Grand Prix*, Automobilia, Milan, 1987.

___, *Ferrari F1 1948-1963*, Editoriale Domus, Milan, 1984.

___, *Ferrari F1 1964-1976*, Editoriale Domus, Milan, 1985.

___, *Ferrari F1 1977-1985*, Editoriale Domus, Milan, 1986.

Cherrett, Angela, *Alfa Romeo Tipo 6C 1500, 1750, 1900*, Foulis, Sparkford, 1989.

___, *Alfa Romeo Modello 8C 2300*, Veloce, Godmanstone, 1992.

Colombo, Gioachino, *Origins of the Ferrari Legend*, Haynes, Sparkford, 1987.

Costantino, Augusto, *Le Piccole Grandi–Marche Automobilistiche Italiane*, De Agostini, Novara, 1983.

Curami, Andrea and Vergnano, Piero, *La "Sport" e i suoi artigiani 1937-1965*, Giorgio Nada, Milan, 2001.

Cutter, Robert and Fendell, Bob, *The Encyclopaedia of Auto Racing Greats*, Prentice-Hall, Englewood Cliffs, 1973.

D'Alessio, Paolo, *Martini Racing Story*, Giorgio Nada, Vimodrone, 1997.

di Ruffia, Carlo Biscaretti et al, *"Fiat"–a Fifty Years' Record*, Mondadori, Verona, 1951.

Dreyfus, René, with Kimes, Beverly Rae, *My Two Lives–Race Driver to Restaurateur*, Aztex, Tucson, 1983.

Fangio, Juan Manuel with Carozzo, Roberto, *Fangio, My Racing Life*, Patrick Stephens, Wellingborough, 1990.

Ferrari, Enzo, *Piloti, Che Gente...*, Conti Editore, Bologna, 1985.

Finn, Joel E., *Ferrari Testa Rossa V-12*, Motorbooks, St. Paul, 2003.

___, *Maserati: The Postwar Sports Racing Cars*, John W. Barnes, Jr., Scarsdale, 1977.

___, *Maserati Birdcage–The marvellous Tipo 60 and 61 sports racing cars*, Osprey, London, 1980.

Fitzgerald, Warren and Merritt, Richard, *Ferrari, The Sports and Gran Turismo Cars*, Bond, Newport Beach, 1968.

Fondi, Pino, *Il mitico Giro di Sicilia*, Giorgio Nada, Milan, 1996.

Frère, Paul, *On the Starting Grid*, B. T. Batsford, London, 1957.

Fusi, Luigi, *Alfa Romeo–All Cars From 1910*, Emmeti Grafica, Milan, 1978.

___, Ferrari, Enzo & Borgeson, Griffith, *Le Alfa Romeo di Vittorio Jano*, Autocritica, Rome, 1982.

Gauld, Graham, *Modena Racing Memories*, MBI Publishing, Osceola, 1999.

Georgano, G. N., editor, *The Beaulieu Encyclopedia of the Automobile*, The Stationery Office, London, 2000.

___, editor, *The New Encyclopaedia of Automobiles–1885 to the Present*, Crescent Books, New York, 1986.

___, with Bochroch, Albert R., *The Encyclopedia of Motor Sport*, Viking Press, New York, 1971.

Hawthorn, Mike, *Challenge Me the Race*, William Kimber, London, 1958.

Herrmann, Hans, *Ein Leben für den Rennsport*, Motorbuch-Verlag, Stuttgart, 1998.

Hodges, David, *A-Z of Formula Racing Cars*, Bay View, Bideford, 1990.

___, *A-Z of Grand Prix Cars*, Crowood, Marlborough, 2001.

___, *The French Grand Prix, 1906-1966*, Temple Press, London, 1967.

___, *The Le Mans 24-Hour Race*, Temple Press, London, 1963.

___, *The Monaco Grand Prix*, Temple Press, London, 1964.

Huet, Christian, *Gordini–Un Sorcier Une Equipe*, Editions Christian Huet, Paris, 1984.

Jenkinson, Denis, *Racing Car Review*, Grenville, London, Editions 1948 to 1958.

Karslake, Kent, *Racing Voiturettes*, Motor Racing Publications, London, 1950.

Lawrence, Mike, *The Mille Miglia*, Batsford, London, 1988.

Lewis, Peter, *Alf Francis–Racing Mechanic*, G.T. Foulis, London, 1957.

Ludvigsen, Karl, *Alberto Ascari*, Haynes, Sparkford, 2000.

___, *Classic Grand Prix Cars–The Front-Engined Era 1906-1960*, Haynes, Sparkford, 2006.

___, *Classic Racing Engines*, Haynes, Sparkford, 2001.

___, *Ferrari–The Factory*, Ludvigsen Library Series, Iconografix, Hudson, 2002.

___, *Ferrari: 60 Years of Technological Innovation*, Ferrari SpA, Modena, 2007.

___, *Juan Manuel Fangio*, Haynes, Sparkford, 1999.

___, *Red-Hot Rivals–Ferrari vs. Maserati*, Haynes, Sparkford, 2008.

___, *The V12 Engine*, Haynes, Sparkford, 2005.

Madaro, Giancenzo, *All the Fiats*, Editoriale Domus, Milan, 1970.

___, *All the Lancias*, Editoriale Domus, Milan, 1993.

Mathieson, T.A.S.O., *A Pictorial Survey of Racing Cars*, London, 1963.

___, *Grand Prix Racing 1906-1914*, Stockholm, 1965.

McDonough, Ed, *Ferrari 156 Sharknose*, Sutton, Stroud, 2001.

Moretti, Valerio, *La Scomessa di Gianni Lancia*, Autocritica, Rome, 1986.

Moss, Stirling with Nye, Doug, *Stirling Moss–My Cars, My Career*, Patrick Stephens, Wellingborough, 1987.

Nye, Doug, *The Autocourse History of the Grand Prix Car–1945-65*, Hazleton, Richmond, 1993.

___, *Dino–the Little Ferrari*, Osprey, London, 1979.

Orefici, Oscar, *Carlo Chiti: Sinfornia Ruggente*, Autocritica, Rome, 1991.

Orsini, Luigi and Zagari, Franco, *Maserati–A Complete History*, Libreria dell'Automobile, Milan, 1980.

___, *OSCA–La Rivincita dei Maserati*, Giorgio Nada, Milan, 1989.

Pascal, Dominique, *Ferrari au Mans*, Editions EPA, Paris, 1984.

Pomeroy, Laurence, *The Evolution of the Racing Car*, William Kimber, London, 1966.

___, *The Grand Prix Car*, Motor Racing Publications, Abingdon-on-Thames, 1949.

___, *The Grand Prix Car, Volume Two*, Motor Racing Publications, London, 1954.

Prunet, Antoine, *Ferrari Sport et Prototypes*, Editions EPA, Paris, 1978.

Rasponi, Simonetta et al, *Fiat 1899-1989–An Italian Industrial Revolution*, Fabbri, Milan, 1988.

Rose, Gerald, *A Record of Motor Racing–1894-1908*, Motor Racing Publications, Abingdon-on-Thames, 1949.

Salvadori, Roy and Pritchard, Anthony, *Roy Salvadori–Racing Driver*, Patrick Stephens, Wellingborough, 1985.

Sheldon, Paul with Rabagliati, Duncan, *A Record of Grand Prix and Voiturette Racing*, Volumes 1 through 13, St. Leonards, Bradford, 1987-2002.

Small, Steve, *Grand Prix Who's Who*, 3rd Edition, Travel Publishing, Reading, 2000.

Surtees, John with Henry, Alan, *John Surtees–World Champion*, Hazleton, Richmond, 1991.

Taruffi, Piero, *Works Driver*, Temple Press, London, 1964.

Tragatsch, Erwin, *Das grosse Rennfahrerbuch*, Hallwag, Bern, 1970.

Trow, Nigel, *Lancia Racing*, Osprey, London, 1987.

Venables, David, *First Among Champions–The Alfa Romeo Grand Prix Cars*, Haynes, Sparkford, 2000.

Wimpffen, János L., *Time and Two Seats–Five Decades of Long Distance Racing*, Motorsport Research Group, Redmond, 1999.

Yates, Brock, *Enzo Ferrari*, Doubleday, London, 1991.

Index